Heaven's Soldiers

ATLANTIC CROSSINGS

Rafe Blaufarb, Series Editor

Heaven's Soldiers

Free People of Color and the Spanish Legacy in Antebellum Florida

FRANK MAROTTI

UNIVERSITY OF ALABAMA PRESS
Tuscaloosa

Typeface: Granjon
Cover: Catholic Knights of St. John keeping memories of East Florida's black martial tradition alive during the era of Jim Crow. Courtesy of the St. Augustine Historical Society Research Library.

∞
The paper on which this book is printed meets the minimum requirements of American National Standard for Information Sciences—Permanence of Paper for Printed Library Materials, ANSI Z39.48-1984.

Library of Congress Cataloging-in-Publication Data

Marotti, Frank, 1954-
Heaven's soldiers : free people of color and the Spanish legacy in antebellum Florida / Frank Marotti.
pages cm. — (Atlantic crossings)
Includes bibliographical references and index.
ISBN 978-0-8173-1784-3 (trade cloth : alk. paper) — ISBN 978-0-8173-8653-5 (ebook)
1. Free African Americans—Florida—Saint John's County—History—19th century 2. Free African Americans—Legal status, laws, etc—Florida—Saint John's County—History—19th century. 3. Slaves—Emancipation—Florida—Saint John's County—History—19th century. 4. Seminole War, 2nd, 1835–1842. 5. Saint John's County (Fla.)—History—19th century. 6. Florida—History—1821–1865. I. Title.
F317.S18M37 2013
306.3'620975918—dc23

2012042395

To the free people of color of antebellum St. Augustine and their descendants, who continue to inspire us.

Contents

Acknowledgments

I owe a huge debt to Dr. Idus A. Newby, professor emeritus at the University of Hawai'i, for devoting a significant amount of his retirement time to assisting me in the early stages of this project. Drs. Marcus Daniel, Margot Henriksen, Robert McGlone, Miles Jackson, and Karen Jolly of the University of Hawai'i also gave me the benefit of their expertise. The late Dr. John P. Harrison of the University of Miami sparked my interest in the history of Latin America, the Caribbean, and the Spanish Borderlands. Dr. John F. Reiger did the same for the history of Florida. The writings of Dr. Daniel L. Schafer, professor emeritus at the University of North Florida, and Dr. Jane Landers of Vanderbilt University moved me to focus on East Florida. My students at Cheyney University, the oldest African American institution of postsecondary education, very much inspired the point of view from which I wrote.

Grants from the National Endowment for the Humanities and the Pennsylvania State System of Higher Education funded my research at the National Archives, where Wayne T. De Cesar was particularly helpful in my quest to locate the Patriot War claims.

Dr. W. Clinton Pettus, the former president of Cheyney University, generously granted me time off from teaching to research and write. My former department chair, the late Dr. Anne S. Jenkins of Cheyney University, believed in me when things were bleak. My colleague, Dr. Warren N. Holmes assisted me with sources on Liberia. Professor Gary Balmer was a great mentor.

Mary Herron, now director of development at the Florida Agricultural Museum, led me to explore many underutilized primary sources at the St. Augustine Historical Society Research Library. Charles Tingley of the SAHSRL was and continues to be very helpful. David Nolan was generous with his time while I worked in the Ancient City. Dr. William T. Abare, the president of Flagler College, allowed his campus to become my home away from home.

Thomas Hambright of the Monroe County Public Library shared his knowledge of Key West history and provided me with a photo of Nelson English. Dr. W. Fitzhugh Brundage, now of the University of North Carolina, graciously assisted my research at the University of Florida, as did Dr. James G. Cusick. Dr. Gail Saunders made the resources of the National Archives of the Bahamas readily available. Sandra Carter of the Heritage Quest Research Library in Sumner, Washington, helped me to make connections between antebellum St. Augustine's free people of color and the Pacific Northwest. Michael Cook generously shared information about his ancestor, Frederick A. Clarke, and guided me to a photograph of him. The staff of the New Kensington Public Library kindly made the Internet available to me.

Dr. Whittington B. Johnson, professor emeritus at the University of Miami, encouraged me to not become discouraged and led me by his example. The late John Hope Franklin fired me up very early on with a great letter of encouragement. Dr. Edward J. Tassinari of SUNY-Maritime University obtained the biography of Jack Smith/Sitiki at the New York Historical Society for me. Independent scholar Michael Finkelman was a constant source of counsel. Dr. Joe Knetsch of the Florida Bureau of Survey and Mapping answered any question that I posed.

Drs. Sherry Johnson, Felice Lifshitz, Brian Peterson, and Victor Uribe were great colleagues at Florida International University. Dr. E. Carter Burrus and Professor Patti Harris were most kind to me at Miami Dade College.

The descendants of the free people of color of antebellum St. Augustine very much encouraged my research and shared expertise that was invaluable, including family stories and materials. James W. Curtis, Dr. Yvonne Daniel, Mrs. Orville Payne, Ms. Jane Ball-Groom, and Ms. Jeanne English bent over backward for me.

Eli Bortz of Vanderbilt University Press steered me to the University of Alabama Press, which I must greatly thank for agreeing to publish my work. The anonymous readers of my manuscript made great suggestions and positive comments.

My friends Chris and Eileen Cortese provided me with much hospitality while I did my writing. My father, Frank Marotti Sr., before succumbing to a rare cancer, urged me to run through the finish line. My mother, a cancer and heart attack survivor, continued to exhort me to finish this project.

Heaven's Soldiers

Introduction

This study focuses on one group of African Americans who struggled to "make it" in an ethnically diverse slave-owning community. It is about agency, memory, and what one historian has called the "hidden transcript of resistance" by oppressed people. It seeks to retrieve "previously suppressed versions of the past" by illuminating interior worlds of the "Inarticulate."[1] The locus is the city of St. Augustine in St. Johns County, East Florida, the time the four decades prior to the American Civil War. My subjects are free people of African descent in the broad sense of the term *free,* that is, not just those who were legally free, but all those who resisted the constraints of legal bondage and otherwise asserted varying degrees of control over themselves and their circumstances.

Historians have long attributed the relatively flexible system of race relations in antebellum East Florida to the area's Spanish heritage.[2] While acknowledging the importance of that heritage, this book gives more than the usual emphasis to the role of African American agency in exploiting the limited opportunities that heritage permitted. In other words, remnants of Spanish rule presented blacks with institutions and customs that talented, ambitious, and fortunate individuals might and did exploit. In doing so, they drew especially on memories of lived experiences and cultural resources of their own.

"Slavery, though imposed and maintained by violence," Ira Berlin has noted, was a "negotiated relationship." That was certainly the case in St. Johns County, and the "negotiators" included free blacks as well as slaves. As Berlin has also noted, Spanish Florida, unlike British South Carolina and Georgia, never made the transition from a "society with slaves," in which bond persons were "marginal to the central productive processes," to a "slave society," in which "slavery stood at the center of economic production." Once the United States acquired Florida in 1821, however, that transition commenced, and the resulting struggle became the focal point of the history of African Americans in Florida. East Florida, it must be noted, was outside the plantation belt, and African Americans there succeeded in following the role Berlin ascribed to "Atlantic Creoles." That is, they mastered the art of cultural brokerage in a milieu conducive to at least limited success, thus taking advantage of their time and place and distinctive cultural environment. This continued a pattern developed in the Spanish period, during which black East Floridians matched the profile, noted by Jane Landers as well as Ira Berlin, of a people of "linguistic dexterity, cultural plasticity, and social agility."[3]

This investigation suggests that that profile continued well into the American period and never entirely disappeared. The profile persisted because the Atlantic Creole mentality endured, sustained in large part by memory, agency, and experience. In that experience, nothing was more important than the role blacks played in the Patriot War of 1812–1813, the memories of which kept alive a determination to resist the imposition of American forms of slavery.

The area that now falls within St. Johns County prospered in 1812. Although racial prejudice and its consequences were not absent, persons of color aspired to and could in fact live lives of dignity, security, and prosperity. Free blacks, many of them fugitives from American plantations, formed a major talent pool. Some of the enslaved were in the process of purchasing the freedom of themselves and loved ones. Others were the offspring and heirs of well-off and influential white fathers. Collectively, they were indispensable to the functioning of the social order.[4]

The dislocations of the Patriot War and the collapse of Spanish authority between 1812 and 1821 winnowed this population. Many fled to Cuba or elsewhere, but others opted to remain and take their chances in the new American order, confident of their ability to turn the risks of political and social transition to their own advantage. Under Spain, they had crafted the boundaries of their liberty; under the Americans, they would endeavor to do the same, with what success this study seeks to delineate.

For East Floridians of African descent, war and social upheaval had always been crucibles of assertiveness and advancement. One or the other—or both—of these conditions would be commonplace in the three decades following the American incursion of 1812. The sheer intensity of the resulting experiences made memory the wellspring of group identity and inspiration. Instability presented opportunity to serve the community, and in doing so further its own well being, to taste the fruits of mobility, responsibility, and freedom. This study demonstrates that black memories of heroic deeds, including those of self-liberation, fueled black hopes and inspired black activities, among them resistance to whites and to the restraints of slavery throughout the antebellum period. The Second Seminole War (1835–1842) was an especially notable example of such activity. But that experience merely expanded the record blacks had earlier made in the Patriot War and repeated later in the American Civil War. This martial heritage produced an oral tradition that sustained the fight against oppression throughout the period of this study and beyond.

Spanish East Florida attracted blacks from the earliest times. Persons of African descent served in the Spanish military forces there as early as 1580 and were participating in raids against nearby English settlements in the 1670s. Such activities were no doubt known in the English settlements, for in 1687, a party of eleven black runaways from South Carolina, including men, women, and an infant, arrived by stolen canoe in St. Augustine, requesting asylum. Cognizant of European political and religious rivalries, and of the convergence of their own interests with those of the Spaniards, these early fugitives offered themselves for baptism in the Roman Catholic faith. It was such activities as these that moved King Carlos II of Spain in 1693 to proclaim a policy that, in the words of a recent historian, "would shape the geopolitics of the Southeast and Caribbean for years to come." The new policy offered religious sanctuary and freedom to slaves who escaped from the British colonies north of Florida.[5]

Subsequent to the king's proclamation, by 1738, the black migrants from Carolina were sufficiently numerous to have their own fortified settlement, Gracia Real de Santa Teresa de Mose, about two miles north of St. Augustine, the presence of which may have helped inspire the famous Stono Rebellion in South Carolina in 1739. During Britain's temporary rule of East Florida, from 1763 to 1784, some Spanish families evacuated to Cuba, while others remained. When Britain returned control of the area to Spain, many of the evacuees returned. In the second period of Spanish control, from 1784 to 1821, the now-abandoned Mose community became a "favorite spot for large Sunday afternoon oyster roasts." Though it is uncertain whether any Mose blacks were among the returning settlers, the persistence of memories of black experience during the Patriot War of 1812–1813 suggests that the recollections of the free black town would have remained strong after 1784. In any case, the tradition of black military service that went back to the earlier period of Spanish sovereignty continued after 1784. Soldiers of color fought on behalf of the Spaniards in 1795, 1800–1803, 1812–1813, and 1817. Also, East Florida blacks were undoubtedly among the forces that battled Andrew Jackson's men at the Negro Fort in 1816 and during the First Seminole War in 1817–1818.[6]

Historians have characterized St. Augustine both before and after the American takeover as "cosmopolitan." "Possibly no small town on the North American continent has ever had such a diverse population," Patricia C. Griffin has written of the years between 1784 and 1821, and Thomas Graham has noted that the town maintained this heterogeneity under American control. The largest group of whites in this cosmopolitan mix was Minorcan. This "diverse collection of individuals and families" from several Mediterranean cultures had been brought as indentured servants to British East Florida in 1768 to cultivate indigo on the New Smyrna plantation of Dr. Andrew Turnbull. After much suffering there, they fled to St. Augustine, where "they became the core of the Hispanic population," the "fabric upon which the [Spanish-speaking] community [was] built."[7]

The Minorcans earned their monetary income from orange growing, construction work, renting slaves, and a variety of small businesses. The resulting seasonal pattern of activity persisted because of St. Augustine's insular location and the absence of alternative economic activities. Not all of the Minorcans were poor. The Perpall family became especially well-off and socially prominent under Spanish rule, and the Cocifacios, Peso de Burgos, Leonardis, and Seguís also prospered through trade, money lending, and performing legal services. In the "personalistic" Minorcan culture, the men of these elite families functioned as patrons to clients of lesser men and families. Perhaps because they had themselves had to toil under black overseers at New Smyrna, the Minorcans reputedly treated their own slaves kindly.[8] In any case, the presence of this sizeable population had a significant influence on people of color in St. Augustine and St. Johns County during the period of this study.

Jack Smith, who had been a quasi-free young man when he arrived in St. Augustine in the spring of 1817, recalled that influence. He remembered especially the joyful and colorful Minorcan religious festivals. During the pre-Lenten carnival season, for example, "a great variety of grotesque disguises, on horseback, in cars, gigs, and on foot, paraded the streets with guitars, violins, and other instruments." On the night before Easter, young men parading door to door serenaded households with the *formatjada* hymn, then ritually demanded a reward, to which householders responded with special cheese-filled pastries. Midsummer brought the festival of St. Johns Eve, marked by dances, flowers, festooned public altars, and masqueraders dressed in the garb of chivalry. "The people were the gayest I can imagine," Smith recalled of the Minorcans in his old age, "serenades, processions, balls, picnics, masquerades came the year round in constant succession."[9]

Catholicism "permeated" Minorcan life as well as public ritual and, like personalism and economic interdependence, helped Minorcans transcend and mediate class differences. The community attended Mass every Sunday, after which its members engaged in "merrymaking" and "trading . . . in the plaza," softening the "hard realities of everyday living." Furthermore, the custom of *compadrazgo* united them. Godparents (*padrinos*) "were expected to provide for the spiritual and material care of the child in the event of the parents' death." The *padrinos* also "establish[ed] a system of reciprocal obligations" with their *compadres* or coparents. Thus, persons who were not blood relatives could become "fictive kin." This practice continued into the American antebellum period and remained "crucial for family and community binding, and even for survival."[10] Local blacks used their own parallel institutions as well as those borrowed from the Minorcans to bolster their own cultural and social circumstances. In doing so, many of them entered into client relationships with Minorcans, cementing their bonds by *compadrazgo* as well as by economic arrangements. The unique Mediterranean-rooted Minorcan population was largely responsible for the persistence of Hispanic culture in St. Augustine after the American takeover.

The Patriot War, one episode in the American drive to control all of North America, shattered a period of economic prosperity in East Florida. Its strategic location on the American frontier and along sea lanes to the Caribbean inevitably drew the attention of expansionist-minded Americans to the area and spelled the end of Spanish control. Turmoil in Europe in the aftermath of the French Revolution and the onset of the Napoleonic wars sparked unrest in Spain's New World empire that also weakened Spanish control. With the assistance of their fellow countrymen north of the border, Americans recently settled in West Florida "rebelled" against their Spanish overlords in 1810, declared themselves independent, and invited President James Madison to annex the territory to the American nation. A year later, Madison obtained secret Congressional approval to seize East Florida should "local authorities" offer the area to the nation, or should the British, then at war with Spain, threaten to take it.[11]

When Britain had retroceded East Florida to Spain in 1783, the rural northern reaches of the province, or the 1,200 square miles between the St. Marys and St. Johns rivers, "remained exclusively Anglo." In this "extension of British America into Spanish Florida," 83 percent of the population had been born in what became the United States, and nine in ten were Protestants. The wealthier among them measured their worth by the number of slaves they owned; the poorer counted their livestock. Both groups placed great value in landholding. Trade for everyone was quicker and cheaper and culturally more inviting with Charleston or New York than with Havana, which led the Spanish governor to countenance the smuggling that developed with the American ports. In an effort to retain the area as well as develop it economically, the Spanish Crown in 1790 had opened it to American immigrants, offering them land on generous terms with minimum interference from local authorities in St. Augustine. Following the invention of the cotton gin in 1793, cotton cultivation spread into the area along with American immigrants, who from the young republic brought American forms of slavery and plantation agriculture with them. An integration of the resulting economic and social systems with those of the American republic was only a matter of time.[12]

When Madison named an ex-governor of Georgia, George Mathews, as his agent for dealing with East Florida, the time seemed ripe for annexation of the area. Due to general prosperity, however, Mathews found little enthusiasm among the immigrant planters for radical political change. He decided, therefore, with Madison's implicit consent, to create an incident that would prompt American intervention. He convinced John Houston McIntosh, an immigrant planter from Georgia who owned substantial acreage in the area and who had sworn loyalty to the king of Spain, to lead a group of the "Patriots of East Florida" in an uprising against Spanish rule. Once the uprising stirred up the local populace, McIntosh and the Patriots, as the responsible local authorities, were to cede their new "republic" to the United States as Patriot forces consolidated their control of the province. With a small force consisting primarily of "volunteers" from Georgia, Mathews lured a few Americans in East Florida to his cause with promises of land and self-government. He nevertheless, aroused little enthusiasm for a military revolt.[13]

In mid-March 1812, on the eve of the "rebellion," the Patriot army numbered perhaps 125 men. Their resolution faltered when the local commander of American regulars, uncertain of ex-Governor Mathews' authority, refused to supply him with men. The Patriots thus had too little firepower to march on St. Augustine, as planned. Instead, on 13 March at Rose's Bluff on the Spanish side of the St. Marys River, nine East Floridians read a list of "grievances" against the Spanish king, proclaimed a republic, and raised a new flag before seventy cheering Georgians. They then offered Rose's Bluff to Mathews in the name of the United States. With the backing of US gunboats, the Patriots seized Fernandina on nearby Amelia Island a few days later, and Mathews accepted the proffered area on behalf of Madison, and the US government.[14]

None of this had much meaning as long as St. Augustine remained under Spanish control, so the insurrectionary forces next proceeded against the town and its fort, gathering "recruits" by compulsion, threats, and enticements as they marched. The town soon found itself besieged and facing food shortages. Blacks in and around the area observed these developments with consternation. Those who lived with and among the Hispanic population had an obvious stake in preventing an American takeover, understanding the threat such a takeover presented to their freedom or to the nature of their bondage. Their fellow blacks who lived nearby in their own settlements under nominal Seminole overlords, and known to history as Black Seminoles, were especially fearful that an American victory would mean their return to slavery. The success of the Black Seminoles in bridging cultural and linguistic barriers had enabled them to influence tribal councils, and the Seminoles had their own reasons for wanting to keep East Florida free of American control.[15]

The Spaniards rallied all of these groups against the invaders. In July 1812, allied Seminole and black units launched a series of rear-guard attacks on the American intruders and "destroyed the Patriots as a fighting and food-gathering organization." In one key action in September, a party composed largely of members of St. Augustine's free black militia, ambushed a group of American supply wagons in Twelve Mile Swamp between the Americans besieging the town and their supply depots on the St. Johns River. They succeeded in breaking the siege and forcing the invaders to retreat all the way to the St. Johns. By this time, too, the Patriots faced resistance in Georgia, where slave owners had become concerned about the impact of the promise by the Spanish governor of liberty to American slaves who deserted their masters and enlisted in East Florida's black or Indian auxiliaries. By May 1813, the United States had withdrawn its regular forces from East Florida, leaving the Patriots to fend for themselves in a "ravaged, despoiled land." Black troops had succeeded in postponing the change of flags.[16] But not for long, and not without leaving a legacy that influenced the history of blacks in East Florida until the American Civil War and beyond.

The portion of East Florida under Spanish control before 1821 ran ninety miles south from the St. Marys River, the southern boundary of Georgia, and twenty-five miles inland between the St. Johns River and the sea. Modern St. Johns County is only about a quarter of what was once Spanish East Florida. After the United States raised its flag over Florida in 1821, Governor Andrew Jackson split the territory, assigning to St. Johns County everything south and east of the Suwannee River. A year later, the territorial legislature created Duval County out of a part of this huge administrative unit. Subsequent division further reduced the size of St. Johns County.[17] These shifting borders complicate the presentation of statistical evidence on matters of concern to this study, including miscegenation, manumission, marriage, baptism, and property holding. The creation of Putnam County in 1849, to illustrate, reduced the acreage of land blacks owned in St. Johns County, but the reduction was not necessarily due to any actual loss of land but may have been due to the new basis of the statistics.

The town of St. Augustine, where the great majority of free blacks in St. Johns County lived in the antebellum era, encompassed slightly less than a mile of the shoreline along a low-lying peninsula on Matanzas Bay. A fourth of a mile inland, María Sánchez Creek marked the town's western border. Beyond this creek, the waters of a grassy tidal basin, the San Sebastián River, ebbed and flowed. One could walk the town's width in fifteen minutes. A perilous inlet to the bay, and thus to the town harbor, choked trade. This hazard diminished somewhat with the commencement of steamship service in 1834, but the search for a more convenient connection to the outside world remained a concern for town boosters throughout the antebellum era.[18]

The town had its differences and tensions. White American Protestants brought with them values and views of the society they had left. They tended to look down on the town's largest ethnic "minority," Minorcans, for ethnic as well as religious reasons. The Minorcans were not only Catholics who spoke a "foreign" tongue, but they also generally had black curly hair and olive complexions. The crassest of the Americans called them "Turnbull's Negroes" and disparaged their lifestyle as a kind of Mediterranean indolence. Still, the Minorcans "posed no challenge" to the American newcomers, though their experiences with black overseers at New Smyrna may have made them suspicious of blacks in positions to do them harm. That at least seems a reasonable way to read the fact that one of the enduring memories of the Minorcans' indenture at New Smyrna involved one of their number suffering "five and thirty lashes from a Negro."[19]

Long before the end of the antebellum period, Minorcans attained preeminence in St. Augustine life. Joseph M. Hernández, for instance, the master of seventy seven bondsmen in 1840, was St. Johns County's largest slaveholder. During a long public career, Hernández served variously as a town alderman, territorial legislator, general in the military, and territorial delegate to the United States Congress. Pedro Benet, whose wealth and prestige earned him the title "king of the Minorcans," was another "influential landowner and taxpayer." He sent his son Stephen Vincent Benet to the US Military Academy, where he became the first Florida graduate. This son in turn fathered three children distinguished by their literary accomplishments, including his well-known namesake, Stephen Vincent Benet.[20]

These examples attest not only to the prominence of Minorcans in St. Augustine, but also to their growing assimilation into American life. In 1843, when Minorcans comprised about half of the town's population, the traditional Easter *formatjada* hymn still resounded in St. Augustine's streets. Yet, unreplenished by new immigration, the population was losing its knowledge of its native Catalan language. In 1850, the town's mayor, aldermen, and marshal all had Minorcan or Hispanic names, a list of them proudly printed by Sylvester Manucy, himself a Minorcan, in the first issue of his newspaper, the *Ancient City*. In 1860, Mathias R. Andreu, another Minorcan, whose weekly *Examiner* had replaced Manucy's *Ancient City*, reminded his subscribers that the "large majority" of St. Augustinians were Catholic; but when he published the *formatjada* hymn, he included an English as well as a Catalan version. Significantly, it was the Catalan version he had difficulty writing out. "Our acquaintance with the language extends only to ordinary conversation," he explained. Andreu provided other evidence that St. Augustine's Latin heritage was fading. Cristobal Bravo Sr., he noted, had recently donated a "coin of the reign of Charles 3rd, king of Spain, bearing date 1707," to the "museum of the Florida Historical Society." Others, he hoped, would follow Bravo's example, and in that way preserve the "relics of olden time" for future generations.[21]

By the time Andreu made this plea, it was possible to speak of at least some Minorcans as Southerners in the sectional conflict then about to engulf the nation. Indeed, one of them, the Reverend A. D. Pellicer, a native of St. Augustine but then the pastor of St. Peter's Church in Montgomery, Alabama, offered the opening prayer at two sessions of the Montgomery convention called to establish the Confederate government. Although Colonel Stephen Vincent Benet cast his lot with the Union during the Civil War, most Minorcans, led by their bishop, Augustin Verot, enthusiastically backed secession and the Confederate cause. This was the culmination of the assimilation of Minorcans into the Southern slave society and into the politics of the national Democratic Party.[22]

Despite this assimilation, the Minorcan presence was a major reason for the persistence of the flexible Spanish style of race relations that influenced black life in St. Augustine well into the antebellum era. The persistence was also due to the racial demography of East Florida. At the time of American annexation, the non-Indian population of the province was perhaps twelve thousand, the majority of whom were persons of color. Under these circumstances, the ethnically distinct Minorcans were counted as whites. That they were counted so may have been a previously unnoticed instance of the "new era in the meaning of whiteness" some historians have recently discerned in explaining the impact of Irish immigration on American constructions of race in the 1840s and afterward. At the same time, however, free blacks would be competing with many Minorcans in an economy that offered limited employment opportunities. Unquestionably, Florida's new American masters considered the Minorcans as white. Self-defense necessitated Minorcan whiteness.[23] Like the Irish, the Minorcans were Catholic, which, like their ethnic distinctiveness, may have prompted their political and economic leaders to encourage the assimilation of "Southern" values, racial and otherwise.

Agriculture was the mainstay of the region's economy throughout the antebellum era. Although some large plantations existed in East Florida, small, diversified farming "was the norm." Despite the pervasiveness of slavery, in all of St. Johns County in 1840, only three individuals owned more than twenty bond persons. Half of the county's slave owners had fewer than four "servants," and only a third of whites were in families owning any slaves. As a result of these patterns, slaves were often jacks-of-all-trades, which led them to develop varieties of skills, with the accompanying benefits of boosted confidence and self-esteem. An "important legacy" from the Spanish era was the task system for slaves, which characterized the labor pattern even among American owners "in the old inhabited places." Most slaves preferred this arrangement because it often enabled them to "complete their assignments well before the day's end" and thus partially control their own time. In the spare time thus afforded them, they had opportunities to earn money of their own.

In addition, many masters permitted their bond persons to hire themselves out, retain a portion of their wages, and even live in separate locales.[24]

Historians have noted and stressed the positive effects of these patterns. In a recent synthesis of their works, Larry Eugene Rivers argues that the enduring influence of Spanish customs "afforded slaves rights not systematically found in the Old South or in other slave systems with European origins." These customs, Rivers continues, influenced the "nature of race relations and slavery well into the nineteenth century." Particularly in East Florida, Latin traditions "survived long enough to impress their image deeply on the institution of slavery" even after the American takeover.[25]

The obvious flexibility these patterns permitted were partly responsible for the romantic views of slavery that appear in some of the historical records of St. Augustine and St. Johns County. William Cullen Bryant, who visited the town in the1840s, described the blacks he saw there as "good-looking specimen[s] of the race, and hav[ing] the appearance of being very well treated." Only "rarely" did Bryant see saw a "negro in ragged clothing, and the coloured children, though slaves, [were] often dressed with great neatness." Years later, at least a few ex-slaves, among them Jack Smith, who has already been cited, and A. H. Darns, who became a physician, echoed Bryant's views. "St. Augustine," recalled Darns of the antebellum era, "was heaven for negroes."[26]

This study examines this "heaven" and the role of African Americans in creating it. It complements the work of historians who have detailed aspects of the story of antebellum black East Florida and fills a significant gap in that work. "The history of the African American experience in Florida has only recently begun to be examined," David R. Colburn wrote in 1995, "and it will take at least another generation of historical research and writing to bring citizens of the state and students of Florida history to a reasonably full understanding of the African American contribution."[27] The chapters that follow hopefully accomplish one part of the task that Colburn defined.

The organization of my investigation is both topical and chronological. I emphasize four pillars of black liberty erected during Spain's rule: family ties to whites, manumission, military service, and landownership. My first chapter surveys black opportunities and liabilities under the Spaniards, in addition to offering a case study that allows a quick glimpse into the American slave society's future workings. The second explores the 1820s, a decade that featured both successful defenses of black rights and chilling statutory attacks on these rights. The first half of the 1830s, another period of mixed blessings, is the subject of the third chapter, and the fourth is devoted to the pivotal Second Seminole War, especially the complexities of that conflict relative to St. Johns County's black community.

My approach to the final two antebellum decades is more topical. Chapter 5 treats black migrations, as well as the impact of the anti-miscegenation and anti-manumission laws of the early 1840s. The sixth and seventh chapters examine African American efforts to preserve Spanish marriage and emancipation customs, in addition to elaborating the strategies by which blacks kept their military heritage vibrant. A concluding chapter explores late-antebellum black landownership. Moreover, because enforcement of antiblack edicts depended on local officials, it also evaluates the workings of white paternalism, as well as black strategies for exploiting the latter. Finally, there is a discussion of the overall impact of laws and ordinances on the lives of people of color in the St. Johns County. I derive the bulk of my evidence from underutilized archival materials and it is my hope that my notes will guide other scholars in their investigations of African American life in Florida.

I
Looking Backward and Forward

In 1868, Eliza M. Whitwell, the quadroon granddaughter of George J. F. Clarke, a former lieutenant governor of Spanish East Florida, critiqued antebellum US policy toward free persons of color in a bitter letter to the prominent St. Augustine physician, John Peck. The "good old Flag of Spain," she wrote, "enslaved none but the slaves giving equal rights & privileges to all as his subjects without distinction. . . ."[1] To Mrs. Whitwell, the republican Stars and Stripes, in contrast to Spain's monarchical banner, had stifled her human potential. This chapter evaluates her bold assertion while at the same time illustrating what could have been. It concludes with a haunting preview of the world that the American regime would create.

Under the Spaniards, Afro-East Floridians, through blood ties with prominent white fathers, could and did attain freedom, property, social standing, material comfort, and in rare cases, "whiteness." These blood ties constituted one important pillar of black liberty. The case of Don Francisco Xavier Sánchez's biracial offspring is illustrative. María Beatriz Piedra, the child of a South Carolina white man and his slave, bore Sánchez, one of East Florida's wealthiest inhabitants, at least eight babies, all of whom were baptized in the Catholic Church. They would come to inherit one-sixth of his ample estate. Three daughters married white Spaniards in formal church ceremonies, and their unions were not recorded in the parish's segregated black marriage book. It was not uncommon for the province's leading men to acknowledge, free, educate, and pass property to their biracial children.[2]

Sánchez, following another common pattern, never married María Beatriz Piedra. Instead, in his fifties, while Piedra was alive, he contracted church nuptials with the teenage María del Carmen Hill. She produced a second family of ten white children. They, not their biracial siblings, became the legal heirs to the overwhelming majority of the Sánchez fortune. The names of Sánchez's octoroon grandchildren, even though the church had proclaimed their biracial mothers white, were entered into the black baptismal registries. Joseph Sánchez, the don's surviving free colored son, was trained as a carpenter. Unlike his sisters, he was not able to take a white spouse. When he was approaching his midthirties, Lucía Isnardy, a government official's teenaged, propertied, quadroon daughter, married him in a Catholic ceremony. Six months later, she died. The widower later established a relationship with Susana Sánchez, whose parents had been his father's slaves.[3] Race relations in Spanish East Florida contained elements of flexible complexity, but whites unquestionably dominated the social hierarchy.

East Floridians of African descent also broke the shackles of enslavement by making incremental payments to their owners. This process, called *coartación*, comprised one piece of a second pillar of black liberty, manumission. Herbert Klein described *coartación* as the "most important" of several emancipation arrangements developed in colonial Cuba, from which Spanish East Florida was governed. Under this arrangement, slaves could request that a tribunal set their price, which they then would pay, almost always in installments, thereby attaining freedom. A bond person's right to own property undergirded the arrangement. After making an initial payment, *coartados* (slaves in the process of buying freedom), could trade masters if they found one who might smooth their way to liberty. Individuals who took advantage of *coartación* were resourceful, industrious, ambitious, talented, lucky, and well-connected. They were likely to be urban slaves. *Coartación* permitted entrepreneurs to obtain skilled workers at low wages and relieved owners of the bother of closely supervising their slaves. Wherever the system operated, many blacks occupied a middle ground between bondage and freedom.[4]

Felipe Edimboro and his wife, Filis, both African born, took advantage of *coartación*, but as in the cases of others who liberated themselves by this process, freedom did not come easily. After enduring the horrific Middle Passage to the Americas, the Edimboros ended up in East Florida. In 1772, Francisco Xavier Sánchez acquired them. Sánchez, a cattle baron, valued Felipe for his butchering. Filis was an excellent domestic. When Sánchez was absent from his main plantation, San Diego, a thousand-acre ranch, he left Felipe in charge. He also assigned the Edimboros to work in St. Augustine, where he held extensive real estate and business concerns. In this urban setting, the Edimboros enjoyed easier access to activities that permitted them to make extra cash in their spare time. They rented space that they transformed into a weekend black dance hall. Filis made toys and baked goods. She earned other funds by washing clothes. Felipe butchered, hunted, fished, peddled firewood, raised hogs, and picked up other part-time jobs as opportunities presented themselves. It took the couple two decades to accumulate their freedom price, notwithstanding an acrimonious court battle with Sánchez, who balked at granting them their liberty.[5]

The Edimboros secured their position in this life and the next through the Catholic sacraments of baptism and marriage. Not only did they solemnize their union within the church, they baptized their children there. They also witnessed a marriage and served as godparents numerous times. Through these relationships and their accompanying obligations, the manumitted couple extended their social networks and increased their community standing, thereby spiritually and materially bolstering their freedom.[6]

Nonetheless, the Edimboros were well aware of the limits of Spanish benevolence. Their son, Sandi, was a hothead. They had tried to teach him his proper social role, but he only learned this lesson through painful experience. At one point, he and a white soldier cast their attentions on the same woman of color. A fight ensued during which Sandi bested his rival, who then took the matter to a military court. This body, after conducting an investigation, sentenced the young black man to toil in chains for one year.[7] The better to instruct him as to show proper deference toward his racial betters.

Prince Witten neither attained freedom from white relatives nor from *coartación*. His liberty was linked more directly to his value as a fighting man. Due to religious and geopolitical rivalries, the Spaniards encouraged slaves from English colonies to the north to flee to East Florida. These fugitives, in turn, eventually impelled their new sovereign to proclaim a religious sanctuary policy for runaways who requested Catholic baptism. Freedom came to men and their families who not only accepted Catholicism, but served in the military. This policy became a point of contention that led to British assaults on St. Augustine in 1728, 1740, 1742, and 1743. Erstwhile fugitive bondsmen helped to repel these attacks, thus creating even more international tension.[8]

Witten, a strapping African carpenter, sought refuge in East Florida with his North American–born wife and children in order to prevent the separation of his family. He subsequently won glory in combat against American invaders in 1795 and against Seminole warriors some five years later. His martial prowess earned him the respect and gratitude of the local colonial authorities. Because Witten had attained freedom under Spain's religious sanctuary policy, Catholicism played an important role in his life. He, his wife, and his children were baptized and married within the church. The Wittens also were among the leading godparents of color in the colony. Through sacramental ties, the family established close linkages to a prominent black general, Jorge Biassou, who had fought for the Spaniards during the Haitian Revolution.[9]

Witten came to own both land and slaves. He also displayed his leadership ability in the civilian realm. He petitioned the government to form a black community outside of St. Augustine. Here, he and his comrades might attain a greater degree of autonomy. In a lumbering enterprise that he conducted part-time, Witten employed black men, thus providing income to them independent of white supervision. At least once, he sued a white employer after the latter had violated their labor contract by ordering Witten's wife, Judy Kenty, to toil in the fields. But, he also learned the limits to which he could push the Spaniards. While waiting in the doorway of a St. Augustine home belonging to Don José Sánchez, Kenty got into an argument with Sánchez's wife, calling her a "damned bitch" in English. This caused Sánchez to physically assault Witten's spouse. The judicial authorities were unsympathetic to Kenty. They sternly reprimanded her for failing to respect East Florida's hierarchy of color.[10]

Judy Kenty's outburst gives a brief glimpse of the repressed anger that she and her husband harbored toward whites, even those who had established policies that made possible their liberty and social standing. One can only imagine what the Wittens thought of their former Anglo-American owners. On 9 September 1812, Prince Witten seized an opportunity to reap vengeance against them within the aegis of royal service, after American invaders from Georgia had besieged St. Augustine. Facing starvation, the desperate Spanish governor dispatched the black provincial militia and some Seminole allies, all under Witten's command, to cut the besiegers' supply lines. In a brilliantly executed surprise attack on that September night, the guerilla unit accomplished its mission, causing the Americans to retreat inland to the St. Johns River. The former refugee had become a savior. Felipe Edimboro also fought with Witten on that heroic night in the Twelve Mile Swamp, northwest of St. Augustine. He too had turned East Florida's desperate need for security to his advantage.[11]

The Americans had hoped to stir up a "revolution" that would lead to an independent East Florida which then would request annexation to the United States. Due in large part to the resistance of men of color loyal to Spain, the so-called Patriot War of 1812–1813 resulted in a US retreat, but not before the invaders devastated the province by plunder and a scorched earth policy. On the eve of the incursion, however, East Florida prospered. Free blacks shared in this prosperity, scrambling to make money like their white neighbors. Because of Washington's ongoing trade war with London, cotton and lumber fetched handsome profits at the port of Fernandina, on Amelia Island, a short distance from the Georgia border. Garden farmers near St. Augustine earned good prices for their produce. Cattle ranching also thrived.[12] These economic good times trickled down to even the humblest free black farmers who surrounded the provincial capital.

In 1812, at Padan Aram, twenty-five miles northwest of St. Augustine, along the St. Johns River's eastern bank, Scipio Fleming planted five acres of corn, peas, pumpkins, melons, sugar cane, rice, potatoes, and other vegetables. Eight or ten hogs, a horse, and a dozen hens roamed Fleming's twenty-five-acre tract that the Spaniards had granted him in 1809. Two log houses and a shed stood on the property. Good rail fencing enclosed seven acres. Although his other possessions were modest—a boat, two guns, a hoe, an axe, an oven, a few pots, and several pieces of furniture—Fleming had distanced himself from his earlier dependence on the white Fatio family's patronage.[13]

Prince Witten lived about ten miles southeast of Fleming's place, on Sweet Water Branch, some fourteen miles north of town. He cultivated ten acres of foodstuffs on land that he rented from the Minorcan John Leonardy. Whereas Fleming's holdings were estimated to be worth six hundred dollars, neighbors assessed Witten's property at double that price. His livestock included four milk cows, a mule, and three horses. The latter were especially valuable because in his spare time, Witten cut cedar for export in the Twelve Mile Swamp. After felling and squaring the logs, he hauled them to a landing. From there, he rafted the timber down the North River to St. Augustine, where he exchanged some of it for merchandise and sold the remainder to John Forbes and Company, which in turn shipped it to New York or Britain. Witten hired as many as twenty black laborers to assist him. He had acquired, among other implements, a cart, a chain, and timber wheels used to transport logs. Like other East Floridians, he had striven, according to the accounts of antebellum witnesses, to make "his fortune, hand over hand, as fast as he could" by engaging in the "most profitable employment or labor" available to blacks.[14]

Two miles closer to St. Augustine, on the west bank of the North River, another man of color, Charles Hill, cultivated several fields, one of which belonged to the Minorcan James Arnau. Hill, like other free black farmers, had constructed his own buildings. He grew the usual food crops, in addition to a small quantity of cotton. Hill's main source of income came from his hauling business, to which he devoted his horses and wagon. Further up the Pablo Road, six miles north of Witten's place, Sancho Davis and his married son Domingo farmed government land and made extra money lumbering. Along the same road, some five miles from St. Augustine, a group of free blacks, which included John Howley, Abraham Rocho, and Abraham McQueen, leased acreage from Don Antonio Yguínez. They collectively fenced the tract and individually farmed plots within the enclosure. Families also constructed buildings and fencing that was theirs to take away once their lease expired. Howley and Rocho supplemented their incomes by harvesting cedar for export.[15]

South of St. Augustine, at Moses Creek, near the mouth of the Matanzas River, other men of color, among them Isaac Bacchus and John Morell, tended small farms and cut timber. Several free blacks worked for Eliza Whitwell's grandfather, George J. F. Clarke, and for her great uncle, Charles W. Clarke, who owned adjoining estates near Bacchus and Morell. George Clarke, a free colored man unrelated to the white Clarkes, farmed and logged in the vicinity as well on land that he rented from the Minorcan Antonio Masters. Toby Herreira, another man of African descent, lived nearby. He planted twenty-five acres in corn, potatoes, pumpkins, and Sea Island cotton. Herreira owned a horse, four cows, four breeding sows, a boar, and more than thirty pigs, plus a hundred chickens, ducks, and turkeys. Decades later, neighbors recalled that he had lived in "comfortable circumstances," holding property worth more than three thousand dollars.[16]

In 1812, Felipe Edimboro owned land on St. Augustine's western outskirts, a "good garden in town," two "prime" slaves, and fifty head of cattle. His son-in-law, Benjamin Wiggins, whose sister was the common-law wife of Charles W. Clarke (a white provincial official/businessman and George J. F. Clarke's brother), had inherited property from his white father, Job Wiggins. The younger Wiggins worked as a "stock keeper & Pilot to those who traveled the country." These activities brought him an income of $500 to $600 annually in cattle and cash, plus another $200 to $300 in fees for his services as a guide. Indeed, one witness recalled that Wiggins "always had money," but "he always kept it private & took care not to let any body know what he had."[17]

From this brief treatment, one can partially understand why Eliza Whitwell defended the Spanish regime so strongly. People of color under the Spaniards could be wealthy and achieve a degree of social prominence. The biracial children of white patriarchs typically inherited their fathers' wealth and a certain portion of his status. Ambitious, hard-working, and talented individuals from the ranks of the enslaved could emerge as respected free subjects of the crown. Men could vie with whites for glory on the battlefield. Free persons of African descent often owned land. Participation in the Catholic Church publicly demonstrated this class's moral and spiritual equality with whites. Black small farmers could aspire to better material circumstances. Still, a proud woman of color like Whitwell surely would have chafed under the racially based insults that the black Sánchez, Edimboro, and Witten families sometimes endured. A glance into the future, however, will more fully explain Whitwell's fond attachment to Spanish days.

During the summer of 1856, Susan Murphy feebly held on to life, drifting back and forth between the present and the past under the influence of senility, brandy, and opiates. Mrs. Murphy was, by some accounts, close to one hundred years old. Her unfortunate final illness, brought on by a broken thigh, promised to increase the fortunes of some of St. Augustine's leading citizens—men such as US Senator David L. Yulee, the physician Dr. John Peck, and lawyer-politician George R. Fairbanks. Murphy's slaves, however, harbored mixed feelings regarding their mistress' impending demise. Belinda, her nurse, stood to gain freedom and an inheritance of $500. Peter, on the other hand, found himself in danger of being separated from his family.[18]

Fifty years earlier, Susan Murphy had been married to James Cashen, who had migrated from Georgia to Spanish East Florida in 1800. Cashen's subsequent career matches the scholar Eugene Genovese's classic description of a paternalist planter. That is, Cashen devoted himself to the "accumulation of land and slaves and the achievement of military and political honors." Within a decade of his arrival, he transformed himself into the "richest planter" on Amelia Island. As many as forty-five "working hands" cultivated the fields of Erin Hall, his cotton plantation near the bustling port of Fernandina. Like other paternalistic slave holders, Cashen funneled much of his wealth into the importation of luxury goods for conspicuous consumption. He lived in a "large fine house," in "good style," having filled it with expensive items "not common in Florida." His table was that of a gentleman, "well-furnished with silver and plate." Cashen adorned his wife, who was "born and raised a Lady," with costly jewelry. The couple entertained overnight guests in their home. They extended their largesse to their less prosperous neighbors as well.

Philip Weedman recalled that Cashen supplied "gratuitously those who were in want of provisions." Moreover, the master of Erin Hall served the Spaniards as a judge and militia officer.[19]

The Cashens' world view enabled them to see themselves as the benevolent protectors of their black "family." Nevertheless, evidence suggests that James Cashen also recognized that his ascendancy rested on violence. In 1810, Cashen imported twenty-eight slaves from Africa on his ship, the *Amanda*. By his own account, the Africans had endured tremendous suffering during the Middle Passage. By 1812, he was employing a significant portion of his labor force in the backbreaking timber industry. This lucrative enterprise was earning money "hand over hand" for East Floridians, black and white. Lumbering, however, disrupted his slaves' domestic lives, forcing bondsmen to live in woodland camps away from their families. Indeed, John G. Rushing, the overseer at John H. McIntosh's Fort George Island plantation, whose male labor force was off cutting timber, recalled that he "had a good deal of trouble with the women on account of the absence of their husbands."[20] Clearly then, Erin Hall had been built on shattered black lives. His slaves realized this, and James Cashen had not fallen entirely prey to his self-deception.

In 1812, the Cashens received a taste of their own medicine. The United States had cast its eyes on booming East Florida, aiming to annex the province by fomenting a "revolution" against Spain. That spring, George Mathews, a Revolutionary War veteran and former governor of Georgia, paid a visit to Erin Hall. Because James Cashen was absent, Mathews presented his wife with an offer that he believed she could not and would not refuse. If her husband would join the planned "revolt," Mathews would safeguard his property and reward him with a high political office. He then reminded Mrs. Cashen that she would then be a "Governors Lady." Although her brother was an officer in the US military, Susan Cashen's aristocratic sense of honor, as well as her haughty disdain for the man standing before her dressed in "garb of the most inferior kind," led her to respond bluntly to "so gross an insult." "Rather would I see my husband stand and be shot at," she snapped, "than should he turn traitor to the Country he got his bread in."[21]

The Cashens' resistance failed to hinder Mathews's land-hungry Georgians (supported by US regulars) from capturing Amelia Island in March 1812. Because of James Cashen's loyalty to Spain, he had rendered himself "particularly obnoxious" to the so-called Patriot invaders. On the night of 19 September 1812, when Erin Hall's fields were "white with cotton," a party of Patriots under the command of the Georgian William Cone exacted their revenge. After the Cashens and their guests had retired, Cone's men seized thirty-three slaves and plundered Erin Hall's stores. Then, they turned their attention to the great house. The raiders first broke open the door to the room in which two female visitors slept. "Pointing their guns," the Patriots "took from them two [slave] girls," threatening the house guests "with an oath" that they would kill the ladies if they made any noise."[22]

The party next plundered the main hall, grabbing from a sideboard several items of sentimental value to Susan Cashen. They also pilfered plates, towels, and table linen. After littering the carpet with sweetmeats, the Americans climbed the stairs leading to the Cashens' bedchamber. Here they demanded to speak to James Cashen, or they would fire his house. When Mr. Cashen emerged, the Patriots dragged him off "like a felon," in his "under cloths." To add insult to injury, Cone's men pulled the rings from Susan Cashen's fingers. If she attempted to follow them, they warned, they would shoot her. Unintimidated, Mrs. Cashen dared them to do so. That night, the Cashens lost property, including slaves, worth over $23,000. "Thus was I deprived of my all," Susan Cashen recalled, and she fell from a "state of happiness & independence to penury."[23]

Despite Cone's threat, Susan Cashen soon found her way to the Patriot camp. Her account of what she observed there illustrates the paternalistic lens through which she viewed her slaves, forty of whom were prisoners, as was their master. "My Negros," she wrote, "were delighted to see me, with the thought that I had come to take them home." She lamented that the slaves could not even give "there Master" a glass of water. "The children," Mrs. Cashen recollected, "continued there [*sic*] cries to come to me, I determined at all events to go & speak to them, as soon as I got in reach of them they clang to me."[24] In Susan Cashen's eyes, she was the beloved mistress of her black "family."

At the same time, Mrs. Cashen's narrative shows that she realized how dearly her bond persons valued their families, for they probably were on the verge of being separated and sold in the United States. She exhibited a special concern for Jenny, a teenaged biracial slave whom she had trained as a seamstress. Jenny seems to have feared her mistress. On one occasion, while "climbing to gather grapes," she fell, dislocating her hip. Until the pain became unbearable, she concealed the mishap from Mrs. Cashen. By the time a physician could be summoned, Jenny had been crippled with a permanent limp. Moreover, Cashen had disrupted Jenny's family life. The young seamstress slept in the great house "in the hall or some other part of the house" with a black girl named June. The night of Cone's raid, Jenny and June likely were reposing in or near the guestroom so that they might wait upon the two white female visitors. Cone's men had captured Jenny's mother prior to entering the Cashen house. Susan Cashen remembered that the mother was so "unwilling to be torn from her child" that she directed the Patriots to Jenny.[25]

James Cashen died in 1823, not long after the United States took control of Florida. For the next two decades, his widow fought to obtain compensation from Washington for the damages that its troops had inflicted during the disorders that rocked East Florida between 1812 and 1819. Susan Cashen also strove to reclaim Lydia, a housekeeper born in a northern state whom the Cashens had purchased in Georgia prior to moving to Amelia Island. When Lydia was the aforementioned Jenny's age, she ran away to the Seminoles. By 1834, she was an old woman who had borne nine children. Now, her former mistress wanted to uproot her and her offspring.[26] Doubtlessly, Susan Cashen justified her actions because she considered Lydia her property. Perhaps she also told herself that she was rescuing the black woman from "savages." Deep in her heart, however, she knew better.

By 1841, Susan was so impoverished that she saw herself forced to rent a house in St. Augustine, near the military barracks. At this time, David L. Yulee became her benefactor and "best friend." Her family in Pennsylvania had deserted her, apparently because they disapproved of one of her marriages subsequent to James Cashen's death.[27] Yulee, a man of influence who soon would become one of the new state of Florida's two senators, may have seen himself as a knight in shining armor, although there certainly were many other St. Augustine widows in distress. As a well-connected politician, Yulee was in the position to have been privy to "inside information" emanating from the nation's capital. Consequently, he may well have known that Susan's situation was about to improve, which, if his intentions were less than pure, would have moved him to maneuver into a situation whereby he could profit.

In late 1841, the US Treasury awarded $5,168 to the woman now known as Susan Murphy, in compensation for damages that she and James Cashen had suffered during the chaotic years of the Patriot War and its aftermath. Three years later, more than $20,000 followed. Another $6,900 came her way in 1846. At this time, she likely purchased at least five slaves, including Belinda and Peter. Her windfall attracted a suitor named Van Hautscher, a man some sixty years her junior. She married him, surely against Yulee's advice. Her new husband soon absconded with much of her fortune. After she divorced the scoundrel, Yulee continued to stand by her. Again, his motives may have been altruistic, but he also stood to gain from his relationship with the lonely, vulnerable, and abandoned divorcee. Murphy still owned a house and five adult slaves, along with land on Amelia Island. Furthermore, she was very elderly.[28]

Susan Murphy thought about all of these events as she suffered through her last months on earth. When she composed her will on 14 March 1855, she left the bulk of her estate to Yulee, while appointing him her sole executor. George R. Fairbanks, Dr. John Peck, and their crony, Judge William A. Forward, witnessed this document. Murphy obviously considered Yulee her guardian angel. She also rewarded her enslaved nurse Belinda's "faithful attentions." Despite the fact that Belinda legally was her property, the dying woman, as the local free man of color Robert Brown had predicted some thirty years earlier, was not free to follow unreservedly the Spanish era practice of testamentary manumission. Therefore, Murphy declared that should Florida not permit Belinda's emancipation, the bondswoman was to go to "any other State she may prefer to live in." Because the woman of color was in her fifties, her working years were coming to an end. In addition, she would have to abandon her family and friends.[29]

As the elderly widow passed in and out of her stupors, more people who had befriended her came to mind. They too, Murphy decided six months after signing her previous will, should be rewarded. Accordingly, in a codicil, she allocated $800 to educate her godson, Oregon Dunham. Her pastor, Father Edmond Aubril, received $100. Friends Mary Strichska and a Mrs. Huertas, respectively, were bequeathed $50 and a portrait. Belinda also benefitted from her mistress's deeper reflections. Fearful that Florida would keep the nurse in bondage, Murphy directed Yulee to "give her her time, at her own disposal," in addition to $200. Belinda, then, was to join the ranks of the quasi-free. Fairbanks and Peck once again served as witnesses, along with the physician F. M. Weems.[30]

A third physician, P. B. Mauran, was a source of concern for Yulee and friends. Dr. Mauran attended Murphy daily for over a year. His bill amounted to nearly $800. Viewing Mauran as an "adventurer" bent on bilking a helpless old widow, the Yulee clique drew up a trust deed, whereby Murphy signed over all of her property to Fairbanks as her trustee. Dr. Peck executed the documentation and read it to his patient "article by article." Yulee was to ensure that all of Murphy's debts were paid. He also was to provide her with a stipend of $60 per month for the rest of a life that promised to be short.[31] In this manner, Yulee and company could protect their future cuts of the Murphy estate.

On 4 June 1856, this careful plan unraveled. Murphy's former feistiness had returned, causing her to experience a change of heart. She told Dr. Mauran that she never had intended to convey all of her property to Fairbanks. Consequently, she defiantly drew up another will, which was witnessed by a group of neighbors. In this document, the ailing, aged woman divided her estate between her estranged blood relatives in Pennsylvania and Belinda, who saw her legacy increased to $500. Furthermore, Mauran informed Murphy's relatives that she also owned a plantation in Cuba, which he had visited. This revelation meant that her estate would be worth $100,000. Then, at 2:00 p.m., on 16 June 1856, Susan Murphy died, leaving a furor in her wake.[32]

In Fairbanks's words, the "Murphy matter" became "disagreeable." The outraged Yulee faction claimed that Mauran had duped a "totally incapacitated" Murphy, whose "mind and memory was much impaired" during her last three weeks of life. They further argued that Mauran could not have accomplished his sordid deed without the assistance of Belinda, who was "ever at her mistress' elbow," and who exerted "an increasing influence upon one of whom liberality was not a distinguishing trait." Voicing an opinion with which Peck concurred, Fairbanks pointedly added that Belinda was "a mulatto woman—belonging to a class proverbially exhibiting the worst attributes of the white and colored race." St. Augustine's white elite, ironically, counted among their clients many free persons of color. In fact, it was they who had sired numerous members of this group that they so despised.[33]

Before the case of Susan Murphy's contested will went to court, Yulee and friends were forced to put out another fire. Daniel Kerr, Murphy's nephew, was inquiring about his inheritance. "Perhaps," Fairbanks advised Yulee, "we had better quit claim [the Cuban plantation] to [Kerr] & the cousins by right of discovery." Kerr's share of the Murphy estate ended up being $2,000. The St. Johns County Circuit Court ruled in Yulee's favor, and Florida's Supreme Court affirmed the decision. Yulee, then, made a killing from his kindness to the unfortunate Murphy. He also saw to it that Dr. Peck received 1,080 acres of Murphy's land in Marion County, Florida, as payment for the latter's medical charges against the estate. As of 1861, on the other hand, the deceased widow's godson still had not received the money that had been set aside for his education. The slave Belinda never enjoyed much freedom. She died about a year after her mistress. In Fairbanks's words, the biracial nurse "followed her mistress to another world." As for the bondsman Peter, who had been whipped at Dr. Mauran's insistence for insolence, Yulee decided to relocate him to Amelia Island. There he worked with another Murphy slave, Anson, who may have participated in the spectacular escape of Andrew Gué and seven comrades from St. Augustine to Nassau in 1843. Peter had striven to protect his family's integrity by taking an active role in the Catholic Church. Years after the Civil War, he angrily recalled his forced separation from his loved ones.[34]

Things had changed for the worse for people of color since Spanish rule, even though, as Susan Cashen's life on Amelia Island demonstrates, the era had featured plantation agriculture that caused constant misery for the slaves who sustained it. Clearly, by the late antebellum period, the black family did not enjoy much respect, whereas under the Spaniards, even slave unions had been protected.[35] Prominent white men who had proven themselves quick to serve as the vaunted patrons of Afro-St. Johns Countians, revealed their disdain for biracial people, along with their disrespect for the basic human rights of the enslaved. And, if white community leaders viewed their mixed-race clients as debased mongrels, they certainly did not hold other free blacks in high regard.

In addition, the government no longer favored the practice of manumission. Racial prejudice, combined with the end of the Seminole Wars, demographic shifts, and geopolitical changes meant that men of color no longer played a critical role in East Florida's security. Instead, those in power now perceived them as potential security threats. Thus, free blacks found themselves deprived of the opportunity for military service, a key route to social prestige and landownership. Regarding the latter, the Susan Murphy case demonstrates how exposed black-owned land was to the cupidity of the well-connected. That is, even an affluent, assertive, white woman's property might fall prone to greed-based machinations, because either the Yulee clique, or their courtroom opponents, were attempting to profit from an elderly widow's death throes.

In her magisterial study of black East Floridians under Spanish rule, Jane Landers suggested that the relatively widespread ownership of real property by people of color would not long survive the advent of American rule in 1821. The Americans, Landers maintained, were bent on the destruction of the region's "intermediate free black class" and soon successfully "pressured many free blacks into selling what remained of their property at rock-bottom prices." Despite a valiant effort to "retain some of their customary privileges," she concluded, landowning blacks were swamped by the racist "tide . . . against them."[36] As we will see, such an outcome was not foreordained, nor did it proceed at a steady downward pace from the inception of US rule. The 1820s, in fact, which will be discussed in the following chapter, demonstrate that many of St. Johns County's free blacks would not have held such a negative assessment of their futures.[37]

2

The 1820s: Anxious Optimism

At least 145 of the Spanish monarch's free black subjects sailed away from St. Augustine to Cuba between 1821 and 1827.[1] They saw the American regime's advent as an impending disaster. Those who opted to remain harbored strong attachments to their land, along with a remarkable faith that they could prosper under US rule, despite the fact that Washington long had regarded the region's free people of African descent as a national security threat. In fact, many of these optimists either had fled from Anglo-American plantations or descended from those who had. Others were the offspring of white patriarchs whom they believed could protect their interests under a treaty of cession that promised them citizenship rights. As we have seen, Spanish East Florida had been far from a racial utopia and some free blacks who stayed may have harbored resentments against the outgoing government. Moreover, the Minorcans also refused to emigrate. Their post-1821 presence constituted a reservoir of Spanish culture that might protect free black interests. This chapter explores the soundness of the choice that a minority of free Afro-East Floridians made to anxiously embrace the new regime.

Free blacks and their white allies braced themselves for an American assault on manumission. Therefore, they made sure that their papers were in order. A month before the transfer of power, St. Augustine mayor Gabriel W. Perpall certified that Nancy, a black woman, had been free since the period of British rule, which had ended in 1783, and that her six children and their children had inherited this liberty. Polly Bowlegs, whose Seminole husband had emancipated her, felt "apprehensive" because of the "late change of Government in Florida" under which "new usages and customs" were "daily gaining ground." Fearing that the "liberty of herself or children may be either jeopardized or called into question," Polly had two white men petition the St. Johns County probate judge in 1821 for official freedom documentation.

The judge granted the request, barring "all persons from molesting or taking possession" of them "under the pretext of their being slaves or under any claim of property on them."[2]

Polly's concern proved well-founded, for during the early years of American rule, blacks who enjoyed freedom among the Seminoles were in danger of enslavement. The circumstances surrounding this peril could be complex. In 1825, for instance, Mary Hanny, a destitute widow with dependent children, offered $300 to any person who would "further the cause of humanity" by retrieving the black Sarah and her progeny from the Indians. Hanny's mother had purchased Sarah for her sometime before 1800, but despite the "deed of gift" proving her ownership, Hanny's father and stepmother sold the slave to the Seminoles. Twenty-five years after that illicit sale, the desperate Hanny pleaded for Sarah's return after hearing that she was alive and now had four children.[3]

Moreover, unscrupulous whites challenged Spanish legal documents. In 1807, the prosperous Connecticut-born planter Ambrose Hull had emancipated his mulatto slave Patience and her children in his will, leaving them a legacy of $200. Five whites had witnessed Hull's will, and George J. F. Clarke recorded it in St. Johns County in 1823. Despite this, the attorney John Rodman had Patience and her daughter Ellen seized by the authorities in 1825, claiming that they were slaves. Clarke, as an agent of Hull's executor, rushed to their defense, forcing Rodman to release them. Two years later when Ellen bore a white man's daughter, she had the infant baptized in the Catholic faith, an act that, in addition to its spiritual benefits, created another permanent record of the baby's freedom.[4] Surely such incidents frightened free blacks. On the other hand, they witnessed the American justice system working in their favor, as well as local whites hastening to assist them.

Those who had achieved their liberty (and that of their descendants) under Spain's religious sanctuary policy, also faced challenges. Lured by Spanish promises, Thomas Primus, his wife, and three children escaped to East Florida from Lucia Braddock Fitzgerald's Georgia plantation. Subsequently, the Spaniards granted them freedom. When the Fitzgerald family later moved to Amelia Island and became Spanish subjects, they encountered the Primuses. Because the Crown had shifted its diplomatic stance and now disavowed the sanctuary policy, the Fitzgeralds petitioned provincial authorities to restore the family to them. Governor Enrique White ruled against them on the grounds that the sanctuary policy had been in effect when the Primuses had reached Florida.[5]

Tony Primus was born free in St. Augustine in 1791. In 1812, when the

Patriot War commenced, he was supporting his mother and siblings by farming and wage labor. George J. F. Clarke was one of his patrons. During the conflict, the Patriots destroyed Primus's modest property and threatened him with enslavement. Primus responded by joining Prince Witten's free black militia unit. He also had inherited a fifty-acre tract that Governor White had granted to his father in 1806. In June of 1825, as "a free colored man," Primus sold this land to another free black, William Hodgeson, and a year earlier, again as a "Freeman of colour," Primus had testified in court on behalf of the sons of the aforementioned black woman Nancy.[6]

Regardless, Waters Smith, the US marshal in St. Augustine, arrested Tony Primus in 1825, inflicting painful injuries on him during the course of the arrest and confining him in a squalid jail cell. Marshal Smith acted under a writ empowering him to confiscate $700 worth of John Davy Braddock's property. Braddock was a member of the Fitzgerald clan. On the basis of the far-fetched claim that Primus was Braddock's "reputed slave and property," Smith confiscated the black man.[7]

The financially strapped Braddocks hoped the American court would overturn the earlier Spanish ruling that the Primuses were free. After hearing the case, Judge Joseph L. Smith instructed jurors that if they were convinced that a sanctuary policy had existed under the Spaniards, and that Primus's parents had been declared free under that policy, and that Tony Primus was therefore born to free parents, then they must find him free. The jury did just that, only to have Marshal Smith appeal the decision, dragging the matter out until 1829, when six whites, including George J. F. Clarke, again testified on Primus's behalf. More than thirty years after Thomas Primus had liberated his family, the US courts definitively confirmed Tony Primus's freedom.[8]

In addition to worrying about whether or not the US regime would acknowledge the liberty that they had attained under the Spaniards, Afro-East Floridians nervously hoped that the Americans would continue Spanish-era emancipation practices. The historian Frederick P. Bowser delineated three ways by which slaves in Spain's American colonies attained their liberty. Masters manumitted, usually unconditionally, their own biracial offspring and their mothers. They also emancipated slaves during their lifetimes or in their wills in recognition of years of devotion or the fulfillment of certain conditions. Slave owners also permitted bond persons to be manumitted in exchange for money.[9] All of these paths to liberty remained viable during the 1820s.

Still, even the white patriarchs of biracial families took no chances. Don

Francisco Richard, for example, had freed his enslaved mistress Eve and their mulatto son Fernando in 1809, but recorded the emancipation only in 1821, when he also registered Eve's six other biracial children, born between 1811 and 1821. George J. F. Clarke had been similarly negligent. When he manumitted his common-law wife Flora in 1797, he had left James, their infant son, off the deed. In 1821, Clarke rectified this potentially dangerous omission. James Erwin, Zephaniah Kingsley, James Darley, and James Ormond also manumitted consorts of color and biracial children within the ensuing nine years, recording their liberty in St. Johns County's deed books.[10]

Spanish colonial culture commonly linked manumission with baptism. In Cuba, for instance, infant slaves often escaped bondage for a standard fee of $25. Toward this end, enslaved mothers sought godparents who they believed might be moved to free their newborns. Willing godparents gained spiritual rewards, along with earthly prestige. The influence of this custom in East Florida is evident in the 1821 baptism of José Pablo Juan Dupon, the son of Clarisa (whose owner was Don Pablo Dupon), and an "unknown" white man, evidently Francis Román Sánchez, a white son of Francisco Xavier Sánchez. The infant bore Dupon's name, as well as that of his godfather, Don Juan González, whose wife was the child's godmother. Clarisa, who was herself of partly white ancestry, thus had attached herself sacramentally to prominent whites who might protect her son's freedom, which, as it turned out, already had been effected shortly after his birth. In December 1820, Dupon had agreed to Sánchez's purchase of the baby on condition that he emancipate him. Sánchez waited until July 1821 to have his biracial son baptized, only days before the American takeover. More than a year later, in December 1822, still apprehensive about how the new administration might view the child's status, he certified before county officials that the boy had been manumitted.[11]

Another variant of the Cuban practice is evident in the case of July, a black Charleston native who John Forrester owned in 1803. July fathered a daughter by Elsy, the black slave of John Leslie, Forrester's business partner. Before the child's birth, Forrester, at his slave's request, struck a bargain with Leslie to bring about the infant's emancipation in exchange for a payment of $50. July then furnished this sum to Forrester, who presumably forwarded it to Leslie. As a result, his daughter Felicia was born free. July turned over his receipt from Forrester to George J. F. Clarke. Several years later, Clarke returned the receipt to July, but by late 1829, it had disappeared. Felicia feared that without the receipt, she might end up enslaved. She prevailed on Clarke to explain her situation under oath to Justice of the Peace Squire Streeter. Felicia's baptismal record served as corroborating evidence.[12]

Several East Floridians manumitted their bond persons by their last wishes during the 1820s. Pompy, the black slave of Chief Payne, a Seminole, purchased Polly, also black, in 1811. On 17 March 1822, Pompy devised his will, which freed Polly upon his death, and transferred his property to her. Later in the same year, Abraham Hudson, a free man of color, honored his wife's last request by liberating Peggy, age fourteen, whom he described as his "blood relative." Likewise, the seven heirs of María Mabrity de Burgos recalled that prior to her passing, she had expressed the desire to emancipate her "faithful servant," the forty year-old Mary. The heirs complied with her instructions in 1824. A year later, Isaac Wickes's executors, as instructed by his will, freed two of his slaves, and gave them $25 each.[13] In short, the American authorities cooperated with deceased slave holders' executors and white patrons of people of color to release favored bond persons.

Jane Landers found that under the Spaniards, East Florida masters rarely freed slaves without monetary compensation. This pattern continued during the 1820s, for the vast majority of the emancipations recorded in St. Johns County's deed books involved cash exchanges. The prices that owners required varied according to the skills, gender, and ages of the slaves, as well as their own generosity and financial needs. Thus, although Isaac Wickes's will stipulated that two of his slaves were to be freed gratis and given small inheritances, his bondsman Boatswain had to pay the Wickes estate $400 for his liberty. William H. Williams manumitted the "coloured man" James Baird for $100 less. Gerónimo Álvarez charged almost as much, $250, to set nine-year-old Juana free. Gerónima Martinelly released Lydia for $100 and Dominga López did the same after the black William Marshall gave her $80 for his son, the child William. On the other hand, the biracial carpenter Harry, a man in his midtwenties, paid Silvester Silva $1,000 for his freedom. People of color as well as whites followed the practice of trading freedom for money during the 1820s. Felipe Edimboro, for example, charged his bondswoman Hannah $350 for her liberty.[14]

Some slaves, prior to and after securing their own freedom, used their funds to purchase loved ones. In 1821, five months before Spain turned East Florida over to the United States, Valentine Pepino offered 275 pesos for his child María Luísa. Pepino was buying his own liberty in installments as a *coartado* at the time and completed his manumission payments four months later. A deed drawn up in 1823 certified that Pepino had paid $475 for another daughter. The next year, as previously mentioned, María Mabrity de Burgos's heirs freed Mary, Pepino's wife. Three years later, Pepino paid $100 for the freedom of a black infant named Tony.[15] All of these transactions took place with the cooperation of white witnesses, agents, attorneys, and executors.

During the initial years of US rule, then, East Floridians of color noticed how Hispanic customs, combined with American justice, worked in their favor. White patrons ensured that the complex records of *coartación* were recorded in St. Johns County's records. On 18 December 1823, George J. F. Clarke entered into the deed books how Peter Seville had gained his freedom. In late 1814, Seville had turned over $100 to William Laurence in partial payment for his liberty. Two months later, in 1815, John Peterson, a free man of color, gave an additional $150 to John Forbes, thus completing Seville's manumission. Another example of *coartación* took place four months before the change of flags. Mrs. Abby Dexter purchased Beck from Sitarky, a Seminole chief's nephew. At the time of this purchase, Dexter's husband and Sitarky agreed that when Beck repaid her price of $300, which she could achieve by working for the Dexter family for seven dollars per month, she would be manumitted. Some three and a half years later, Beck had accumulated this sum. Seetake, probably a variant spelling of Sitarky, made a similar arrangement with the "Blackman" Nero. The Seminole, on 10 March 1822, stated that he was freeing Nero under the condition that Nero pay him, "from time to time" in such amounts that Seetake wanted or needed, a sum of $200. Although Nero was conditionally free in 1822, his final emancipation only took place in 1824.[16] During the interim, then, Nero was a quasi-free man.

The quasi-free status of *coartados* confused some white officials. Prior to the 1821 cession, Sarah Petty struck a bargain with her slave Cyrus, whom she owned apart from her husband, George Petty. She agreed to rent Cyrus to Horatio S. Dexter for $13 per month until he earned $200, at which point she would manumit him. Cyrus apparently leveraged this arrangement himself, taking advantage of the fact that George Petty owed $200 to a Mrs. Falk. Petty wanted Dexter in effect to pay Falk for Cyrus's toil because Petty himself could not coax Cyrus to labor efficiently. "Cyrus does not seem willing to go to work," Petty wrote, attesting to the slave's agency in Petty's arrangement with Dexter. Do not, he warned Dexter, "acquaint Cyrus that I have wrote to you respecting him."[17]

Subsequently, Dexter listed Cyrus as his slave in an inventory of his Volusia plantation, perhaps to increase the value of his holdings for credit purposes.

Then, probably to protect Cyrus from being seized by a creditor, Dexter executed a manumission deed for him in late 1825, stating that the black man had paid him $400. The following year, however, a judge issued a writ of attachment against Dexter in a creditor's favor, whereupon Marshal Waters Smith arrested Cyrus, and held him until he obtained a bond from two white patrons, George J. F. Clarke and Joseph M. Sánchez.[18]

In late 1827, Cyrus's situation deteriorated, for Marshal Smith demanded that Clarke and Sánchez deliver Cyrus to be sold. Clarke refused, insisting that Cyrus had been Mrs. Petty's slave, not Dexter's, and that Cyrus had paid her $200 for his liberty. Clarke delayed the case for a time, but a jury eventually ruled against Dexter and an appeal against the ruling failed. Because Sánchez had died by this time, Clarke must have forfeited the bond and in the process acquired Cyrus, because in 1835, the latter paid Clarke the final $5 of his $400 self-purchase price, a sum that perhaps recovered the cost of the forfeited bond. Still, Cyrus received no freedom papers from Clarke, and in 1848, long after the latter's death, the question of Cyrus's status arose again. This time, Clarke's executor, John M. Fontané, formally manumitted him. The 1860 census lists Cyrus Forrester as an eighty-four-year-old farmer living across the St. Johns River in Clay County, owning real and personal property worth $2,400.[19]

The intricacies of Cyrus Forrester's case may be linked to George and Sarah Petty's manumission, in January 1822, of a man listed in the record as Simon Forrester and described as a black man around forty years of age. By his "industry," Simon had earned his freedom price of $450. Twenty years later, however, in legal testimony on behalf of George J. F. Clarke's biracial heirs, Simon Forrester swore that he had purchased himself from John Forrester prior to 1816. The discrepancy in dates may have been due to a *coartación* arrangement under which Simon Forrester had commenced his freedom payments in 1816 or earlier and completed them in 1822. Simon Forrester may have paid John Forrester $250 before coming into Mrs. Petty's possession, and the 1822 manumission may have been conditional upon final payment of an agreed-on purchase price by working for Dexter. In the cases of Cyrus and Simon Forrester, two white men, Dexter and Clarke, had acted honorably to prevent a gross injustice.[20]

Some of the quasi-free acted audaciously. In early 1826, Jack Forrester, who belonged to George J. F. Clarke, stole a boat and made his way to a plantation near St. Mary's, Georgia, where he carried off Maria, her six children, and four other slaves. The owner soon recovered all but one of them, a nineteen-year-old African named Tom Sterret, who he assumed had accompanied Forrester back into Florida. The master described Forrester as passing for a free man, but Clarke did not manumit him until 1828, when Forrester paid him $400. Evidently, Forrester's bold escapade, which calls to mind Spain's former sanctuary policy, did no harm to his own freedom arrangements. What became of Sterret is unknown. After Forrester's manumission, he lived with Fanny, whom he had purchased a short time before. It is likely that he had bought Fanny and himself by making incremental payments.[21]

Free people of color living in St. Johns County during the transitional 1820s, besides their concerns regarding manumission, also worried about their land holdings. Landers documented Spanish grants totaling 5,940 acres to thirty-three blacks between 1784 and 1821. After 1821, American officials validated titles to 3,695 of these acres in the names of fifteen persons of color. They also confirmed substantial acreage to the white fathers or husbands of free blacks. Felicia Garvin received title to three thousand acres at Youngblood Hammock and along the Indian River that had been owned by her deceased white spouse. Federal officials also awarded five hundred acres to Mrs. Garvin's mother, Flora Leslie. The biracial heirs of Job Wiggins, who were, like Garvin, members of the extended Clarke family, received title to 1,200 acres at Rollestown.[22]

The white patriarchs of the biracial Clarke family, George J. F. Clarke and Charles W. Clarke, had been among the founders and leading citizens of the settlement of Fernandina during the boom years prior to the Patriot War and had relocated their families there in 1808. Eight years later, persons of color owned forty-four lots in Fernandina. Some they sold before the American takeover. After the cession, federal land commissioners rejected the claims of thirty black petitioners to Fernandina lots on the grounds that they lacked "any evidence of title." The Spaniards customarily had permitted such lot holders to keep their titles in their personal possession, so it is easy to understand how they could have been destroyed during the violence that plagued Amelia Island during the final decade of Spanish rule. Moreover, it is important to note that blacks alone had not suffered the pain of seeing their land titles denied. Joseph Simeon Sánchez, a white son of Francisco Xavier Sánchez, lost six parcels in Fernandina because he too had no written proof of ownership.[23]

Federal authorities followed due process when they considered real estate claims of people of color. The wording of these claims suggests that free blacks considered themselves citizens of the United States and therefore entitled to the use of its administrative and judicial agencies. In his successful petition for title to 210 acres fronting the Hillsborough River, Joseph Sánchez called himself a "citizen of the United States and resident of East Florida," as did Felipe Edimboro, whose petition also was granted. In a document that he submitted for a biracial nephew, however, George J. F. Clarke was more cautious, crossing out "citizen" on the form and substituting "native" of "E. Florida" for it. Despite this caution, this claim was denied. Historian Charlton W. Tebeau concluded that the United States, in general, "dealt reasonably with claimants, many of whose documents were fraudulent as to origin, location, and extent."[24]

During the 1820s, as in Spanish times, free people of color continued to buy and sell land. Joseph Sánchez had purchased a St. Augustine marsh lot containing a little over seven acres in 1810. A decade or so later, he sold it for $600 to a Charleston man. Also in 1821, Sánchez parted with another city lot in exchange for $400 from his white kinsman, Francisco P. Sánchez. The biracial Sánchez was not pessimistically dumping tracts because he feared that the Americans aimed to strip him of his real estate. Instead, he bought his deceased father's Capuaca plantation from his white half-brother, Joseph Simeon Sánchez, for $2,000. He then acquired property in town for $700 from María Puello.[25]

As under the Spaniards, the taint of illegitimacy permitted some whites to quash the dreams of Afro-East Floridians to inherit land. In Spanish times, Jesse Fish Jr. lived with his black common-law wife Clarissa and their seven children on the ten thousand acres that he owned on Anastasia Island, across Matanzas Bay from St. Augustine. Fish's property included an "ancient and venerable" manor house as well as "El Vergel," an expansive citrus plantation that his father had cultivated as early as 1763. One visitor who passed a night in the manor house recounted that he was "very politely entertained by two handsome young ladies (mulattoes)." Tragically, in 1812, lightning struck Fish. His sudden death and lack of a will meant that Clarissa and her children did not inherit his estate, which passed instead to his nearest legally recognized relative, a white niece.[26]

This situation was partially ameliorated under the Americans. Fish's mother, Sarah Warner Fish, in 1823, deeded five hundred acres that her son had owned in Graham's Swamp, on the Matanzas River, to a "certain black woman named Clarissa now free, formerly servant to my son Jesse Fish and commonly called Clarissa Fish," and to Clarissa's "seven coloured children," who in actuality were her grandchildren. In 1825, one of Sarah Fish's relatives, Gabriel W. Perpall, sold a town house to Clarissa Fish for $500. She, in turn, conveyed her Matanzas tract to John Perpall for $1,000.[27]

James Darley, perhaps with the example of Jesse Fish in mind, meticulously planned for the economic security of his black enslaved consort and his biracial children. In early 1829, Darley emancipated Maria and her offspring. Shortly thereafter, he made a will bequeathing most of his estate to them. The estate included fifteen slaves, who were to be hired out to support Maria's family. The heirs of color also were free to cultivate as much of Darley's Tomoka plantation as they wished. Within six months of his death, his executors were to construct a comfortable dwelling for Maria inside the fence surrounding his existing home. He also willed furniture, bedding, cooking utensils, and a weekly allotment of corn to her. Darley's sister in England was to inherit the remainder of his property.[28]

Other people of color acquired land from whites or blacks who were not family members. William Hodgeson, "a free coloured man," bought fifty acres from Tony Primus for $25 in 1825. The previous year, the biracial William Wanton had purchased a hundred acres from the Havana-based company, Arredondo & Son. Toward the end of the decade, Tabb Smith, who was of African descent, traded his rural tract west of St. Augustine to John Drysdale in exchange for the latter's urban orange grove.[29] The point is, that the dawn of US rule did not automatically end free blacks' aspirations for landownership in St. Johns County, nor did the regime change result in the confiscation of their acreage or end the possibility that they could expand or acquire real estate.

The optimism of free people of color manifested itself in the businesses that they established on the real estate that they owned in St. Augustine. When William Garvin, Felicia Clarke's white husband, died in 1823, George J. F. Clarke purchased $400 to $700 of goods from New York so that his widowed daughter could establish a store at her residence. The elder Clarke's sons, George and James, were "keeping a tailor shop" in 1826. Sprig Mosby, born a slave in Virginia, was a free man and a landowner in St. Augustine who maintained close ties to the extended Clarke family. In 1825, Mosby, along with John Fish, the mulatto son of the deceased white citrus grower Jesse Fish, operated the Laffeyete Coffee House, where patrons played cards and billiards, ate, and drank coffee or spirits. The name of the tavern reflected their patriotic identification with the American republic and cleverly exploited public sentiment, for a grateful Congress had just granted the Marquis de Lafayette a huge tract in Florida, where the popular Revolutionary War hero planned to establish a "slave-free utopian community." Mosby and Fish thus had chosen a name whose appeal crossed racial lines. Indeed, the tavern's clientele included whites as well as blacks.[30]

Although the Laffeyete Coffee House proved to be a popular place of diversion, the black proprietors soon had trouble collecting from their customers, which in turn, led to problems with their suppliers. To prevent their principal creditor from taking over one of his properties, Mosby conveyed his Marine Street lot to fellow black businessman Tabb Smith. Smith immediately mortgaged the lot to Mosby, who transferred the mortgage to his wife in trust. The scheme failed, however, for the creditor, the white Dirk Fleischman, successfully sued Mosby and Fish for $185.95, obtaining a writ of attachment against their real property, which included the Marine Street lot and the home on St. Francis Street in which Fish and his family lived. Fish sold the personal property he had available, including a cow and a bull, for cash to make payment on the "judgement rendered against him."[31]

The legal battles between Mosby and Fish and Fleischman were acrimonious and long. The latter accused the two black proprietors of "secreting and disposing" of their real property to avoid their debt payments, and they in turn claimed that he owed them $400. The outcome of the litigation is unclear, but the dispute commenced a downward spiral in the fortunes of the two free black entrepreneurs. Both men were listed on the tax rolls as delinquents in 1826. Fish thereafter faded from the historical record, an indication of his death or migration. Mosby evidently never again owned taxable property and was unable to pay his assessments for being a free man of color between 1829 and 1835.[32] Still, as in Spanish times, free men of color could sue and be sued in a court of law. Moreover, as players in the American marketplace, they were subject to the risks that whites also faced.

Discriminatory taxation policies, however, threatened both black land holdings and small businesses. These taxes also revealed the American intention of barring men of color from military service. Taxation stirred episodes of heated controversy among all St. Augustinians throughout much of the antebellum period. In 1826, the local *East Florida Herald* attributed the origin of this spirited and persistent debate to the change of flags. Under the Spaniards, the newspaper explained, "no regular[?] system of taxation was adopted either for this city or any part of the country. Hence the strong repugnance of the old inhabitants to any sort of taxes." As the 1820s drew to a close, the conflict over taxes intensified. In December 1829, the "Grand Jury for the Eastern District of Florida" called the Legislative Council's "highly unconstitutional, impolitic, and oppressive" territorial levy a "grievance" that "cannot be tolerated in this free country."[33]

Under the Spanish crown, free blacks frequently had petitioned the provincial authorities for redress. The treaty of cession, as mentioned earlier, promised all former free subjects of Spain the rights of US citizenship. These legacies, in addition to the rhetoric of white tax protest, encouraged the bucking of racist statutes in the name of the republican principles that East Florida's new rulers espoused. Indeed, St. Johns County's free people of color and their white allies were quick to paint their efforts to preserve the most beneficial aspects of Iberian culture with the brush strokes of the incoming regime's ideology.

The Americans, from the inception of their rule in 1821, gave black Floridians plenty of reasons to utilize this strategy. They quickly barred free colored men from voting, jury duty, militia service, and public office.[34] These prohibitions set the stage for taxation policies that aimed to reinforce the racial marginalization process. Because of the ambience of tax resistance that pervaded St. Johns County, however, blacks there perceived an opening through which they could strike a blow against their oppressors. Sympathetic whites would assist them in their battle.

When the county government, in 1824, charged a discriminatory tax of $5 on free blacks, Robert "Brown Bob" Brown vented his anger to the *East Florida Herald,* which agreed to give him a public hearing. His origins are obscure. Brown identified himself as a biracial family man and landowner native to East Florida. He may have been related to Isabel Felicia Brown, a black whom Isaac Wickes manumitted at the end of 1818. Approximately four years earlier, she had borne a mixed-race daughter to the free biracial Antonio Rivas, who purchased the girl from Wickes for 200 pesos in 1821. Another relative of Robert Brown's may have been George Vanness. Born in St. Augustine as Wickes's slave sometime around 1810, Vanness began life as George Rivers, possibly a corruption of the Spanish "Rivas." His surname seems to indicate that his father was free. He eventually became the property of Nehemiah Brush, who permitted him and his wife to live quasi-free lives as custodians of orange groves across the river from the St. Johns River port of Palatka. Robert Brown later would sell land to Brush, which hints at some connection to Isabel Felicia Brown and Antonio Rivas.[35]

In his 1824 letter to the *Herald,* Robert Brown, citing the treaty of cession, claimed US citizenship. He complained that in addition to a St. Johns County poll tax of $5, he had to pay another $3 to the city of St. Augustine. Whites, on the other hand, only owed a poll tax of $1 to the county and nothing to the city. Moreover, whereas free blacks saw themselves obligated to pay their county and city poll taxes at the ages of fifteen and eighteen, respectively, whites did not pay their minimal sum until they were twenty-one. Brown also attacked the sophistry that the authorities proffered to justify their racist levies. Free men of color, they argued, did not serve as jurors, public officials, or militiamen. Therefore, they enjoyed more freedom than whites and should compensate the government in order to do their fair share for the community. Brown maintained that free blacks should not have to pay for being deemed incapable of performing the duties of citizenship. He pointed out that because of their humiliating "degradation," it was impossible for them to enjoy trials by juries of their peers, or the monetary and honorific rewards accruing to "civil and military offices."[36]

The free man of color summarized his objections by employing republican principles. He categorized the local levies as "unequal taxations" and therefore "unconstitutional, as the wise framers of that grand National Charter . . . made no difference in persons and person's colors." In order to reinforce his points, Brown raised the Revolutionary-era specter of a surreptitious government plot against liberty. Georgia's discriminatory poll taxes, he explained, had led to racist legislation that became so onerous that whites' property rights eroded, since the state eventually forbade them to manumit their own bondsmen. "[O]ne evil begets many," Brown wrote, and in the entire world, he added, "there will not be found another spot where the slave holder cannot on any terms emancipate his slave."[37]

Two weeks after it published Brown's letter, the *Herald* reported that the local federal court had agreed to consider the constitutionality of the county government's race-based poll tax. Editor E. B. Gould noted that the upcoming case, "must, from the nature of it, be very interesting." Gould mentioned other "irregularities" in county assessments and recommended that under the circumstances, "it is better that the Taxes should not be collected, than that the officer, whose duty it is to make the collection, should be involved in difficulty." In court, James F. Clarke, a biracial son of George J. F. Clarke, who had married a white woman, Mary Dulcet, spearheaded the resistance. His efforts resulted in a victory, as US Judge Joseph L. Smith ruled that a "discriminatory tax was unconstitutional." Municipal ordinances suggest that the $3 poll tax likewise was repealed.[38]

The *Herald* may have been referring to the latter event when, on 26 July

1825, it informed its readers that, "at the last Legislature, the City charter was repealed, and with it fell all the laws of blood that had previously disgraced our city statute book, and we hope that they will not be renewed." In the same issue, Gould reprimanded the city marshal for what he characterized as illegal actions in relation to a curfew on free blacks' movements. The editor wrote that "many of a different complexion have been more offensive to the slumbering citizen, and committed greater outrages upon the laws of society in their nightly peregrinations than the colored population of our city has done, or will ever do." He pointedly advised the marshal to "ask the advice of counsel before he carry his operations much farther." Gould also expressed his hope that the "City Council, instead of adding to the weight of our evils, will afford that protection which humanity gives all a right to ask for." In the *Herald*'s next issue, he promised to publish a letter from "A Friend of Freedom and Florida," which made "certain strictures upon several acts of the City Council concerning free persons of color."[39]

During the 1820s, the pillars of manumission and landownership remained intact, but military service was in serious jeopardy. The Catholic Church, which had traditionally protected the rights of the offspring of interracial relationships, also faced troubles. According to historian Michael Gannon, after the United States came to power in East Florida, the church "found herself adrift" and it "would not reach safe harbor for another thirty-seven years." St. Augustine "went months, sometimes years, without seeing a priest." Despite this instability and turmoil, black Catholics, when they had the opportunity, continued to avail themselves of the sacraments. Through the record of his baptism on 6 October 1822, Tomás Jaime O'Neill y Pons, born a month earlier, entered history. His parents, Jayme O'Neill and Catalina Villalonga, were bond persons, respectively, of D. N. Fitch and Agueda Pons, and his godparents, Anselmo González and Ysabel, were slaves of Don Antonio Giraldo and Don Bartolomé Villalonga. Significantly, the recorded surnames of the infant's parents were not those of their owners, and the child was named for his father.[40] Thus, the baptismal registry documented the date of the child's birth, along with his genealogy. The ritual also bestowed him with a support network that stretched beyond the bounds of his parents' working locales. Finally, after his baptism, he became the spiritual equal of his owner.

The same advantages are apparent in the baptismal records of Honora, Susana, and Jorge Clarke, the children of James and Mary Clarke. The priest noted that James was the free biracial son of Don Jorge [George J. F.] Clarke and the black Flora Clarke. He added that Mary's parents, José Dulcet and

Francisca Rosy, were white. The godparents all were free: Juan and María Dorrington (probably whites); James's brother, Tomás Clarke; the biracial sisters Sofia and Isabel Fish; and another man of color, Sprig Mosby. Dorrington had acted as an intermediary for Mosby when the latter purchased a city lot on Marine Street for $300. Isabel was the wife of John D. Clarke, James's brother.[41] Through the sacrament, then, propertied people of color reinforced their ties to each other and to the white community. In short, many blacks in St. Johns County viewed membership in the Catholic Church as advantageous, and they continued to follow Hispanic religious traditions.

American Protestantism, on the other hand, presented African Americans with religious choices they that had not enjoyed under the Spaniards. Protestant missionaries, the historian Janet Duitsman Cornelius wrote, "gave special privileges to those slaves who were literate, encouraged blacks to teach each other, and even surreptitiously taught those slaves who were eager enough to learn." The enslaved Jack Smith obtained the rudiments of writing from his mistress before coming to St. Augustine, and after he arrived there, a Presbyterian bondsman, Caleb Simmons, as well as a white elder in this church, E. B. Gould, continued to instruct him. In addition, the free colored preacher Tabb Smith came to St. Augustine, giving blacks a type of social and religious leadership they did not see in Catholicism.[42]

Smith, like Mosby and Fish was a free man of color who believed that he could succeed in American East Florida. Born free in Georgia during the 1790s, Smith had married a free woman and established a reputation as a "man of approved moral and christian character." A Baptist, he was "appointed by the proper authorities of that denomination to administer Christian ordinances" and "preach to the Baptist church of blacks" in St. Augustine. In that capacity, he "ministered to a colored congregation" for "some time" prior to December 1831, raising the ire of local Catholics in the process. Smith, however, did not limit his activities to religion. He hired a white man named Ashman to tutor his children, boarding him in his home. He also acquired real estate, owning by 1832 at least "four city lots with dwelling houses upon them, and an orange grove, facing on Marine Street," in addition to a slave.[43]

Moreover, the free black immigrant retailed liquor and groceries, and kept a "cart for public hire." His slave, a man "of a yellow or mulatto complexion," John Fleischman, "alias John Solana," probably was Smith's drayman. Smith conducted business with influential whites such as Waters Smith, Joseph L. Smith, Joseph Simeon Sánchez, and Gabriel W. Perpall. Nevertheless, he soon found himself in trouble with municipal authorities. In the spring of 1828, he accused a city official of illegally selling some of his loose-running hogs. The aldermen accepted the complaint but made Smith pay $2 before he could recover them. A few months later, the city sued Smith for physically interfering with another animal control officer who was discharging his duty to sell roaming hogs. Smith agreed to return the hogs and to pay the court costs. His temper also manifested itself when he caught John Hammond, his white employee, loafing. When the latter blustered that he would return to work when he felt like it, Smith grabbed him, leaving Hammond's throat so tender that he had difficulty swallowing for a week.[44]

The justice of the peace who heard the case resulting from this spat found Smith guilty of assault and battery. He then sentenced him to be whipped under a recently passed territorial ordinance of 19 January 1828 that imposed a maximum of thirty-nine lashes on any black convicted of abusing a white person. Smith appealed this sentence in November 1828 on the grounds that the ordinance was unconstitutional, as Florida's criminal code made no distinction between whites and free persons of color in the allocation of punishments. The federal judge who heard Smith's appeal refused to address the constitutional issue, but dismissed the case on the grounds that Smith had been "charged with one offense and sentenced to be punished for quite a different one."[45]

As discussed in the previous chapter, the Spaniards had allocated punishments designed to enforce the colony's racial hierarchy. Significantly, during the first decade of US rule, a Washington-appointed jurist refused to castigate an assertive man of color who had assaulted a white man. In addition, local aldermen had exercised restraint with Reverend Smith, who skirted the limits of St. Augustine's tolerance for blacks attempting to exercise the prerogatives of whiteness. Smith's status as a minister of the gospel, along with his efforts to educate his children, his entrepreneurial activities, his position of authority over white employees, and his fearless challenges of municipal and territorial ordinances, vividly illustrate the sense of guarded optimism that prevailed in St. Johns County's black community as Americanization commenced.

Scholars of antebellum history disagree about whether or not discriminatory laws seriously affected the daily lives of free people of color. Some experts argue that these oppressive statutes arose during periods of crisis. At other times, they contend, such laws were either unimplemented or laxly enforced. In East Florida, however, antiblack measures deeply disturbed persons of color and their white allies. Free blacks, in 1823, hoping to fend off statutory assaults, petitioned Florida's Legislative Council, and in 1826, Zephaniah Kingsley did the same. These efforts seemed to have paid off, for prior to 30 December 1826, Kingsley wrote, "happily . . . little has been done as yet by Legislative provisions, of a permanent character, to influence the condition of the colored population either for good, or for evil."[46] But, things were about to change.

On 30 December 1826, Florida's legislature passed a bill that, effective 1 March 1827, banned free blacks from entering the territory. Those violating this law faced a fine of $500. If they could not pay it, they were to be auctioned as slaves for a year. Matters soon worsened. In 1828, the Legislative Council approved "An Act Relating to Crimes and Misdemeanors, Committed by Slaves, Free Negroes, and Mulattoes." Only Peter Mitchell, who represented St. Johns County, dissented. This law featured certain sections that did not differentiate between free persons of color and the enslaved. For example, as Tabb Smith had learned, both had to be respectful when dealing with whites. When they failed to be properly deferential, they were subject to whippings or having their ears nailed to a post. During the next year, lawmakers attacked manumission. Any owner freeing a bond person had to forfeit $200. Those emancipated had to leave Florida within thirty days.[47]

These strictures floored Zephaniah Kingsley, who, after having served in the legislature, had penned, circa 1826, his "Address to the Legislative Council of Florida on the subject of its Colored Population," which St. Augustine's *East Florida Herald* published in a series of letters under the pseudonym "Rationalis." In this essay, Kingsley stated that he aspired to "promote the welfare & happiness of the people of Florida." Doubtlessly, he wished to protect his biracial children too, but the fact that he owned some two hundred slaves, along with multiple plantations in East Florida north of St. Johns County, gave his words a certain gravitas. Geography and demography, Kingsley maintained, dictated that for agriculture to be profitable, black slaves must cultivate the territory. The same two factors also made free people of color crucial to securing the plantation economy. Whites, he explained, by necessity, had to foster the loyalty of this class by ensuring their rights to land, slaves, education, wealth, and respect. Although he did not recommend that free blacks should hold public office, he heartily endorsed a major role for them in military service, citing Prince Witten's heroism during the Patriot War in support of his assertion. Kingsley implied that as long as slave systems existed, masters would sire children by their bondswomen and subsequently free them. Oppressive laws would alienate these freed persons, thus endangering Florida's internal security and damaging its relationships with its West Indian neighbors.[48]

Zephaniah Kingsley expanded his ideas in "A Treatise on the Patriarchal, or Co-operative System of Society," which he first published in 1828. Here, he enlarged the scope of his mission to the entire South. Using foreign slave systems as his model, Kingsley advocated flexibility. For purposes of productivity, morale, and security, masters, he asserted, must dangle before the enslaved the possibility of self-purchase, and allow them to own property. As far as possible, slaves should run their domestic lives. Reasonable labor assignments should be set. Once these were completed, bondsmen should be able to tend to their own gardens and activities. In short, owners should rely on the carrot rather than the stick. Because of their ancestral ties to whites and blacks, Kingsley regarded free persons of color as the "grand chain of security by which the slaves are held in subordination." Therefore, it was essential that the law protect their property and rights, including suffrage. If not, they would cast their lot with those in bondage. Moreover, free people of color descended from seven white great-grandparents should be considered legally white. Such policies, besides safeguarding the South from insurrection, would blunt domestic and international abolitionist critiques. To reinforce his points, Kingsley reminded his readers of how the British, during the War of 1812, had recruited to their ranks, by promises of freedom, slaves who "became regular soldiers of good discipline and appearance."[49]

Clearly Kingsley saw discriminatory laws as a very real threat to free people of color. So did Robert Brown, who decided that he had had enough of East Florida. In November 1828, he was a carpenter living in New York City. Brown and his wife had sold their five hundred acres located in Florida's Alachua region to Nehemiah Brush. Robert and Ann Brown had voted with their feet. They did not merely shrug off these statutes as unenforceable, nor did they derive comfort from the idea that they might be mere temporary expedients in times of crisis. Kingsley lamented that "those who enact laws to regulate slaves, and free people of color, are often obliged to consult popularity rather than policy and their own good sense." "Liberty," he maintained, "is merely nominal, without any constitutional protection." And, Kingsley added, "partial, exorbitant, and tyrannical taxes or fines" were unconstitutional. Indeed, "these severe enactments against color" already had driven "several of the most respectable and enterprising young men" out of the United States and into the Haitian navy. Again using the lessons of history, in this case by invoking the bloody Haitian Revolution, Kingsley predicted that "more will undoubtedly follow" the disgruntled young free black emigrants.[50]

On 2 September 1829, "Juridicus" echoed Kingsley's serious concerns in St. Augustine's *Florida Herald*. The writer excoriated Florida's lawmakers for their "little respect" for the Constitution when they passed bills that enacted racially based taxes, banned free blacks from entering the territory, and severely punished free people of color who physically or verbally abused whites. In the latter instance, he elaborated on the Legislative Council's "wanton stretch of power." Because the accused were tried before a justice of the peace, they could, without a trial by jury, suffer as many as thirty-nine lashes. "This class of persons," Juridicus thundered, had "rights and privileges secured to them, as much as to any white person, by the Constitution of the United States." In fact, he declared, "this Constitution makes no distinction of colour." Then, Juridicus made a statement that must have made many readers' blood boil. Nearly two centuries before Barack Obama's presidency, he provocatively argued that a "black or yellow-skinned man, if a freeman . . . if the people choose to elect him he has as good a right as any white man in the country to be president of the United States."[51]

Daniel Schafer has attributed Spanish East Florida's "relaxed racial system" to its "geopolitical situation." That is, the colony owed its security, in large part, to local free soldiers of color. Spain's legal system viewed slaves as victimized persons who had rights that its courts must defend. Bond persons could buy their liberty, marry legally, or be emancipated for a variety of reasons. They could work in their spare time to accumulate funds to free themselves or their loved ones. The government viewed manumission favorably. Freed persons could, as Schafer notes, "participate in the Spanish colonial system." Free blacks could and did earn money, land, and fame as craftsmen, farmers, and militiamen.[52] Men such as Robert Brown, Zephaniah Kingsley, and "Juridicus," in this sense, wanted to turn back the hands of time. Yet, they also looked forward, for they couched their arguments in constitutional terms and used republican rhetoric, staking their reputations on appeals to American political principles. In Cuba (the destination of most East Florida free blacks in 1821), Schafer reminds us, the "relaxed racial system . . . was vanishing."[53] Only time would tell whether or not it would disappear in St. Johns County as well.

During the 1820s, however, blacks in the county could and did buy freedom and land. They started businesses. They harbored hopes for better lives under the American flag. They could count on the assistance of powerful white allies. The local press publicized their plight and supported their struggle for liberty. At the same time, people of color experienced well-founded anxieties. But, although their social and economic environments were in flux, many persons of African descent still believed that they could stave off the worst effects of racist legislation as the 1830s dawned.

3
The 1830s: Manumission, Property, and Family

National, local, and international events conspired against St. Johns County's free people of color during the 1830s. In 1829, a black man, David Walker, sanctioned servile insurrection in his *Appeal to the Coloured Citizens of the World*. The Virginia bondsman, Nat Turner, led his followers to slaughter more than fifty whites in 1831. Additional slave unrest followed in the South. The abolitionist William Lloyd Garrison commenced his newspaper, the *Liberator,* in the same year. Four years later, the American Anti-Slavery Society flooded Charleston, South Carolina, with its literature, provoking white violence and raising frightening constitutional issues. An economic depression plagued the nation in 1837. Meanwhile, Middle Florida, the region between the Suwannee and Apalachicola rivers, became a cotton kingdom whose planters dominated the territorial legislature. An unusually cold spring devastated St. Augustine's important citrus industry in 1835. At the end of the year, the Second Seminole War erupted, causing an influx of refugees into the city and generally disrupting the economy. To make matters worse, an insect infestation further damaged the orange groves. In 1839, yellow fever struck St. Augustine, disease killed the silkworms imported to spark a substitute source of income, and the aftershocks of the Panic of 1837 reached Florida. Across the Gulf Stream, in the British Bahamas, abolition was proclaimed, black troops guarded the archipelago, and slaves on American ships that foundered in the colony's waters were liberated.[1]

Despite what historian Daniel Schafer categorized as the territorial legislature's "aggressive" 1829 attack on manumission, influential patriarchs from the Spanish era openly defied these new laws in St. Johns County, as in northeastern Florida generally, by continuing to issue emancipation papers without requisite security bonds, by accepting the validity of freedom documents that had no legal standing, and by not enforcing the mandatory emigration of newly liberated slaves. Many owners continued the tradition of freeing their biracial children and emancipating other favored bond persons in their wills. The numbers of manumissions, however, dropped dramatically. Sixty-four took place in the 1820s, but there were only twenty-six manumissions recorded in the 1830s. Still, except for 1838, at least one was certified each year in this tumultuous decade.[2] These statistics must be used with caution because sometimes emancipation deeds in the 1820s reflected the anxieties of already free blacks seeking to more fully guarantee their safety. This being said, the numbers do illustrate a disturbing downward trend.

Nevertheless, in this increasingly repressive atmosphere, even blacks could and did free other blacks. On 12 November 1830, James F. Clarke, for $400, emancipated John Sivelly, a twenty-five-year-old "mestee or coloured man of small stature." In 1837, Clarke's brother, George P. Clarke, liberated his slave, George Sevelly, who was described as a dark, thirty-year-old biracial man standing five feet five inches tall. Census and church records suggest that neither of these freedmen left the territory as Florida law required. Elizabeth Wiggins, the Clarke brothers' free colored aunt, declared in 1839 that upon her death, her slave Fanny would be free, if the latter served her faithfully during the remainder of her days. Wiggins, to ensure that there would be no legal dispute over the matter, authenticated the deed with her seal. Two white men sanctioned this arrangement by witnessing the instrument.[3]

Sometimes, runaways as well obtained their legal freedom by the actions of fellow persons of color. In June 1821, before departing for Cuba, Don Francisco Xavier Sánchez's daughter, Anna, sold the "yellowish" José Rafael, whom she had inherited from her father, to the free man of color "Don Jose George" for $323. José Rafael subsequently fled to the Seminole nation, so George sold his rights to him to the white Bernardo Seguí, who hoped to retrieve the slave. Frustrated in his efforts, Seguí, incurring a loss of $100, later transferred these rights to Gad Humphreys in 1835 for $300. George Santos, José Rafael's brother, whom Don Fernando de la Maza Arredondo had manumitted some two years earlier, then bought the rights to his sibling. Humphreys quit-claimed the slave in September 1835.[4]

Furthermore, by the decade's end, the custom of *coartación*, though extralegal, still survived. George Gibbs was leaving St. Augustine in 1839, much to the distress of one of his slaves, Jimmy, whose family belonged to another owner. Jimmy prevailed on Gibbs to agree that he could remain in St. Augustine if he could find someone who would pay $700 for him and free him when he had repaid that sum.[5] The distraught slave, facing separation from his loved ones, appealed to the Spanish past to rescue him. In effect, he unofficially had his price declared and was permitted to find a master to emancipate him on an installment plan. Jimmy Gibbs hoped that *coartación* would preserve his domestic life.

Such practices ensured that some St. Johns County slaves continued to live in a quasi freedom that could baffle their white neighbors. In 1834, about a decade before Gerónimo Álvarez officially emancipated Petrona and her two children, one white St. Augustinian who complained about Petrona's abusive language toward him thought that she was a free woman. James Roberts declared in his will written in South Carolina in 1814 that his slave Phoebe should receive free food and clothing, along with an income of $14 per year for life from the proceeds of his estate. Roberts insisted that she be kept at home "as free," doing nothing more strenuous than sewing or tending to her wardrobe. Phoebe lived in this middle ground between freedom and slavery from 1814 until 1835, when, now residing in St. Johns County, she was discharged from all responsibilities as a slave so that she might work as she pleased. Patty Harrison, a teenager, absconded in 1837 with "what was and what was not her own." In advertising for the runaway, whom she called María Rodríguez, her owner warned that Harrison had "reported herself throughout this city as free born, and sent to me not to work but to be educated."[6]

Stepney Morris, also called Stepney Bulow, had his month-old daughter, Donata Morris, baptized in St. Augustine's Catholic church in March 1826. Her mother, Amelia Nichols, was a free woman. The fact that Morris had a surname that whites recognized, and that he passed this surname to his daughter, is one indication of a free status. Other records suggest that Morris was an ambitious, hard-working man of an entrepreneurial disposition. In January of 1837, he deposited $8 in a bank, the Southern Life Insurance Company of St. Augustine. He also owned a horse and cart, for which he rented a slave, Caesar, as a drayman. In 1838, he opened the Washington Beef-Steak and Oyster House next door to the store of B. E. Carr, with whom he maintained a business relationship. The eye-catching newspaper advertisement announcing the opening of his restaurant featured open oyster shells flanking a pearl, and promised "suppers at the shortest notice . . . in a style of elegance and comfort unsurpassed in St. Augustine."[7]

Rather puzzlingly, he does not appear on an 1838 list of free persons of color required to select white guardians. Amelia Nichols and her children, however, were on the list, and the census of 1840 lists no man in her household. Morris's name is also absent from county tax rolls between 1829 and 1835. He did appear in 1842 church registries when his son Alexander was baptized and in probate records as owing money to the estate of the recently deceased merchant Isaac W. Avery. These contradictions are cleared up in records generated after Morris migrated to Key West in the 1840s. It turns out that John D. Clarke, one of George J. F. Clarke's biracial sons, had at some point purchased Morris, promising to emancipate him as soon as he paid the remainder of his manumission price, plus a portion of his earnings. In 1847, Morris completed his self-purchase and obtained his freedom.[8]

As in Spanish days, self-purchase was a long, arduous process. An incident reported in 1839 in the St. Augustine press reflects how onerous *coartación* was for the enslaved. William Henry Shadgett, a visiting Englishman suspected of being an "Abolition Emissary," on one occasion publicly chastised Donato Andreo for cursing a black man who was late for work. After Shadgett's rebuke, Andreo overheard two men of color, Marcellino and George, who were standing nearby, comment on Shadgett's remarks. The slaves obviously knew that the British had emancipated the bondsmen in their empire, which included the neighboring Bahamas. "Well George," said Marcellino, "good news. We will all soon be free, and shall not have to ask a white man any favors . . . we shall all be free without paying for it."[9] Although they surely savored the opportunity to do so, bond persons resented being forced to pay large sums for their liberty.

In reality, despite the best hopes of Marcellino and George for the British liberation of American slaves, Florida's antebellum legislation sought to drive free black men away or make them irrelevant, nonthreatening, and docile. These statutes severely challenged St. Johns County's African American community. Though it is true that it was up to local whites to enforce the laws, their mere existence placed men of color in positions of dependency, subjecting them to the whims of mercurial and self-interested patrons who, even when they found it suitable to choose the quality of mercy, made debtors of the objects of their forbearance. On the night of 16 May 1837, for example, civilian patrollers under John C. Cleland's command seized the free man of color George Seville in a drunken state. Cleland recommended that Seville be whipped like a slave in adherence to the law. The patrol apprehended another free black man, James Williams, who was going to a merchant's without a pass. White men did not require passes. Joseph M. Hernández's slave, Alex, also was nabbed. He had been on his way home after "shutting the office of the War Department." Because Cleland felt that Williams and Alex had "behaved very orderly" and were "decent and well behaved negroes," he decided that they should only be fined. Otherwise, if whipped, he feared that they might become "careless and unprofitable servants."[10]

Discriminatory taxation was another tactic used to marginalize free people of African descent during the 1830s. Besides humiliating free blacks, these levies aimed to deprive them of their property. As we have seen, in 1825, James F. Clarke led a successful effort to invalidate a St. Johns County racist impost. Afterward, a territorial revenue act passed in 1828 again taxed free blacks at a higher rate than whites. When the tax collector demanded payment from the brothers James, Joseph, George, John, and William Clarke in 1829, they refused to satisfy any "color tax." When the collector would not accept partial payments, the Clarkes' white father, George J. F. Clarke, settled their accounts. But, he warned the official not to deposit the portion assessed for race, because his sons intended to challenge it in court. When they initiated the challenge, Justice of the Peace E. B. Gould, in 1830, ruled against them. Disregarding the issue of constitutionality, he declared the case moot because they already had paid the disputed tax. Therefore, Gould would not refund their individual assessments of $0.50 and he charged each of them $2.12 in court costs to boot.[11] The Clarkes next appealed to the Superior Court. Tax returns indicate that this challenge likewise failed. In fact, by 1832, Florida for a time increased the discriminatory levy tenfold and assessed free black women as well. That same year, the tax collector seized a cow worth $102 from William R. Clarke's wife, Louisa, along with a horse of the same value from his brother George, presumably for nonpayment. Whites in the county were similarly opposing an ordinance to raise revenue for a free school. Goods were confiscated, returned, then seized again. One irate white complained that $20 of property might be taken to satisfy a $2 tax liability, due to the characteristically low bids offered at tax auctions.[12]

This situation threatened all county property owners. It was especially ominous for free blacks, however, for it constituted a vehicle by which whites might legally rob them. That is, statutes and ordinances could demand higher and higher taxes from the community of color and then confiscate large amounts of land or other holdings in order to recoup government losses at public auctions featuring tight-fisted bidders who might collude so as to reap material gain from black misfortune. The previous discussion of Susan Murphy illustrates the vulnerability of an elite white woman to predatory neighbors. Members of the free colored class shared Mrs. Murphy's plight, but to a greater extent because of their race.

William and Louisa Clarke, on their part, complained to the Superior Court about the confiscation of their cow. The matter dragged on until 1841, when it was dismissed. Clearly, it was not 1825 anymore. The couple had officially protested their treatment at the hands of the territorial government and lost. In 1833, some of the Clarkes' land, including fifty acres just beyond the city gates, was advertised for public auction. The sale was to take place in 1834 if two years of back taxes were not forthcoming. As the family still held the advertised tracts in 1840, this auction seems to have never taken place.[13] Nevertheless, the Clarkes possessed plenty of other land that the authorities could confiscate in the future if the family could not pay their taxes.

George J. F. Clarke had sensed a shift in Florida's racial climate that he realized did not bode well for his biracial children. Accordingly, he made provisions to help them weather the storm in the wake of his passing. In August 1829, he conveyed five hundred acres to his son George for $300. It is unclear whether any money actually exchanged hands. A year later, the aging patriarch paid Waters Smith $1,500 for fifty acres just north of the city gates. Two months afterward, seven of his biracial children "bought" this land for $2,100. Clarke deeded it to them in seven contiguous tracts. On the same date, he "sold" 150 acres on the Matanzas River to his above-mentioned son George for $300, the identical price that he had "charged" each of his other children for their urban plots. By these and additional transactions that the Clarke children carried out with other whites, they gained titles to 3,650 rural acres, thirteen lots in St. Augustine and its immediate environs, and two slaves, in some forty months between 1829 and early 1833. Moreover, by the provisions of their father's 1834 will, they stood to inherit 33,950 rural acres, two St. Augustine lots, and two half-shares of two city marsh lots. In Fernandina, they would inherit two homes, five lots, two half-lots, and a wharf lot.[14]

Other free blacks added to their real estate with the assistance of white patrons. The quadroon Sampson Williams took advantage of his bonds to the wealthy Hispanic Sánchez, Hernández, and Perpall families. Fabiana Fish, Gabriel W. Perpall's wife, was a white aunt of Williams's biracial bride, Harriet Fish. His white father, William Williams, was a kinsmen of Samuel Williams, the deceased husband of Joseph M. Hernández's spouse, Anna Marie Hill, who was the sister of Francisco Xavier Sánchez's young wife, María del Carmen Hill, and the aunt of Venancio Sánchez. The latter wed Carlotta Perpall. Sampson Williams's father had died in 1807. His estate, appraised at $10,557, included thirty-nine slaves. He held tracts of 180 acres on the St. Johns River and 220 more acres at Spring Garden, south of St. Augustine in the Mosquito district. At the latter location, he raised cotton and corn. The planter never explicitly acknowledged his paternity regarding his quadroon children Sampson, Susanna, and Eliza. But, in his will, he declared that they and their biracial mother, Angelica, were to be freed. The patriarch also gave his colored heirs three slaves, five cows and calves, cooking utensils, and sufficient food to support themselves until they could make a crop on his Mosquito tract. They were to be permitted to live there as long as they wished. The remainder of his property went to three white nephews: Abner Williams, William Williams, and William Henry Williams.[15]

In 1830, Angelica Williams and her children, along with seven slaves, lived in rural southern St. Johns County. She had taken further steps to protect her family's freedom by extending her kinship ties to other landed biracial families through Roman Catholic sacramental rituals. On 1 December 1828, her son Sampson was a godfather, along with John and William Clarke, to the mulatto daughters of the Mosquito planter James Darley. The godmothers were Angelica Williams and the biracial daughters of Jesse Fish. Maria Darley, James Darley's black common-law wife, and her children, soon would inherit slaves and land. She, like Clarissa Fish, also moved into town. Three weeks after this christening, John Clarke and his wife, Elizabeth Fish, baptized their daughter Carolina. Sampson Williams and Sophia Fish were the godparents. A few years later, Williams married Harriet Fish. George P. Clarke then took Phoebe Fish as his bride. Another propertied biracial man, James English, wed a fourth Fish sister, Maria.[16] Just as the nuptials of the white Hill sisters had united the Sánchez, Williams, and Hernández clans, the marriages of the biracial Fish sisters joined the free colored Clarke, Williams, and English families.

Sampson Williams's real estate dealings illustrate the advantages of his connections to Joseph M. Hernández and Venancio Sánchez. By 1835, in conjunction with his nuptials, he had moved into St. Augustine, having purchased a house in the Barracks Ward for $100 from John C. Huther, who had acquired it for the same sum from Hernández. The latter never had recorded the sale to Huther, so he quit-claimed the property in order that Williams could finalize the deed of conveyance. A couple of weeks later, in return for a loan of $484.44 and future advances of goods and groceries, Williams mortgaged this recently acquired property, along with two enslaved young boys, to Sánchez. On 1 November 1836, Joseph Papy conveyed a home to Angelica Williams for $550. Sánchez's loan may have made this sale possible. After her death, Sampson Williams, as his mother's executor, mortgaged her home to

Sánchez for $590 in December 1839. The following February, Sánchez quitclaimed it when Williams repaid him. Because his mother had owed $816.64 in debts at her passing, Sánchez's assistance ensured Williams's retention of two town lots.[17]

Indeed, victimization was not the entire story of black landholding. Other African Americans held on to their land, and some actually expanded their holdings. In 1833, George P. Clarke, for example, gained three thousand acres from Thomas Douglas, a white man, for $3,000. Statistical evidence indicates that during the 1830s, free people of color had more opportunity and means to acquire real estate than in any other decade of the American antebellum period. They acquired twenty-two lots in St. Augustine, fifteen of which had belonged to nonfamily members, and 8,025 acres outside the town, 3,000 of which they bought from nonrelatives and for which they paid a total of $8,829.[18] The success of these efforts against spreading racial constrictions is certainly a positive part of the story of antebellum black landownership in the county.

The county's free blacks also had another occasion for optimism in the 1830s. When Spain officially ceded Florida to the United States by the Adams-Onís Treaty, Washington pledged to compensate Spanish subjects for damages caused "by the late operations of the American Army." Congress implemented this provision by an act passed on 3 March 1825, authorizing federal judges in Florida to hear evidence and make awards. The secretary of the treasury was then to review the awards and pay those he found "just and equitable." Not until 26 June 1834, however, did Congress decide that "losses occasioned in East Florida, by the troops in the service of the United States in 1812 and 1813" should fall under the 1825 act. All former free Spanish subjects, including blacks, could file claims. The biracial children of wealthy whites potentially might win large sums from the federal government. George J. F. Clarke, for instance, was pressing for compensation totaling $45,015. In the end, the federal government awarded $12,468 in the names of fourteen free people of color and another $262,142 to blacks as heirs of the estates of eight white patriarchs. The individual awards ranged from $157,146 to the free black children of John Fraser to $102 for Tony Primus. The average settlement given in the name of a free black was $983. The figure for black heirs of whites was $33,582. This illustrates the economic potential of these African American elites, for according to a formula that historian Daniel Schafer has devised, this average approximates $1.2 million in current purchasing power.[19]

Blacks continued to run small enterprises during the 1830s. William Clarke and his wife, along with Sampson Williams, operated food service and hospitality businesses. At one point, Clarke and Williams ran a bar, while Louisa Kerr Clarke baked cakes. Their customers included soldiers, slaves, free persons of color, and elites such as Joseph Simeon Sánchez's wife. Evidence of the patronage that the Clarke couple enjoyed from prominent whites evinces itself in an 1834 receipt connected with a "Court Ball" that local dignitaries attended. It featured music, champagne, wine, whiskey, brandy, chicken, beef, shrimp, raisins, almonds, and baked goods. At this function, Clarke's wife earned \$5, while he garnered \$3. Their supervisory role may be discerned from the pay of other "servants" in attendance—between \$0.37 and \$1.25. Some 160 winter visitors came to town during the mid-1830s, and because of the Second Seminole War, St. Augustine boasted a significant military presence, as well as refugees from the countryside.[20] These influxes meant potential opportunities for free blacks running restaurants, taverns, boarding houses, and catering businesses, along with those employed in such activities.

At least a few free women of color supported themselves wholly or in part through economic endeavors of their own. The widowed Felicia Garvin is one who did so. She had a slave, Peggy, as well as an apprentice, Charlotte Irwin. Mrs. Garvin busied her two charges with cooking, washing, baking cakes, and breading oysters for sale. She sometimes made as much as \$3 per day selling cakes. Garvin also took in sewing and rented rooms in her home, where her daughter Eliza established a school. Prior to 1832, a white tutor named Ashman ran a "humble school" that St. Augustine's blacks supported "out of their slender means." Ashman taught twenty to thirty pupils, "the greater part of whom were coloured children." This integrated educational enterprise combined local Hispanic tradition and the new Protestant influx. As a result of such efforts, by 1832, there were, according to a newspaper account, "but few of the children of the free people of color" in town "who have not been taught to read." Moreover, a number of enslaved children, "too many perhaps," also were literate. Eliza Garvin, then, continued a practice that reflects blacks' optimism and ambitions for success. After she left town in the early 1840s, her quadroon cousin, Honora "Nora" Clarke, continued her work.[21] Free black men also pursued a variety of occupations. William Clarke and Sampson Williams, for example, added lumbering and selling oyster shells to the city for public works projects to their hospitality enterprises.[22]

Running businesses, as in the 1820s, entailed risks of lawsuits and indebtedness. Melvin Patrick Ely, in his study of an antebellum free black community in Virginia, discussed a "cash-poor" economy "chronically battered by vagaries of the national and international markets" that made "everyone . . . a debtor, and almost everyone at least sometimes a creditor." Ely pointed out that in "relatively prosperous times" a "string of lawsuits" might erupt "if someone in the chain of debt defaulted." In hard times, these suits, along with "forfeits of property to satisfy court judgments," became "epidemic."[23] Similarly, antebellum inhabitants of St. Johns County, as even a casual perusal of legal actions archived at the St. Augustine Historical Society's research library indicates, found themselves constantly enveloped in litigation. This became more acute during the economic troubles of the 1830s.

James F. Clarke's varied business ventures further demonstrate the adaptability required of free blacks who earned a living in St. Johns County and the frequent recourse to the courts that these ventures necessitated. Besides tavern keeping, hauling, and carpentry, Clarke at one time or another engaged in lumbering and real estate rental. He even raised an experimental tobacco crop, in hopes of making money by crafting "segars." Like other businessmen, he was sued and he sued others. In 1830, Aaron Kemp, a white man, held Clarke responsible when the latter's slave, John Sivelly, ran a cart containing Kemp's goods over a wharf's edge. Less than two years later, the Minorcan Joseph Manucy hauled Clarke to court. Manucy had lent the free man of color $124. Clarke secured the loan by mortgaging two slaves. When he did not receive the sum back on the due date, Manucy initiated foreclosure proceedings. In 1835, on the other hand, Clarke sued another Minorcan, Gabriel W. Perpall.[24]

Only a very few free men of color earned part of their livelihood from skilled crafts. At various times, William Clarke, as well as his brothers James and George, worked at tailoring. This brought them into competition with the city's Minorcan residents. In Pensacola, the former Spanish capital of West Florida, there were no Minorcans and fewer Hispanic holdovers than there were in St. Augustine. There were many more free black craftsmen there during the 1830s and 1840s. In St. Augustine, wrote historian David J. Weber, "Minorcan residents kept control of the trades for themselves."[25] This circumstance constituted a significant obstacle to black advancement.

Licensing requirements presented free blacks with another occupational hurdle. To wit, municipal authorities in 1830 rejected Jack Forrester's petition to open a tavern on Charlotte Street, contrary to the wishes of six of Forrester's white neighbors. Another free man of color, José de Regla, received a permit for his tavern in the same year. The fate of these and similar applications for businesses seems to have rested at least in part, on nothing more concrete than official whimsy. Under such conditions, free blacks were forced to curry the favor of the city fathers. Furthermore, they had to contend with periodic outcries, like one in 1837 against the allegedly deleterious effects of the "numerous receptacles of vice and iniquity kept by free Negroes."[26]

William Clarke and Sampson Williams knew well the pitfalls of the liquor business. On 29 July 1830, Squire Streeter swore before Justice of the Peace E. B. Gould that Clarke had sold a "half bits worth of rum" to Streeter's slave Tom at Clarke's grog shop. This was contrary to an 1828 Florida statute. When the case went before the Superior Court, Clarke's attorney objected that his client had a license from city council to sell spirits. The judge overruled this objection, but dismissed the case on the grounds that the punishment called for in the Legislative Council's act was unconstitutional.[27]

A few years later, William Clarke was in trouble again because of a matter connected with his business. In 1835, Clarke retailed liquor and sold other goods. Together with Sampson Williams, he applied for a license renewal for 1836. Following city council's dictates, Williams gave Venancio Sánchez as his security for the requisite bond. He was planning to "keep his shop in his house in Marine Street next door to the residence of J. Riz Esqre." Six white male neighbors (excluding Riz) attested to Williams's "good moral character." They also opined that the establishment would contribute to the "comfort of the neighborhood." After fulfilling these requirements and with the knowledge that white allies R. D. Fontané (the brother of George J. F. Clarke's executor) and Joseph Simeon Sánchez (Venancio Sánchez's relative) served as aldermen, Clarke and Williams believed that approval of their application would be routine.[28]

In fact, when Clarke and Williams asked if they needed to do anything else to secure their license, the city council replied that the application was complete, but that it had not yet acted on it. Believing that there would be no objection to their business, the partners commenced retailing alcoholic beverages. As 1836 began, a white man, Philip Weadman, felt that they were violating a municipal ordinance. Weadman rebuked them by reading the ordinance aloud to them. The free colored proprietors, assuming that Weadman was not aware of their application and that he had no authority for his actions, continued to serve customers. Not long afterward, to their shock, the city shut them down. In a letter to the mayor and aldermen, which Clarke and Williams both signed, they explained their reasoning, apologized, and requested that their license be issued. At the same time, they followed protocol by promising to respectfully submit to whatever decision might be rendered. They poignantly added that "they have always endeavored to conduct themselves as good citizens and entitle themselves to the good opinion of the community."[29]

Unfortunately, on 5 December 1835, unbeknownst to them, their application had been rejected. On 23 December 1836, William Clarke once more applied for a liquor license for the same Marine Street location. Again he was rejected. On 23 September 1837, he tried another time. No council action was recorded, but given the complaints about black-run taverns in that year, approval appears unlikely. Clarke experienced other financial difficulties as well. On 27 February 1837, he had deposited $50 in the Southern Life Insurance and Trust Company, the second-largest bank in Florida. It soon collapsed. By 21 February 1839, "Williams & Clarke" were offering their "shop on Charlotte St. near the wharf and the Oyster House connected therewith" for a two-year lease.[30] The bottom line was that the St. Augustine authorities could restrict the already limited economic opportunities for free blacks at will. White patrons could giveth and taketh away.

The free black community of St. Augustine and its environs, it will be recalled, was distinguished by the blood ties of many of its members to whites. This pattern had its roots in the Spanish system of slavery and race. According to Jane Landers's study of Spanish East Florida, between 1784 and 1821, one-fourth of all blacks baptized were of Afro-European descent. Such unions were "common and accepted in Florida," Landers explained, "much as they were on the African coast and in other areas of Latin America."[31] Consequently, a gradual "whitening" of "elite" elements of the free black population occurred. Not only did a handful of white patriarchs have a disproportionate influence among the free black (and slave) population, but that population included a disproportionate number of mulattoes (half whites), quadroons (three-quarter whites), octoroons (seven-eighth whites), and persons of other shadings of racial intermixture. Many persons of mixed racial ancestry were slaves for a part or all of their lives, or were manumitted at stages in their lives that ranged from infancy to maturity, and were either married to and/or produced progeny with slaves and were thus related by blood and/or marriage to whites, blacks, slaves, and free persons of color at the same time.

Among the eighty-eight names of whites appearing in the baptismal registries prior to the US takeover who admitted siring children of color were men of several nationalities and some of the province's most prominent citizens, including Francisco Xavier Sánchez, Francis P. Fatio, Jesse Fish, George J. F. Clarke, and Mateo Solana. Other men of stature, such as Francisco Gué, Francisco Marín, Andrés Papy, and Pablo Sabate came from families with long histories in St. Augustine. These white fathers included planters, military officers, and government officials, as well as soldiers, sailors, merchants, urban craftsmen, small farmers, and physicians, and there is no evidence that any social, economic, or political stigma was attached to them. Of the eighty mothers whose white partners admitted their paternity, one-third were themselves of mixed racial ancestry and slightly more than a third were free. An additional 116 women of color produced children by white men whose paternity is not recorded in church registries. Only about one in eight of these women were free, and less than one in seven was biracial, which indicates a relationship between the mother's skin color and/or social status and the willingness of white fathers to acknowledge the relationship.[32]

The territorial legislature, in 1832, aimed to sever future interracial blood connections by prohibiting white men from marrying or having carnal relationships with "coloured" women. It was in the aftermath of this act that Zephaniah Kingsley announced his intention to leave Florida, "where the base suspicion of sexual intercourse, renders every person liable to pay a fine of one thousand dollars," and where "every free colored female no matter how decent or how respectable" found herself in danger. In 1833, eleven other white men, including the St. Johns County luminaries George J. F. Clarke, Charles W. Clarke, and Roque Leonardi, joined Kingsley in sending a memorial to Congress. These leading men characterized the new territorial policy as "political quackery" originating "in the illiberal prejudice of a local government totally at variance with the liberal spirit and generous policy" of the United States.[33]

The memorialists accused the legislature of calculating "materially to disturb the peace and happiness" of Spanish-era inhabitants whom the treaty of cession protected. Reminding the Congress that in all slave-holding societies, "not a very inconsiderable part" of white men "have without the formalities of Marriage ceremonies, children by colored women," the petitioners declared that in Hispanic countries, these children "were free and admitted to most of the rights of Spanish subjects." The territorial legislators' effort to deny these rights to persons protected by treaty rights was inquisitorial as well as unconstitutional, the product of a "moral or political fanaticism" that sought to sever "virtuous and sacred ties of domestic life and parental affection."[34] Like Robert Brown in the 1820s, the petitioners cast their protest in terms of republican ideology. Moreover, by using the word *inquisitorial,* they took a pointed shot at a culture that regarded itself as superior to Spain's Catholic heritage.

According to the historian Daniel L. Schafer's analysis, by 1829, Florida, in place of the Spaniards' "three-caste system," had established a "two-caste system of race relations on the statute books." Still, as Schafer pointed out, there remained that bone of contention among current historians: the issue of enforcement. In other words, the extent to which discriminatory laws actually affected black lives. After the American takeover, evidence of interracial relationships in Catholic baptismal records diminished sharply. This is partially due to the loss of stature of the Catholic Church, though about two-thirds of the people of St. Augustine were still Catholic at the time of Florida statehood in 1845.[35]

Also, Catholic records after 1821 include much less racial and genealogical information than in the Spanish period, and the records themselves cease altogether for periods when no priest was present in the city. Of the Protestants, only Episcopalians documented baptisms, confirmations, and funerals. These entries provide minimal information. Nevertheless, it is significant that after the passage of the 1832 antimiscegenation law, no father was identified as white in the black Catholic baptismal books, and no distinction was made between blacks, mulattoes, quadroons, and octoroons, as had theretofore been done. Another indicator of a shift is that the phrase "unknown white" disappeared from notations of the paternity of biracial children in Catholic baptismal entries.[36]

The tightening racial restrictions of the 1830s made continued residence in St. Johns County unbearable for some free blacks. Early in the decade, Tabb Smith saw the handwriting on the wall. When Florida's legislature, in 1832, approved a measure forbidding preaching by people of color, except for integrated services held in white churches, "a strong desire to emigrate to Liberia with his family & as many as he can induce to accompany him," seized Smith. He sold his slave for $500, appointed a white man to take charge of his property in St. Augustine and "throughout the Territory of Florida," and at the end of the year, sailed with two of his children from Charleston to Africa. Frances, his wife, remained behind until her husband's real estate affairs were put in order. She finally joined him in Liberia in 1835. The next year,

George J. F. Clarke, the leading patriarch-protector of the county's people of color, died. Around 1837–1838, Charles W. Clarke also seems to have passed away.[37]

At the same time, religion promised to be a potential ally to blacks, as it had been under the Spaniards. Beginning in 1836, devout Catholic masters in St. Johns County had their consciences pricked by clergymen who maintained a continuous presence in St. Augustine. After a long period of instability under US rule, Bishop Michael Portier, from his see in Mobile, Alabama, assigned Father Claude Rampon to St. Augustine as its pastor. The Frenchman remained at his post until 1843, the longest tenure of a priest since 1821. Under Rampon, as historian Michael Gannon observed, Catholicism "waxed strong once more" and "parishioners [became] . . . assiduous in the practice of their faith."[38] People of color would sorely need the church's support in the face of the legislature's insidious attack on the African American family.

In short, the noose around the necks of free blacks in St. Johns County tightened as the decade of the 1830s reached its midpoint. Nevertheless, ominous portents did not extinguish the hopes of the free colored class as a whole. Nor did they quash slaves' dreams of liberty. As it had so often in East Florida's past, frontier violence reared its head as 1835 drew to a close. Such chaos traditionally had enabled persons of African descent to prove their mettle and gain or buttress their freedom. War might well halt or reverse the crystallization of an American-style slave society.

4
The Second Seminole War

When the Second Seminole War (1835–1842) erupted, free blacks were able to enlist in the militia. Between 1835 and 1838, in accordance with family and Spanish East Florida tradition, William Clarke joined his white neighbors' struggle against the Indians and their black allies. From 14 November 1835, until 20 February 1836, he volunteered as a private in Captain Benjamin Putnam's Independent Company A of Colonel Joseph Simeon Sánchez's Second Regiment of the Florida Mounted Militia. He appears on Captain George Phillips's Company's muster rolls in the same regiment as a musician from 29 June to 29 October 1836. Here he wore out "two drum heads." Clarke went on to sign up for hitches in David Levy's and E. B. Gould's units from late 1836 until early 1838.[1]

It appeared that, as under the Spaniards, security needs once more would open the door to the enhancement of black prestige through military service. At this critical juncture, Florida's new rulers might have chosen to integrate free blacks into the social system as soldier-defenders. Indeed, like William Clarke, other St. Augustine free men of color demonstrated their willingness to fight under the Stars and Stripes. Historians have largely overlooked this willingness. The best documented of these black volunteers was the biracial Benjamin Wiggins, whom the scholar Kenneth W. Porter characterized as "probably the most active Negro partisan of the whites in the early days of the Seminole war." Shortly after the outbreak of hostilities, Wiggins was "engaged in the highly hazardous occupation of riding express," and was soon "employed as a principal guide to Colonel Brisbane's regiment of South Carolina volunteers" in US service in Florida. In July 1836, at Dunlawton plantation south of St. Augustine, Wiggins took part in an encounter in which he killed three Seminoles and was himself seriously wounded. Before his death in August 1837, Wiggins served in three different companies of Joseph Simeon Sánchez's Second Regiment of Florida Mounted Militia.[2]

Like his white Indian-trader father and African-born mother, Wiggins displayed a talent for languages, which the Spaniards had used in frontier diplomacy. He also had served the Spanish as a pilot and militiaman in what Jane Landers described as the "many disturbances which shook Florida," including the Patriot War, earning whites' respect in the process. E. B. Gould, a judge, newspaper editor, and public official in St. Johns County, characterized Wiggins as a "long standing" resident of "unimpeached integrity and veracity." With no mention of Wiggins' African ancestry, Generals Duncan L. Clinch and Joseph M. Hernández included testimony by him in support of their compensation claims for losses that they suffered during the Second Seminole War. No other African American's depositions were included in the lengthy proceedings.[3]

In assessing Wiggins's loyalty to the United States, Porter suggested that as a "frontiersman," Wiggins's interests were "naturally about as much with the whites as if he had been of unmixed European ancestry." Having grown to maturity under Spanish colonial rule, Wiggins had benefitted from policies that, in Frederick Bowser's analysis, "rewarded every step taken" by free blacks toward self-improvement and which in that sense "approximated the white ideal." In such a society, "only under the most extreme circumstances did the advantaged person of color identify with those beneath him." In Wiggins's case, something else may have been equally important: In 1797, Indians had killed his eldest brother Billy.[4]

Other free men of color also fought against the Seminoles. Besides William Clarke, George P. Clarke, Thomas Clarke, John D. Clarke, Sampson Williams, Jack Forrester, Peter Seville, and possibly Carlos Manuel Clarke, all served in militia units as musicians, guides, and privates. The Clarke family, white and black, had a distinguished record of military service in East Florida. Wiggins and Williams were linked to the Clarkes by marriage. Peter Seville was a protégé of the family as well as the son of Don Juan Sivelly, an Italian artillery sergeant in the Spanish army; Jack Forrester had once been the property of the family patriarch, George J. F. Clarke. This combination of family and militia ties represented continuity from Spanish times.[5]

Unlike the Spaniards, the Americans permitted no persons of color to serve as commissioned or noncommissioned officers, nor did they form separate black militia units. Moreover, the veterans would receive no land grants as compensation for military service. The fact that some of those who served did so as musicians was another reflection of the erosion of free black status. Paradoxically, at the same time, whites publicly acknowledged the bravery and martial skills that men of African descent had displayed some twenty-five years earlier. In August of 1836, the *Florida Herald* reported that Benjamin Wiggins and two other free blacks had arrived in St. Augustine from New Switzerland with news that Seminoles were lurking in the vicinity of the Twelve Mile Swamp. The *Herald* reassuringly reminded its readers that Wiggins's father-in-law (Felipe Edimboro) and perhaps Wiggins himself had "figured conspicuously" in Prince Witten's storied attack on American troops during the Patriot War. Later, the *Herald*'s weekly rival, the *News,* praised the "commendable zeal exhibited by the negroes" in combating a suspected fire by arson that erupted at J. C. Clelland's "very handsome building." Both editors, because their purpose was to comfort nervous whites, failed to draw appropriate lessons from this historical record of black martial skill and loyalty, as they stopped short of advocating the formation of a free colored unit to combat the Indians. In fact, when free blacks were discharged from service, they had to endure the humiliation of being forced to select white guardians.[6]

Outside St. Johns County, some men from at least one biracial family with St. Augustine roots fought against the Seminoles. William, Charles, and Phillip Wanton, quadroon sons of Edward M. Wanton, who had suffered greatly for his service to the Spanish during the Patriot War, moved to Alachua County in the early 1820s. At that time, the Seminoles held the elder Wanton in high esteem, but by the 1830s Wanton had become involved in disputes with some of them over debts owed to him and over his accusations that they had encouraged his slaves to abscond. Soon after the Second Seminole War commenced, the Americans ordered Wanton out of the village of Micanopy and destroyed the buildings on the property that he owned there to keep them from falling into Seminole hands. His three sons then enrolled as privates in American units, serving from 1837 to 1840, long after their St. Johns County counterparts ceased to be accepted for enlistment. Interestingly, one of the sons, Charles Wanton, in his early fifties, later fought for the Americans during the Third Seminole War (1857–1858).[7] Perhaps it was their light skin color and/or frontier conditions that enabled the Wantons to be accepted in the US military when other men of color were denied the opportunity.

The American failure to more effectively rally blacks to their cause resulted in harrowing security problems for St. Johns County's white community. The controversial role that Luís Fatio played left whites fearfully guessing at the loyalty and sympathies of their most trusted slaves and free black neighbors. Fatio grew up as a slave at New Switzerland, Don Francisco Fatio's huge estate encompassing ten thousand acres and fronting twelve miles of riverbank in northwestern St. Johns County. The son of the planter's slaves Adam and Juana, Luís was born in 1800 and baptized nine months later in the Catholic Church. His parents' favored standing is indicated by the fact that he had two godparents at his baptism. Other plantation slave infants typically had a single godparent or, as was often the case, shared common godparents in a joint baptismal ceremony during the course of priests' circuit visits. Luís's godparents were bond persons not of Fatio but of Don Francisco Xavier Sánchez,[8] a circumstance that suggests something of the paternalism of the Spanish society as well as the sense of community that existed among the slaves. Luís Fatio's family, in short, must have been esteemed by Don Francisco Fatio in ways that are not evident in the historical record.

That is at least suggested by the fact that Don Francisco Fatio's daughter, Susan Philippa Fatio, gave him the gift of literacy, perhaps in the Fatios' "splendid" manor house, which dazzled antebellum whites. It surely fired the impressionable black youngster's imagination, fueled his ambitions, and expanded his world. The mansion displayed "several valuable oil paintings," all gilt-framed. One of these, "representing a battle," measured five to six feet long and two to three feet high. Besides containing a "great abundance" of the "very best quality" furniture, the great house also boasted a "Choice Library [of] over 1200 Vols.," "mostly English, French, German & Spanish publications." Luís Fatio not only gained the ability to read and write, but he eventually learned to speak English, French, Spanish, and a Seminole tongue. At a young age, he married a town slave, a woman who later bought her freedom. Soon thereafter, he ran away from New Switzerland and made his way to the Gulf of Mexico, most likely with the assistance of siblings, who lived among the Seminoles. His freedom flight ended at Tampa Bay, where he was apprehended and sold to the commanding officer at Fort Brooke. There, he served as an interpreter for a succession of commanders until the early 1830s, when he was purchased by Don Antonio Pacheco. Pacheco entrusted him with a number of responsibilities at his Sarasota trading establishment, forty miles south of Tampa. By 1835, then, as Luís Pacheco, he possessed multicultural skills which permitted him to move easily in and out of Florida's African American, Anglo, Hispanic, and Indian worlds.[9]

At the end of that year, Pacheco's widow rented him out as an interpreter to Major Francis Dade, who with a hundred troops, marched inland from Fort Brooke to reinforce Fort King, near modern Ocala. Along the way, Dade frequently sent the black man ahead of the advancing column to scout. The Seminoles ambushed Dade on 27 December 1835, in what is commonly called the start of the Second Seminole War. Only Luís Pacheco and three whites survived the attack. The whites accused him of complicity in the ambush, but he denied the charge, insisting that the Indians had captured him and held him against his will. Whatever the truth, General Thomas Jesup considered the polyglot slave as a bad security risk and, in 1837, forced him into exile with the Seminoles who were removed west of the Mississippi River.[10] He now was a free man.

That is not the end of Luís Pacheco's story, however. He remained an enigmatic figure, even as an elderly man. In 1892, in his nineties, he returned to Florida to live under the care of the woman who in her girlhood had taught him to read and write. There, he attended church regularly and continued to deny any complicity in the Indian ambush of 1837. When he died in 1895, he was interred at New Switzerland after a funeral (according to a contemporary obituary), "attended by representatives of the old families of Jacksonville." Kenneth W. Porter concluded that "the pious, devoted nonagenarian, with his eyes fixed on the beyond," may not have been guilty, but the scholar was not as certain about the "roving restless man in his thirties, the erstwhile incorrigible runaway, with a brother and sister among the hostiles."[11] Luís Fatio/Pacheco's life demonstrates the exceptional human and military potential that the Americans might have more effectively tapped from St. Johns County's African American community.

The successful attack on Dade's troops that made Luís Pacheco's name notorious rallied many slaves in East Florida to the Seminole cause. Large numbers deserted from the Tomoka and Mosquito regions south of St. Augustine, where slaves during the Patriot War era had been left to fend for themselves and from whence many of them fled to the Negro Fort on the Apalachicola River in northwestern Florida, or the Tampa area, and where those who remained became troublesome workers. Some had even borne arms in defense of the Spanish government. Now, two decades later, Indian emissaries, including two Black Seminole diplomats, Abraham and John Caesar, appeared in Tomoka and elsewhere, actively soliciting volunteers to serve their cause. Thus it happened that in the immediate aftermath of the Dade Massacre, blacks from "Tomoka & Smyrna" were again in the Tampa region besieging Fort Brooke.[12]

At the same time, other blacks, enslaved and free, joined the exodus of refugees pouring into St. Augustine, provoking white fears of traitors within their midst. Many of these refugees, as one antebellum writer asserted, "had wives among the Indian negroes, and the Indian negroes had wives among them." Within the town, therefore, were people of color with blood connections to the Seminoles, individuals who might furnish supplies or intelligence to that enemy. Even before hostilities commenced, General Duncan L. Clinch had warned his superiors in Washington of the danger of a black–Seminole alliance. The warning proved well-founded. "These coloured persons are giving us much trouble and there is scarcely a doubt that some of them have . . . given important information to the Indians," Benjamin Putnam, an officer in the Florida militia, complained in July 1836.[13]

By August, the *Florida Herald* reported that the Seminoles had demonstrated their ability to penetrate into St. Johns County, appearing at Moultrie Creek, "within five miles and in sight of town," and at the Canova and Papy plantations, "within a stone's throw" of St. Francis Barracks on St. Augustine's southern edge. Rumors circulated that Indians were moving about the town market under cover of darkness. Most of the "several hundred Negroes concentrated within the walls of the city" had picked up an Indian language as a consequence of lifetimes of contact with the Seminoles. Some whites were especially fearful of arson, afraid the smoke would signal the Seminoles to attack. Indeed, on 22 September 1836, a St. Augustine federal jury convicted Castillo, a slave belonging to "Messrs. Cruger & Depeyster late of Mosquito Co.," of that crime. He was sentenced to ninety-nine lashes. Indeed, some of Depeyster's bondsmen, to demonstrate their solidarity with the Seminoles, had gone so far as to adorn themselves with war paint. By October, the Grand Jury of St. Johns and Mosquito Counties was lamenting the "total ruin" the war had already brought to the countryside around St. Augustine.[14]

Ironically, the territory's increasingly repressive race laws gave blacks wiggle room. As in the 1820s, the St. Augustine press critiqued laws aimed at free people of color. A major target was the legislature's Act Respecting the Hostile Negroes and Mulattoes in the Seminole Nation, which declared that any captured free colored belligerents would be enslaved. Whites whose slaves were apprehended also faced sobering consequences. Because East Florida's bondsmen lived in close proximity to the Indians, as opposed to the relatively secure slaves of Middle Florida's plantocracy, the measure was deeply resented in St. Johns County. For weeks in late 1836, the *Florida Herald* reflected this anger. "Linguet," for instance, sarcastically upbraided lawmakers for failing to list punishments for "quarteroons and quinteroons," a "privileged class" to which he felt "some of the members of the [legislative] council have themselves given rise." The *Herald* also protested a recent statute barring free blacks from immigrating to the territory, citing the case of a recent arrival from New York who came with the intention of working as a "domestic servant in the house of a highly respectable gentleman." Blacks could exert leverage in this divisive atmosphere. Thus, when the lawyer John Rodman was called to task because Rebecca, one of his house servants, had sheltered in her home blacks who had "held communication with the Indians," he asserted that "every person accused, white, mulatto, black; free or slave . . . is entitled . . . to an indictment by a grand jury and a regular trial by a petit jury." When a critic took him to task for his defense of slaves accused of aiding the enemy, an anonymous defender noted that Mayor Frederick Weedon had permitted two bondsmen who had been apprehended after running away to the Indians, to "go at large," even though they faced more serious charges than did Rodman's Rebecca.[15]

The celebrated case of Randall Erwin takes on an added significance within this charged atmosphere. By the beginning of 1837, the recently named general in charge of US operations in East Florida, Thomas S. Jesup, had the Seminoles on their heels. To counter these victories, the Black Seminole leader John Caesar decided to bring the fighting as near as possible to St. Augustine. In January 1837, the *Florida Herald* reported that three men of color, Andrew Gué, Joe Merritt, and John Bicenty, had contacted Erwin, a free mulatto, at his home on Anastasia Island, some four or five miles south of St. Augustine. They told Erwin that during the previous summer, when only "an inefficient patrol" of eight to ten civilians kept watch, two Seminoles had ridden "through the town and went out at the gates." Therefore, Gué and the others contended, it was safe for Erwin to assist them. Erwin then purportedly provided cloth, needles, thread, and tobacco, promising to pick up other supplies for them in St. Augustine. The following night, Erwin's conspirators helped raid the Hanson plantation, just outside of town, in the aftermath of which they were caught in a surprise attack during which Merritt was fatally wounded. Gué, also wounded, managed to escape.[16]

In a manner not revealed in the sources, the authorities soon learned of the raiders' contacts with Erwin. As a result, he, along with Stephen and Tomasa Merritt, Joe Merritt's father and sister, faced charges of treason. As Kenneth Porter noted, the affair "revived something of the panic of the early days of the war." The dread of an impending slave uprising, which it fueled, drew the militia back to the city, thus relieving military pressure on the Seminoles and their black allies operating in rural areas. More than one hundred white men signed a petition calling for the exile of the accused. The terror resulting from the US decision to enhance its national security by conducting a war against free men of color (blacks as well as Seminoles) hit home hard, as John Caesar had surmised. In the words of a local newspaperman, the Erwin affair vividly demonstrated the potential for a "consequence . . . had it been permitted to ripen we well may shudder at."[17]

An investigation into the family ties of the accused sheds light on the outcome of the trio's trial. Randall Erwin was the biracial son of James Erwin, a white South Carolinian who owned a plantation on the Little St. Marys River. George J. F. Clarke, the elder Erwin's friend, described him as an "ingenious man." A neighbor called him "an honest and correct man." The Clarkes were close to the Erwins. In fact, Charles W. Clarke, administered James Erwin's estate. Randall Erwin also may have been tied to another prominent white, George Center, who was serving as a St. Augustine alderman in 1838, when he was "appointed sole trader with the Indians." Contemporary accounts cited Center's "high character" and "experience in the Indian character." Erwin's connection to Center would have been through his sister, Charlotte, who for a time had lived in Felicia Clarke Garvin's household and who would, in the near future, according to some evidence, bear three children to the white man.[18]

Stephen Merritt was similarly well-connected. Also known as Stephen Wright, Merritt had been born around 1786, the son of an Englishman and a free black South Carolinian, Emilia Wright. He was baptized into the Catholic Church at the age of six as Estévan Roque Mery y Right, with Don Roque Leonardy standing as his godfather. His brother, Francisco Joseph Wright, received the sacrament the same day. The latter's father was John Wright, a free black from Carolina. It is likely that he and Emilia fled south to obtain their liberty under Spain's sanctuary policy. In 1803, the Spaniards granted 145 acres to John Wright and he also acquired a Fernandina town lot.[19] Stephen Merritt and his brother apparently married sisters, the daughters of the Africans Tomás Herrera and María Dolores, who, even as slaves, legitimized their nuptials in a church ceremony. After he attained his liberty, Herrera, who seems to have been called "Toby," suffered serious wounds while fighting for the Spaniards circa 1802–1803 against the Seminoles. In 1812, he owned a small farm south of St. Augustine, in the Matanzas area and again defended his sovereign during the Patriot War. Antebellum whites remembered him as being "industrious" and "thrifty." When Stephen Merritt and his wife, Josefa Herrera, baptized their children, including José Márit Herrera, prominent whites served as their godparents. Before succumbing in the aforementioned raid, Joe Merritt had carried out a deception that shocked St. Augustine's whites. He disguised his defection to the Seminoles by feigning his own drowning, which had "called forth sympathies of the people [of St. Augustine] much in his favor."[20] This sympathy was a consequence of the many years that the Merritts had worked to gain whites' esteem.

Randall Erwin, like the Merritts then, sported biracial ancestry and could take advantage of blood and patronage ties to whites. Through inheritance and marriage, he was an heir to land and other property. Although ambition, intelligence, and assertiveness were aspects of his basic character, his successful maneuvers through the racial minefields of an increasingly repressive society also can be partly explained by his relationships to whites and his community standing. These advantages, together with his personal abilities, enabled him to harness the ameliorative features of antebellum paternalism, of the conviction of many whites, for example, that in dealings with the law, respectable blacks should enjoy, in the words of the historian James Denham, the "same procedural safeguards as whites." White attorneys did not hesitate to defend blacks and often enhanced their professional prestige in doing so.[21]

Randall Erwin's statements to his accusers, as well as those that Stephen Merritt and other witnesses uttered, reveal rifts in the black community, reminding us of history's complexity, and the layers of human motivation. Erwin, like his sister Charlotte, clearly was a client of the Clarkes, who had volunteered to fight the Seminoles. He bought rice and sugar from William Clarke. When Erwin came into St. Augustine to see a doctor because of "pain in the ear" that made speaking difficult, John Clarke accompanied him to two stores and purchased cloth, thread, needles, and tobacco for him. Erwin claimed to have been at odds with Stephen Merritt, as well as John Bicenty, Joe Merritt, and Andrew Gué. Regarding the latter three, he swore that on a Saturday about midnight, they came to his house while he was ill and his family slept. "Had he been well," he continued, "he meant to have shot them." They were part of a group of ten or twelve men, which included John Caesar and an "Indian chief." Their goal was to obtain "six dollars worth things." When they saw tobacco and calico atop a "Bureau," they took it from the defenseless Erwin. Then they told him that they would be back. Erwin stated that he "intended to inform against them," but he did not because he was "ashamed of being caught in such a situation and had not been able to do something with them."[22]

Stephen Merritt, on his part, informed the court that he too was a family man living with his wife and four daughters on Anastasia Island, some five miles south of Erwin on land that he occupied with Gabriel W. Perpall's consent. His son Joe had run away because he had beaten him some three to four months previously "for bad conduct." He had not seen him since. It is unclear whether or not Merritt was referring to Joe when he added that he had "a son in the Indian nation" who he had "not heard from for a long time." Merritt reported that there was tension between his family and Erwin's "which was occasioned by Toby [Herreira?]." He complained that "Randall [Erwin] took his family away from him." Perhaps Erwin was his son-in-law, since Merritt's daughter Tomasa also had been charged. Regardless, he denied any knowledge of Erwin's encounter with his son, Bicenty, and Gué. Interestingly, he declared that he "heard that Randall had bought a Rifle of Ben Wiggins." Regarding his relationship with the Seminoles, Merritt admitted that they had "taken" him a year previously, but that after two hours, he "made his escape." Although he "had frequent intercourse with the Indians," he deposed that he never had seen John Caesar.[23]

Another free man of color, James Edinburg, however, contradicted Stephen Merritt's testimony, just as John Clarke had contested Randall Erwin's initial deposition. Edinburg recounted how he had known Merritt for "a number of years," including "in the Indian nation." Moreover, he had "frequently" seen Merritt and John Caesar "talk with each other." Therefore, Edinburg had "every reason to believe that John Caesar and Stephen Merritt were well acquainted with each other." A white man, Antonio Pellicer, agreed with Edinburg. He related how two years previously, Caesar had asked him for directions to Merritt's place, informing Pellicer that the latter "owed him ten dollars." He went on to describe how Merritt had "promised to give [Caesar] a Saddle in payment," but instead of doing so, he had returned empty-handed from St. Augustine. He then essentially promised to give Caesar a check instead. The Black Seminole was so enraged, Pellicer chillingly added, that he "said he would take one of Stephen Merritt's children."[24] In summary, under the pressure of serious charges in the midst of a war that raged in St. Johns County and reached the very streets of St. Augustine, witnesses waffled, lied, and took issue with one another. Then again, this may have been a clever tactic for the protection of the black community as a whole.

Although white popular opinion ran squarely against Erwin in 1838, there was no cry for blood vengeance, only that he be exiled. The following year, a former federal judge defended Erwin in court, persuading an all-white jury to declare on 18 March that Erwin was not guilty of the charge of "attempting to excite and exciting slaves to insurrection." Erwin's attorney, Joseph L. Smith, had convinced the jury that "no law . . . authorized [black witnesses] to testify in a United States case." Therefore, "many negroes who were to have testified as to the facts, against the negroes on trial, were excluded." The *St. Augustine News* reported this verdict matter-of-factly. Tomasa Merritt avoided a perjury conviction the following week. It appears that her father likewise was exonerated. Subsequently, Erwin evidently placed himself under the protection of the white patriarch Zephaniah Kingsley and sailed to Haiti, where Kingsley had earlier evacuated his own biracial family. In July, a ship carrying 113 free black emigrants departed for Hispaniola from the St. Johns River. Four years later, Erwin was back in East Florida.[25]

Andrew Gué's role in the episode also very much troubled St. Johns County's whites. In the summer of 1836, when he was no more than twenty-one years of age, Gué fled to the Seminoles. Early in the war, he and two of his fellow runaways had been "in the habit of coming into town at night and being harboured aided and fed." On his nocturnal visits to St. Augustine, he recruited slaves to the Indian cause by convincing them that he held a position of confidence with the Seminoles and "only wanted a white man's scalp to make him a great man." In Seminole culture, according to the scholars John Mahon and Brent Weisman, "personal bravery and stealth," demonstrated in raids on the enemy, won "increased prestige among the warrior's peers, the privilege of wearing a tattoo, and the opportunity for a young man to earn an adult or warrior's name." Wounded thrice in the attack in which Joe Merritt (and John Caesar) died, Gué hid among sympathizers until his capture in March 1837. "The notorious Andrew Gue taken," the *Florida Herald* headlined. Newspapers in faraway places such as South Carolina and New Hampshire reprinted the story. There is no record of his punishment, although Gil Wilson has surmised that it consisted of "rather light" jail time.[26] Thus, it also appears that Andrew Gué had been able to manipulate white paternalism and probably his master's economic self-interest.

The patrol regulations designed to protect whites during the troubles developed into a source of conflict among them, and blacks took advantage of this dissension. Florida's draconian slave code reflected whites' worst fears, but generally speaking, the patrolling of slaves and free blacks was poorly planned and even more poorly executed. A city ordinance of 1836 made all able white men subject to patrol duty from eight o'clock in the evening until "broad daylight." The ordinance required at least ten patrollers each night, and those neglecting the duty risked fines or imprisonment. Even during the tense May nights of 1837, in the midst of the Second Seminole War, patrol records reveal scores of absences. On one night, for instance, Abraham Dupont commanded only four men—the other five failed to report for duty. In fact, the prescribed ten-man detail was the exception rather than the rule.[27]

Men who did perform patrol duties often had unpleasant experiences on St. Augustine's dark streets. Patrollers were as likely to have to deal with unruly soldiers as with slaves lacking passes, again illustrating a rift in the white community that blacks could exploit. In 1837, the slave patrol caught a soldier breaking into a home. On another occasion, a mounted trooper fired at a slave patrol from the St. Sebastian Bridge. Soldiers were often found drunk in the street. People of color saw such soldiers as allies in their struggle against increasing repression. In May 1837, Patrol Captain Abraham Dupont and two of his men (the other seven having failed to report for duty) entered the tavern run by George P. Clarke, a free man of color and son of George J. F. Clarke, at 11:00 p.m. There, Dupont discovered Clarke's brothers James and John "drinking and smoking segars," with soldiers and a white man who claimed to be temporarily minding the tavern. One of the soldiers, who was armed, threatened the patrollers, causing Dupont, who lacked "a sufficient guard to take the party without shedding of blood," to order the soldiers back to their barracks. Seizing the Clarke brothers and their nephew, James D. Garvin, whom they encountered in the street, the patrol escorted the them to the guardhouse. The short-handed Dupont soon had to release them, however, when he learned of a drunkard staggering through one of St. Augustine's narrow passageways who was creating a disturbance. To Dupont's frustration, the offender turned out to be one of the soldiers he had just reprimanded at Clarke's grog shop. In his inebriated state, the soldier was praising the Seminoles, "speaking in behalf of the rights of the Indians," and bellowing that "he wished every ball that the Indians fired would take effect."[28]

A week later, Patrol Captain Matthew Solana spotted five soldiers leaving James F. Clarke's bar, soon after midnight. The soldiers "commenced yelling and making a great noise," and to elude Solana, they disappeared into the tavern of Sampson Williams, another free man of color related to the Clarkes, threatening the patrol from behind locked doors. A determined Solana gathered reinforcements and returned to the tavern, only to learn that the offending soldiers had returned to Clarke's place, where they pledged to "turn out" the "garrison" against the patrol if it troubled them further. When Solana indignantly followed the soldiers to the barracks, and demanded to speak to the sergeant of the guard, the sentry snapped that the civilian Solana had "no business here." Two months after this incident, in August 1837, the mayor dispatched Patrol Captain Bartolo Maestre and his men to the home of Thomas W. Clarke, a free black, where they found not only the corpse of Clarke's father, Ben Wiggins, but also a white man, John B. Suárez, "making a great noise and being drunk [causing] much disturbance in the house."[29]

Other after-dark black activities seemed to more seriously threaten St. Augustine. In May 1837, the merchant Emanuel Águiar reported that he had overheard a group of slaves plotting insurrection. Another white, Francis Andreu, had observed several black men armed with "large sticks or clubs" walking through the dark streets. He too suspected that the "negros were preparing to rise." Águiar attested that he had heard blacks say that the uprising would coincide with the departure of a steamboat from town. He singled out the slave Jimmy Gibbs, alleging that Gibbs, while referring to a political barbecue, had said, "let them go on—let them frolic—our time will come. I have got things fixed."[30]

The authorities interrogated Gibbs and the bondswoman Betsey, both of whom belonged to the Methodist congregation. The latter claimed that she, Gibbs, and two other slaves were discussing "religious matters and the gospel." She also recollected complaining to Gibbs about the ill treatment she had received from his wife, Venus. Gibbs replied that Betsey should have mentioned the problem earlier so that they could have resolved the matter before the church. The suspects' good standing in the Protestant body evidently convinced their accusers of their innocence. Moreover, a witness, Emanuel Garrido, added that Gibbs bore a consistently respectful demeanor.[31] Thus, the slaves' pious reputations caused cooler heads to prevail, even during the Seminole War's bleakest days, when whites felt threatened by enemies both outside and inside the city.

As 1839 faded, the *St. Augustine News* found much to praise in its hometown. The paper boasted of three churches, two cemeteries, six physicians, two printing presses, twelve attorneys, two ice cream parlors, "sundry places where gentlemen may take brandy and water," a bank, a reading room, and a soda fountain. Moreover, it painted a promising future. Construction projects included new homes, housing developments, a bridge, and repairs to the fort. When a planned railroad became reality and regular steamship service linked the city to Savannah, Georgia, the economy would grow. The county's population was expected to boom along the St. Johns River when the Seminoles finally succumbed. Meanwhile, a farmer's market opened for several hours each business day, its stalls displaying meat, fish, fresh fruit, and vegetables. Peddlers balancing baskets on their heads hawked seafood and produce along the sandy streets. In 1830, 1,108 whites, 474 slaves, and 126 free people of color resided in St. Augustine. A decade later, the population included 1,476 whites, 863 slaves, and 120 free blacks, although these numbers surely reflect the influx of military personnel and rural refugees as a consequence of the Second Seminole War. African Americans had considerable freedom in this setting, despite white security concerns, earning their own spending money, learning and using a variety of skills, worshiping, and otherwise participating in a rich social life.[32]

Other evidence from the newspapers reveals a seamy side of the story. It portrays an urban locale rife with mayhem and political rancor. Early in 1839, one mile north of the city, a "careless servant" set a blaze that leveled Thomas Douglas's farmhouse. Somebody broke into T. S. Hewlett's store in July. Yellow fever struck between September and November, sickening 700–850 inhabitants and killing 39–50. A mentally ill New York native hung himself at the beginning of December. A week later, a suspected arsonist destroyed J. C. Clelland's uninsured, "very handsome" dwelling at the North City wharf's entrance. As 1840 unfolded, another arsonist struck A. J. Noda's mercantile establishment. During the following month, the bloated corpse of a psychologically disturbed man was discovered floating near the Anastasia Island lighthouse. The summer brought news of the malicious knifing of a horse and the drowning of an "insane" soldier near the North City Beach, along with a duel attributed to editorials in St. Augustine's *Florida Herald & Southern Democrat*. Indeed, on the pages of the Democrat *Herald* and the Whig *News,* vicious political mudslinging so poisoned the atmosphere that federal judge Robert R. Reid decried the "very dreadful consequences which party will lead to" and the "want of unanimity and brotherly love among us."[33]

And then, there was the Seminole War that would not go away. In February 1840, warriors killed two wagoners transporting mail from Jacksonville to St. Augustine. Three tense months later, a party of Seminoles ambushed a theater troupe seven miles from town. Next, they conducted a midsummer assault on Indian Key in South Florida, along with an attack on Edwin Jenckes's homestead twenty-five miles north of the city, which multiplied white fears. Florida's new governor, Robert R. Reid, pledged to tighten security and "immediately offer rewards for the apprehension of all whites & blacks holding intercourse with, or aiding the Indians." On 14 September, George L. Phillips again echoed white nightmares when he spoke of the "traitorous designs of some of our coloured population." Other whites petitioned Congress for assistance, citing dangers they feared from the British West Indies, where they accused officials of threatening to "incite" "savage foes" to "deeds of outrage." London, the petitioners warned, was threatening the South by "causing to be disciplined for war the coloured population of her American Colonies."[34] The memorialists understood history well. From as far back as the seventeenth century, colonial times, settlers in the English-speaking Southeast regarded foreign black troops as security threats.

The climax of the Seminoles' terror campaign occurred when more than a score of warriors attacked the Hanson plantation, two miles west of St. Augustine, on 25 October 1840. Guards stationed at the city gates, as well as townspeople, could hear shots that they fired. The Indians plundered the plantation, but before they could torch the buildings, loyal slaves warned whites, who succeeded in dispersing the raiders. This raid badly frightened the American forces. During the ensuing night, rattled sentinels posted around the plantation fired on approaching US troops, killing a sergeant and wounding an officer. In the excitement thereafter, George and Joe, two Hanson bondsmen, were "arrested on a charge of treasonable intercourse with the Indians." The case against the bondsmen was pursued vigorously. By late November, a grand jury had "examined upwards of 30 witnesses, embracing officers of the Army, negroes, and captured Indians," and took note of the "extraordinary zeal for [George and Joe's] conviction" on the part of some witnesses. Still, the members of the jury "were uninfluenced by the malignant prejudices of several of the witnesses, and no bill was found against the slaves."[35] Once again, as in the 1830s, whites resisted the temptation to circumvent the justice system by taking blood vengeance on blacks accused of treason.

Whether George and Joe were guilty or innocent, many blacks did in fact ally themselves with the Seminoles, and, as Kenneth Porter concluded, they played a major role in the Indians "winning control of the St. Johns River valley up to the gates of St. Augustine in the early days of the war." By keeping "that region terrorized," they forced commanding General Thomas S. Jesup to allow scores of runaway slaves who had joined the Indians to leave Florida. On the other hand, the 1840 Hanson raid constitutes an example of historical complexity. Jesup had decided, in the historian Larry Rivers's words, to employ a "divide-and-conquer" strategy in 1838 that traded black freedom for black support, or at least neutrality. Afterward, "many Black Seminole leaders," shifted their allegiance to the US military, rendering critically important services as guides and interpreters. Feeling betrayed, the Seminoles "took revenge when they could."[36] Hence, at the Hanson plantation, by 1840, bondsmen had reason to inform on the Seminoles.

Historian Larry Rivers has characterized the Second Seminole War, particularly from 1835 to 1838, as "probably . . . the largest slave uprising in the annals of North American history." At the war's commencement, some 1,600 African Americans, the Black Seminoles, called the Indian nation their home. More than 1,100 slaves labored nearby. By some estimates, a thousand bond persons may have run to the Indians during the fighting. The guerilla conflict cost Washington $40 million and the lives of 1,500 American troops.[37] The war also may be viewed as a major episode in the ongoing effort of the enslaved to thwart the United States' imposition of an American-style slave society in the former Spanish territory. To be sure, in this respect, it may be considered as an extension of the Patriot War of 1812–1813, when blacks and Indians sided with the Spaniards against American invaders. Moreover, it constituted the culmination of the Anglo-Hispanic struggle over both sanctuary in Florida and the presence of black fighting men there. Now, the closest freedom destination for St. Johns County's enslaved was across the Gulf Stream in the Bahamas.

St. Johns County's people of color saw the ocean as the remaining path to liberty. In 1839, the *St. Augustine News* reported that a "negro belonging to J. HERNANDEZ, Esq., of this city, secreted himself on board of the Southerner, just before she left the wharf for Charleston, on her last trip." The *Southerner*'s skipper discovered the stowaway after he had embarked, and though "put to a great deal of trouble on account of the slave," returned him to Hernández.[38] Much more significant black migrations would take place by sea in the 1840s.

5
Restricted Manumission, Migrations, and Antimiscegenation

Florida lawmakers sought to complete their victory against black fighting men by launching a vigorous attack on manumission in 1842. The sad outcome of the slave Jimmy Gibbs's freedom bid (which began in 1839 when his owner agreed to sell the black man to a master who would emancipate him so that he could remain united to his St. Augustine family) vividly distinguishes the American regime's attitude from that of the Spaniards. That George Gibbs, the owner, was willing to part with Jimmy Gibbs likely was due to his family connections with Zephaniah Kingsley, who was especially notable among whites in antebellum East Florida for his concern for free blacks' well-being. George Gibbs was Kingsley's brother-in-law and spent a great deal of time at the Kingsley plantation on Fort George Island, near modern Jacksonville. "The door of liberty," Kingsley believed, should always be "open to every slave who can find the means of purchasing himself." A planter who followed this precept would be better able to control his labor force, he theorized, for "hope creates a spirit of economy, industry and emulation to obtain merit by good behavior, which has a general and beneficial effect."[1]

Jimmy Gibbs faced the task of finding a buyer he could trust. He eventually located such a man in Andrew Pow, who once had been the Minorcan Pablo Sabate's slave and had purchased his freedom a decade earlier for $400. Pow had at least two children by Juana (also called Jenny), a slave of Francisco Gué, and a daughter by Francisca, a bondswoman of Doña Marianna Gué. All of Pow's children were baptized in the Roman Catholic faith, and all officially bore the surname Gué. A year after Pow purchased himself, Francisco Gué emancipated Pow's wife, Jenny, then about thirty-five years of age, for

$350. Three years later, in 1833, Pow paid $173.50 for a lot on St. George Street in St. Augustine next to the Presbyterian church.[2]

Jimmy Gibbs and Andrew Pow were friends who worshiped together in a Baptist congregation. After a long discussion in the presence of other black church members, Pow agreed to buy and then manumit his friend on condition that the latter repay his $700 purchase price. When Gibbs asked Pow to draw up a contract, however, he refused. "You know brother Jimmy," Pow responded, "you and I are [Christian] brethren and . . . not of this world . . . our [oral] agreement is more binding than any in writing." In a weak bargaining position, Gibbs reluctantly assented. As a free man of color, Pow had to secure the approval of his white guardian, Joshua Joyner, for this arrangement. With the explicit understanding that Gibbs would be freed upon paying Pow $700, Joyner consented. Only George Gibbs is known to have voiced any objection, complaining that on the open market, his bondsman would have brought $900.[3]

In Andrew Pow, Jimmy Gibbs had a master whose talents, ambitions, and energy matched his own. Once a slave himself, Pow had purchased his own liberty and probably that of his wife Jenny, in addition to accumulating property, including a town lot. Furthermore, Pow had rejected his slave surname, as well as his former owner's religion. Thus, Pow was an attractive role model for the Protestant Gibbs. Inspired by the prospect of freedom, Gibbs worked hard, in time earning his market value of $900, more than the agreed on freedom price, which he duly handed over to Pow. The latter, to Gibbs's dismay, refused to execute the legal paperwork necessary to certify Gibbs's freedom.[4]

Meanwhile, Andrew Pow was taking measures to solidify his own precarious liberty. In April 1841, he married Jenny Gué in the Presbyterian Church, and some time thereafter purchased his son Francisco, then about twenty years old, from Francisco Gué for $700, mortgaging his town lot to do so. Meanwhile, his relationship with Jimmy Gibbs deteriorated. Seeing Pow's expenditure on his son, the slave pressed Pow for his freedom papers, only to have his black master threaten him with the whip and have him jailed on 9 November 1842.[5] It is evident that for Pow, blood proved thicker than the waters of baptism.

A day after Jimmy Gibbs's arrest, the American legal system initially worked in his favor. The slave's lawyer had him released on a writ of habeas corpus made possible when Joshua Joyner, Pow's former guardian, entered a deposition supporting Gibbs. The latter, sensing a victory, expressed the desire "to be liberated by process of law," as he would have been under the Spanish regime. Federal Judge Isaac H. Bronson, who heard the case on 10 November, ordered that another hearing take place on 28 November, remanding Gibbs in the meantime to the custody of James Gould, Pow's current guardian. The results of this second hearing are unknown, but it is clear that Gibbs lost his freedom bid, for in September 1844, with Gould's approval, Andrew Pow sold Gibbs to Rafael Fontané, who in turn conveyed him to George R. Fairbanks, who seems to have owned Gibbs's wife, Venus. Less than a month after parting with Gibbs, Pow manumitted his son Francisco.[6] There is no record that Jimmy Gibbs ever was emancipated in St. Johns County.

By 1850, Andrew Pow was dead. His wife Jenny seems to have preceded him in death, and his son Francisco apparently left St. Augustine in 1848. At the time of Pow's passing, he owned a lot appraised at $100 and personal effects worth $40. He also left two hogs and twenty-five chickens. The census of that year listed "Andrew Sabata" as an illiterate black laborer living alone, birthplace unknown. In his final days, he may have converted to Catholicism, for on 10 January 1849, a free man of color, aged fifty, named Andrés Sabate, was baptized.[7]

Jimmy Gibbs's fate illustrates the decline of *coartación* by 1842, and the increased precariousness of the status of blacks caught in Florida's transition from a Spanish society with slaves to an American slave society. As a bondsman, Jimmy Gibbs had no standing in court under US law. Even if he could have negotiated a written agreement with Andrew Pow, it would have carried no legal weight, for it was impossible for a slave to make a binding contract. The arrangement between Pow and Gibbs, therefore, was a private affair, unenforceable by law.[8] Pow, from his standpoint, surely understood that manumissions were becoming increasingly difficult in Florida. Therefore, he placed the liberation of his family before the emancipation of a fellow church member. From this perspective, the legislature's assault on the pillar of manumission had significantly affected both Gibbs and Pow, albeit in different ways.

Because of St. Augustine's Spanish past, American Florida's antimanumission policy was especially repressive. As a result, some bondsmen, unlike Jimmy Gibbs, decided to employ extralegal measures to attain their liberty. On 2 July 1841, Ned or Edward Dixon, a twenty-three-year-old enslaved carpenter, fled from his owner in a small boat. Dixon, a "bright Mulatto or Quadroon" with straight hair and the "letters E D on his arm in Indian ink," could pass for a white man. On 19 November 1842, James Keogh announced a "liberal reward" for the recovery of his missing yawl, which he believed had been stolen by Amos, Sandy, and Brass, fugitive slaves of William H. Williams. Slaves in other areas took similar measures. At Key West in early July 1843, seven slaves stole a boat and though "closely pursued," they managed to reach the Bahamas, where a St. Augustine newspaper reported that "they have ever since been sheltered and have no doubt been made free."[9]

On Tuesday morning, 25 July 1843,[10] the daring, intelligence, and skill of seven enslaved men convulsed St. Augustine "into a state of unusual excitement." Before daybreak, Robert Williams, Joe Williams, Gasper Mickler, and Henry Fontané, "the negroes composing the crew of the U.S. Transport Sch. Walter M," along with Andrew Gué, William Hernández, and Jim Ashe, commandeered the schooner's boat, loading it with "plenty of provisions." Besides "a quantity of bread, pork, and water," the bondsmen took the federal vessel's "spy-glass, compass, and lead line," along with "about 400 rounds of cartridges" and "seven stand of muskets." They then rowed some two miles south to Fish's Island, opposite the city, where they abandoned the *Walter M*'s boat and loaded themselves and their supplies into "a large whale boat belonging to the [harbor] pilots which had been hauled up and repaired."[11] Thus began a migration and manumission that would create international repercussions.

One might imagine the shock of St. Augustine's white residents as they discovered the theft from the *Walter M* in the morning, its abandoned boat in the afternoon, and the missing pilot boat "towards night." Moreover, "with one or two exceptions [the fugitives] were thought to be most faithful negroes and stood high in the estimation of their owners." One of the "exceptions" was "the notorious" Andrew Gué, who "made some noise in the beginning of our Indian troubles." Gué's name appears at the top of the subsequent reward list for the runaways. Below him is William Hernández, who may have been the other exception. Perhaps he is the slave of Joseph M. Hernández who unsuccessfully stowed away on a ship bound for Charleston, South Carolina, in 1839.[12] Those employed as crewmen on the *Walter M* certainly had been deemed trustworthy, which made the bondsmen's bold gambit for self-liberation an especially bitter pill for whites to swallow.

We know that in 1839, Andrew Gué had worked for the city, presumably on his own time. Three years later, the enslaved Henrietta Boyé bore him a daughter whom the couple baptized in the Catholic Church. During this time, he apparently enjoyed a close relationship with Antonio Fontané, a bondsman highly regarded by whites for his fidelity. Fontané stood as godfather for Gué's infant girl. To all appearances, Gué had integrated himself into St. Augustine society, and he probably was en route to purchasing his freedom. If that was indeed the case, something went wrong in the summer of 1841. In July, his owner, Francis Gué, warned St. Augustinians not to hire or do business with Andrew Gué without first obtaining written permission. The bondsman chafed under this restriction. He ran away for a time in June 1843. The mother of his child, moreover, may either have died or was separated from him around this time. Records indicate that her owner's family left town between 1842 and 1850.[13] In short, his hopes for a happy future were rapidly shrinking.

The fugitives' owners must have felt angered, disappointed, and duped by bondsmen like Andrew Gué, whom they believed they had treated well, even mercifully. On a much more mundane level, however, St. Augustine's bond persons adeptly manipulated white paternalism. For example, in a letter that Joseph Simeon Sánchez wrote on 14 August 1843, he complained that his slave Ben, whom he had permitted to work independently, "regularly cheated" him by withholding a portion of his wages. Consequently, Sánchez rented out Ben to help build the city's seawall. Another slave, John, Sánchez groused, "began to play me the same game being either sick or pretending to be so." When Sánchez put him to work on the seawall, he "upon one excuse or another . . . never worked a whole month." The frustrated master added that John "reported himself sick early on this month and today[?] has reported himself well." Because construction was scheduled to halt on 20 August, Sánchez ended up "allow[ing] him to find work on his own account."[14] Hence, although slave owners viewed themselves as benevolent because they allowed their "servants" to exercise degrees of autonomy, such "lenience" was rooted both in white self-interest and black shrewdness. One can discern both of these factors in the escape of Gué and his companions.

Because of the whale boat's seaworthiness, the quantity of provisions taken, and the navigational instruments carried off, St. Augustine officials quickly surmised that the fugitives were headed to the British Bahamas, from whence one of the men of color hailed. Whites suspected that outside influences had impelled them to do so. They could not fathom the notion that local slaves, on their own accord, would cause such trouble. In slave owners' minds, their "people" must have been corrupted. Joseph Simeon Sánchez blamed his slave Ben's intransigence on abolitionist influences, hinting that Andrew Gué and his comrades had fallen under the same spell. In fact, Mayor Abraham Dupont and his aldermen, Pedro Benet, Manuel Crespo, E. J. Midicis, and Matthew Solana, found "good ground for believing that there exists in some quarter, and probably in the Bahama Islands, a regularly organized system for the abduction of our slaves—or for aiding and abetting them in escaping from their owners."[15]

Black St. Augustinians gladly fueled this paranoia. "A few days" after Andrew Gué and his companions escaped, "a suspicious sail appeared on the coast and continued for several days "to lurk on and off" of St. Augustine's harbor, causing "excited general attention" among the inhabitants. The harbor pilots boarded it and discovered "a rather numerous crew . . . but otherwise [it was] unusually light, or only in ballast." The mysterious ship was from Rum Key in the Bahamas and when the pilots departed, it "immediately put about, and steered in the wake of the Walter M—the vessel from which a portion of the negroes escaped, and which had just previously left [St. Augustine] for Key West." Afterward, a slave informed his master that one of the fugitives, "a few nights before he absconded, observed to some of his comrades, that a British vessel would soon be off the Port; and that there would then be a good opportunity for those who wished it, to obtain their freedom.[16]

To be sure, it seemed like the seven runaways had vanished into thin air. Although on Tuesday, when the escape was discovered, a "detachment of soldiers were despatched in boats to Matanzas bar," some twelve miles south of town, to "intercept them," the party "returned on Thursday without success." They were not spotted again until Sunday, 6 August, when they suddenly appeared ten miles north of St. Augustine on John Seguí's farm. "Suffer[ing] much for want of water," they "filled a three gallon jug" and "supplied themselves with a quantity of Water Melons" before returning to sea. They told Seguí that they had made it to Key Biscayne, three hundred miles to the south, but could not cross the Gulf Stream because of the "adverse winds" and strong current that "drifted them to the northward." Because Seguí was a "simple man" and alone when the fugitives approached him, he dared not challenge them. The Minorcan did send word to town, causing the authorities to send one search party south by land and another by water. The next day, St. Augustine's *Florida Herald & Southern Democrat* published an offer of a reward of $350 for black men's apprehension.[17]

The fugitives must have become increasingly desperate and disheartened. Their luck seemed to be running out. On Wednesday evening, 9 August, a scout spotted their fire on a beach across from the abandoned Bulow plantation, more than forty miles south of St. Augustine. As he awaited "the advance party from General [Joseph M.] Hernandez's," the slaves discerned the scout and quickly extinguished their fire. Trapped by high surf, their only escape route was via the Halifax River to Mosquito Inlet, and then out to sea. To reach the river, the black men had to carry their whale boat 150 yards across the beach.[18] Although they once more eluded their captors, their plight would become even more precarious in the coming weeks.

Fergus Bordewich's description of a contemporary whale boat provides a sketch of the circumstances under which the runaways labored. Whale boats were small, perhaps twenty-five feet in length, quite capable of ocean voyages, and equipped with "fore and main spritsails." When the wind was not blowing, they could be rowed. But, they provided no protection from the sun, saltwater, and rain. Sleeping would be difficult. Wet clothing, thirst, and "claustrophobic" conditions would cause "extreme" discomfort. Moreover, the mariners would have to keep a constant watch for potential captors eager to administer "sure and swift punishment." At times, they might have to land in order to dry their clothes, cook, and gather water.[19] Just as in the cases of slaves who, under the Spaniards, were able to purchase their liberty by paying cash installments, it would take a mixture of talent, determination, perseverance, and luck to attain freedom in the Bahamas.

Yet, the historical record demonstrates that these seven men thirsted for freedom even more than they thirsted for water. In early August, during their second voyage to Key Biscayne, whites spotted a "suspicious fore-and-aft schooner" at New Smyrna, some 60 miles south of St. Augustine, and then again "off the bar at Fort Pierce, 120 miles south of New Smyrna. On 22 August, Captain Russell of the sloop *Seagull* observed this schooner at anchor, off Hillsboro Inlet, eighty miles south of Fort Pierce. When the *Seagull* landed at the inlet, the schooner "moved about a mile out." The next morning, "a brig hove in sight" and headed toward the schooner, which "immediately" weighed anchor "and made off to the Southward, and after beating away from the brig, made her way back Northwardly." The brig left the schooner "tacking about" off Hillsboro Inlet on 23 August.[20]

On the morning of 24 August, "near Lake Worth," about twenty miles north of Hillsboro Inlet, settlers noticed "a whale boat with 4 oars." "From the manoeuvres of those on board," Russell reported, the settlers "supposed them to be negroes who ran away from St. Augustine on the 24th July last, and were now connected with the schooner." When the whale boat was hailed, "no answer returned." As a result, "two shots were then fired at [the whale boat], but by lusty pulling she escaped." When the US revenue cutter *Crawford* visited Lake Worth, its commanding officer, Captain Day, after hearing about this encounter, left "in pursuit of the negroes and vessel."[21]

The relationship between the schooner and the whale boat in which the seven St. Augustine fugitives absconded has not come to light. Nevertheless, it points to a lingering "conspiracy theory" that had emerged from the initial discovery of the escape. Between 24 August and 1 September, the fugitives seemingly made the final sixty miles from Lake Worth to Key Biscayne. According to the scholar Marvin Dunn, "escaped slaves from Georgia and other southern states" used the island, which "stands nearer to . . . the Gulf Stream, than any other piece of land," as a way station to the Bahamas. Cape Florida, on the southern tip, was a well-known source of fresh water. Because they were short of supplies, Andrew Gué and his comrades tried to take them from the settlers along the Miami River, but they "were made to retreat." With the settlers following them, the runaways "landed, hid their boat, and made good their retreat to the thick mangrove hammocks" on Key Biscayne.[22] The black freedom-seekers had once again outwitted their befuddled opponents. The burning need for provisions, however, would seriously jeopardize their bid for liberty and in the process illustrate history's complexity.

On 1 September,[23] around 5:30 p.m., three armed fugitives entered the home of John Henry Geireen, a German immigrant who had left his wife in New York and had settled on Key Biscayne with his daughter and son some nine months previously. Alone in the house was Anna, a girl between the ages of five and seven. The intruders did not threaten or use violence against her, but one of them placed his hands over her mouth to keep her from crying. They made off with flour, biscuit, "wearing apparel," and a rifle. Then matters went horribly awry. Anna quickly ran to her father, who was fishing nearby on the beach. Geireen grabbed his gun, giving chase to the black men. "A few moments later," Anna "heard two shots in quick succession and her father's cries immediately after." For half an hour, the German settler writhed in pain from four six-inch buckshot wounds to the left chest and neck. At six o'clock, he died. Anna and her brother, a boy two years older, hid in terror during the night, "enduring intense suffering, from the stings of myriads of mosquitoes." The next morning, "a small boat with some white men from the Miami [settlements] came there but would not remove the children though they were entreated to do so." Finally, at noon, a Mr. Ferguson rescued the traumatized youngsters.[24]

Andrew Gué and his companions continued to be daring and elusive foes of the United States after this most unfortunate incident. The fugitives were seen leaving Key Biscayne in the direction of the Miami River. "Several days later," they returned to the island. On 3 October, the "master of a fishing smack" informed the authorities at Key West that he had spotted the runaways at Key Biscayne's abandoned lighthouse. In addition, the captain of "a small schooner," reached Key West the same day, reporting that after landing on Key Biscayne, he saw the black men, who ran after him until he safely reached his vessel. These accounts prompted Captain E. A. Ogden to send Lt. Hetzel, with twenty soldiers carrying twenty days' rations, to Key Biscayne on the *Walter M*. The *Nautilus*, a revenue cutter, also was despatched.[25] The nooses were tightening around the fugitives' necks.

Hetzel reached Key Biscayne on the afternoon of 6 October. Lt. Davis, of the US schooner *Flirt*, also landed on the island the same day. For the next two days, the military "thoroughly" searched "all the coves, and creeks, where a boat might easily be concealed," but "discover[ed] no traces of the negroes." The manhunt expanded to "both shores of Key Biscayne Bay, Fort Dallas, the Miami, Little River, McGregor's Island, and a great portion of the tract of country called the 'Hunting Grounds.'" On 10 October, when the *Nautilus* arrived, a reinforced search party under the command of Lt. Woodward "proceeded a second time to the Miami, giving the country a more thorough examination." The federal troops "scoured" some sixty to seventy miles of "the old hunting grounds," for they believed that "in lingering about the Miami," the fugitives "intended joining the Indians." To forestall this possibility, General William Worth enjoined the latter to capture the black men and deliver them "for punishment."[26]

The fruitless manhunt continued until at least 13 October. When the soldiers returned to the Miami settlements, they received shocking news—"the negroes . . . had . . . returned." Moreover, the seven fugitives, still manning the pilot boat that they had taken from St. Augustine, had added two more men to their number. One, Anson Murphy, another St. Augustine slave, as well as the second new man, some time afterward apparently lost heart and abandoned the original runaways. In any event, the terrified Miami settlers claimed that they "were not strong enough" to subdue the nine blacks, who had "passed up and down the Miami." Because the weather had been "calm and favorable" during the "five or six days succeeding the return of the negroes down the Miami," the US officers believed that the bondsmen had "ma[de] their way to some of the Bahamas."[27]

Indeed, a new drama was about to unfold. Nassau's *Royal Gazette* reported that on 10 October 1843, the *Springbird*, a schooner returning from a "wrecking or droghing voyage," carried "seven persons" from a "whale boat" that had "fallen in with" the Bahamian vessel. Upon reaching their long-cherished sanctuary, Andrew Gué, along with his companions, William Hernández, Joe Williams, Robert Williams, James Ashe, Gasper Mickler, and Harvey (alias Henry) Fontané, whose official surnames indicated that they belonged to different owners, made a statement pregnant with meaning. That is, they claimed to be the property of only one man, "a Mr. William Williams, of St. Augustine, E. F."[28]

By doing so, they acknowledged their bonds both to each other and to blacks in the Bahamas. Andrew Gué seems to have been born a Williams slave, although the case for his origins is circumstantial and far from certain. A list of human property belonging to the Samuel Williams estate at Tomoka dated 1814 contains a family consisting of the biracial John, his wife Hester, and their newborn son Andrew. Also enumerated were William, a son of Friday and Lucy; Bob, the child of Boatswain and Nancy; and Harry, whose parents were Long John and Betty. Perhaps these were the men who whites called William Hernández, Robert Williams, and Henry Fontané. James Ashe, another fugitive, was married to a Mickler family slave. He may have had blood or kinship connections to another runaway, Gasper Mickler.[29]

Under the Spaniards, East Florida's black militia often were related to one another or had established fictive kinships through Catholic sacraments. Gué and his comrades, by raiding a federal vessel, operated as a military unit. They seem to have exhibited some of the region's traditional martial kinship patterns. The Williams family also had held slaves in the Bahamas, blacks who in 1843 were free and who, because of the Williams connection, might sympathize with the fugitives more personally. The runaways from St. Augustine astutely surmised, as Alan Cobley explained, the fundamental importance of kinship in "small, 'people-sized' communities in the Caribbean, where everyday life is negotiated through a series of deeply imbedded local networks."[30]

On 13 November 1843, the Grand Jury of the Counties of Monroe and Dade indicted the fugitives for robbery and murder. A week later, the United States requested that London order a warrant for their arrest, and "upon the exhibition to the proper British Colonial authorities . . . of such evidence as may be deemed sufficient under the provisions of the 10th article of the Treaty of Washington," to deliver the prisoners to Joseph B. Browne, the US marshal from Key West. The British minister in Washington, Henry S. Fox, sent instructions to the governor of the Bahamas, Sir Francis Cockburn, in duplicate packets, one of which Marshal Browne received at Key West on

17 December. There the local federal judge and the district attorney advised Browne that in addition to Fox's instructions, certified copies of the grand jury's indictments, along with a person who could identify Andrew Gué and his companions, would constitute sufficient evidence for the extradition. Browne set sail for Nassau the following day, arriving at his destination on Christmas Eve. The lawman had a private axe to grind as well. Seven months previously, in May 1843, Coleman Royal, one of his own slaves, with a party of four men and a woman, stole the pilot boat *Mary Neavis* from Key West and sailed to Andros Island with a "considerable amount of property in money and goods" of Browne's. These fugitives subsequently were declared free in Nassau.[31]

Besides placing abolitionist Great Britain in a quandary over the extradition of runaway bond persons, the St. Augustine runaways compelled the United States to walk a foreign policy tightrope. On 9 August 1842, Washington had signed the Webster-Ashburton Treaty, which settled a simmering border controversy with Canada that had threatened to erupt into war. Moreover, the agreement had endowed Anglo-American relations with a much more positive tenor, holding out the happy prospect of future cooperation between the two nations. Because British animosity constituted the top threat to US security, this promising state of affairs was no mean accomplishment. At the same time, however, sectional controversy over slavery's expansion, especially in regard to Texas, raged within the Union. Edward Rugemer has argued that at the time of Andrew Gué's flight, London's policy of liberating those American slaves who made it to its colonial ports either by accident or design, generated severe "Anglophobia in the South, which became the dominant factor in the push to annex Texas to the United States."[32] This US preoccupation with Texas, along with a healthy respect for British military power, paved the way for the fugitives' freedom.

They also were assisted by an intricate transnational network of allies. Governor Cockburn received a copy of Fox's instructions on 10 December. Cockburn was "particularly careful" that "its contents should not transpire, as had its purport been known it might have induced to such of the Fugitives as were at the time in Nassau quitting the place." He well-understood the power of local black opinion regarding the liberation of US runaway slaves. Despite his precaution, he could not stifle the black maritime communication network. A vessel arriving at nearby Harbour Island from Key West already had reported that the *Nautilus* was waiting at the latter port to transport Browne to Nassau. Consequently, Cockburn suspected that "as soon as the 'Nautilus' was seen off the few of [the fugitives] who might previously have been here, were on their way to quit the Island." Their plight, as in previous cases of a similar nature, had generated sizeable black community support, which pressured British authorities in Nassau to hold firm in their policy of liberation. In addition, a "Friendly Society" in the colonial capital "composed of emancipated Negroes," hired an attorney on behalf of the black St. Augustinians. Marshal Browne responded by employing his own barrister.[33]

Meanwhile, the fugitives' white supporters, exploiting recent advances in printing technology and postal service, also mobilized. Annie Abel and Frank Klingberg described how the British and Foreign Anti-Slavery Society (BFASS) had "its means of ferreting out information and this in the most remote places." The US abolitionists "aimed and managed to keep their British friends thoroughly well informed of all conditions at home likely to affect the cause they mutually had at heart." Ironically, the anxious, detailed reports that St. Augustine's newspapers furnished, placed the runaways on a vast Atlantic world stage. From Boston, circa 15 November 1843, Joshua Leavitt informed Thomas Clarkson, the BFASS president, of the presence of the black Floridians in the Bahamas. By 6 December, Leavitt's letter had reached London and was forwarded to the Earl of Aberdeen, Britain's foreign affairs secretary. In this note, Aberdeen was reminded of the "intense anxiety" of the "British public" regarding such matters. Eight days later, Reverend J. H. Hinton of the BFASS relayed information concerning the runaways to Reverend Henry Capern in Nassau, requesting that he lobby the local colonial authorities and asking him to keep his English counterparts apprised. Next, in early 1844, the *British and Foreign Anti-Slavery Reporter* chided the Americans for conducting a "national negro hunt." Although federal officials maintained that Andrew Gué and company were "fugitives from justice," the *Reporter* lionized them as refugees "from oppression."[34]

Evidentiary matters were of utmost importance. The US indictments were not based on eyewitness accounts of the shooting on Key Biscayne. The dead man's two young children merely heard shots. For this reason, although Marshal Browne brought people to Nassau who could identify the black men who had fled St. Augustine, they could not place them on Key Biscayne nor determine if Geireen's homicide, because of "self-defense," was justifiable. This point was crucial, because for extradition to take place, the defendants' actions had to meet the definition of murder in the Bahamas as well as in the United States. Moreover, indictments coming from slave owners, who had a vested interest in ensuring that human property was recovered, were suspect in British circles. Thus, the Florida grand jury was perceived as being prone to fraud and capable of corrupting local colonials. Also, when runaways were extradited, even if they were found innocent, they still were reenslaved. Because the case of the Florida fugitives was the first to fall under the new extradition agreement, the nervous Hinton asked Capern if the black men could be moved to "any spot where they would be safer than at Nassau?"[35]

The *New York Evangelist* opined that the Bahamian authorities' decision would "have an important bearing, and disclose[s] more fully than any other decision which has yet occurred, the determination of Great Britain with regard to our fugitive slaves." Marshal Browne and Governor Cockburn treated the affair with urgency. Although it was Christmas Day and Cockburn was scheduled to attend "Divine Service at St. Matthews Church" at 10 a.m., he agreed to meet Browne and the US consular agent at Government House at 9:30 in the morning. The following day, Cockburn caused a warrant to be issued to Chief Justice J. C. Lees for the arrest of the fugitives. On 28 December, Lees and his two associated justices received Browne's evidence. After the "most mature consideration," they "reluctantly" decided the next day that it was "quite impossible" to issue a warrant based on "mere Indictments without any evidence upon which they were framed." That is, they refused to accept indictments from a "jury in Florida" without "*viva voce evidence*" or copies of the depositions on which the original warrant was granted. The judges pointedly reasoned that what constituted murder in Florida might be "very far" from the definition of the crime in Great Britain or the "Northern States of America." Browne departed on 30 December, genteelly thanking Cockburn "for the Courtesy and good feeling evinced toward him personally, and in his official character." Despite vigorous protests on the part of the United States, London stood its ground. Andrew Gué and his comrades finally were officially free men, although, by 1 January 1844, Cockburn believed that they had "left this Colony." The still-wary *Boston Daily Advertiser* advised them to "take care of themselves."[36]

International abolitionists had viewed the affair as a "test case." Accordingly, Reverend J. H. Hinton advised the Earl of Aberdeen, that "the eyes of nations . . . the eyes of the world . . . will be fixed on the proceedings which are taken in respect to [the case of the seven Florida fugitives]."[37] In the late seventeenth century, English slaves fleeing to Spanish East Florida also had created "test cases." Furthermore, bond persons in St. Augustine under Spain's rule had grown accustomed to appealing to the judiciary for their liberty. In 1843, geopolitically astute black runaways from the "Ancient City" essentially opted to press a "freedom suit" before British judges. By taking such drastic measures to do so, Andrew Gué and his companions personified the deep-seated yearnings of enslaved St. Augustinians for their liberty. In time, this pent-up volcano would explode. That is, the Civil War would fully expose the short-sightedness of Florida legislators' draconian racial policies.

By acquiring Florida, the historian John Lewis Gaddis explained, Washington sought to quash security concerns emanating from what twenty-first-century commentators would call a "failed state." But, the republic now had another problem: "how to keep that expansion itself from generating new sources of insecurity." As Florida's territorial period came to a close, its lawmakers increasingly perceived the British Bahamas as a menace to the system of bondage that was the foundation of the peninsula's wealth. Likewise, in 1842, Secretary of State Daniel Webster viewed the Bahamas as a threat to the entire nation's security. These fears were reflected in newspaper reports from St. Augustine relating to the 1843 escape. Furthermore, on 14 August 1843, St. Augustine's city council implored the federal government to initiate naval patrols between their locale and Key West.[38]

With the spectacular flight of their own slaves fresh in their minds, St. Augustine whites soon saw further evidence of the lengths to which African Americans would go to free themselves. Sometime during the summer of 1844, eight blacks employed as oarsmen by "an association of Pilots" at the mouth of the Mississippi River, near La Balize, Louisiana, seized the pilot boat *Lafayette* and headed toward the Bahamas. En route, the Louisiana fugitives became stranded on a reef, where a Key West wrecking schooner encountered them. The blacks told the wrecker's captain that they had been without water for over three days, and that they were bound to Jamaica from Boston. After carrying the castaways to Tortugas Key, the suspicious skipper, noticing the pilot boat's freshly lettered name, rubbed off the paint, thus revealing the vessel's true identity. The runaways then confessed. Because the US magistrate at Key West was absent, the wreckers brought the *Lafayette* to Judge Isaac H. Bronson in St. Augustine, seeking salvage rights.[39]

Two of the captured fugitives claimed to be free mariners. Judge Bronson, therefore, allowed them the opportunity to prove their claims. The other six prisoners he ordered sold at auction, along with the *Lafayette*. Forty percent of the net proceeds was earmarked for the wreckers. About two weeks later, however, on 10 August 1844, the *Vigilant*, a US revenue schooner, arrived in St. Augustine with a "demand from the Governor of Louisiana" for the return of all eight runaways, six of whom had been sold four days previously.

Apparently, the *Vigilant* left St. Augustine with only the two men whom Bronson had delayed auctioning. The revenue schooner later perished in a "tremendous" October hurricane that slammed Key West. Among the passengers presumed dead were Robert Cooper, one of the Louisiana pilots who had employed the apprehended runaways, and "two of the negroes who deserted with the Pilot boat from the Balize." This matter, especially as it had followed on the heels of Andrew Gué's escape and his subsequent freedom in the Bahamas, generated quite a controversy in St. Augustine.[40]

Another significant exodus of blacks from St. Augustine took place as a consequence of Tallahassee's hostility toward biracial people. By the early 1840s, St. Johns County politicians sensed an advantage in calling an opponent a "race-mixer." The *Florida Herald & Southern Democrat,* on 8 October 1841, for example, ridiculed a local political opponent, Peter Sken Smith, by calling him "*Tab* Smith," after the free man of color who had tweaked white sensibilities some ten years earlier. On 17 December 1841, the same newspaper chided another opponent, Daniel S. Gardner, for "hardly [being] considered . . . as a white man, inasmuch as he lived with his negro wife and children." The prominent politician David Levy Yulee, who was born in the Virgin Islands, also was victimized by the town's growing racism. His enemies spread a rumor that he was a man of color. In 1842, at the "public dinner table" in St. Augustine's Florida Hotel, none other than Zephaniah Kingsley, the patriarch of a multiracial family and defender of free black rights, perceived the expediency of bowing to the prevailing rhetoric against people of mixed African and European ancestry. Kingsley, defending Yulee's "whiteness," noted that he had known his father on St. Thomas and was "intimately acquainted" with Yulee's mother's family. It was, Kingsley paradoxically asserted, "one of the most respectable in the Island."[41]

St. Augustine's extended Clarke family also felt the sting of the growing entrenchment of negative American attitudes toward those of Afro-European descent. By the 1840s, persons of color in St. Johns County who "flaunted" their white ancestry encountered stern rebukes. The marriage of George J. F. Clarke's quadroon granddaughter, Eliza M. Garvin, reflected the shifting ambience. Under the Spaniards, Garvin's mother and uncle had legally married whites. However, even in Spanish society, as we have seen in the cases of Francisco Xavier Sánchez's mixed-race daughters, these unions had ruffled feathers. Thus, informants living in the early twentieth century recollected how the white fiancé of a biracial Clarke drank some of his blood so that she could swear before a priest that "she had negro blood in her veins."

Still, these interracial marriages at least had been tolerated in Spanish days. But Eliza Garvin's marriage to the Bostonian William H. Whitwell, a white Army hospital steward who was stationed at Fort Pierce, Florida, during the Second Seminole War, was another story. In order to evade Florida's antimiscegenation law, the couple contracted a Catholic marriage in Kingston, Jamaica, on 10 July 1842. There was so much opposition to this union back in St. Augustine, however, that the newlyweds felt compelled to move to Philadelphia, where William Whitwell subsequently practiced medicine.[42]

Matters soon worsened for the Clarkes. In 1845, the new state of Florida levied a discriminatory poll tax of $3 on free persons of color. Whites only had to pay $0.50. Because of territorial legislation passed in 1842, which (honoring the terms of the Adams-Onís Treaty of cession), exempted blacks who had been free Spanish subjects in Florida, the Clarkes launched a challenge. Eight men of color banded together under the quadroon James D. Garvin's leadership. They also had white allies. The white widow of James F. Clarke, Mary Dulcet Clarke, agreed to serve as a witness, as did the Minorcan Peter Triay. Joseph L. Smith, who, when he was a federal judge, had ruled in favor of the Clarkes in the 1820s, and the lawyer O. M. Dorman, took up the cudgels in court. The backgrounds of local officials gave them hope of success. The tax collector, Joseph S. Sánchez, had biracial siblings. The justice of the peace who would hear their appeal, George L. Phillips, an immigrant from British St. Helena, had sought letters of administration for Charles W. Clarke's estate in 1842. In that same year, as foreman of St. Johns County's Grand Jury, Phillips characterized St. Augustine's patrol system as "onerous" to whites and "unnecessary."[43] Upstanding white patrons, the Clarkes hoped, once again would shield them.

The quadroon George W. Clarke, son of Charles W. Clarke and Patty Wiggins, appeared before Phillips on 28 March 1846. Triay, through a translator, and the widow Clarke testified that he had lived in Fernandina before Spain ceded East Florida to the United States and had continued to reside in the territory ever since. Justice Phillips was not impressed. He declared that a "Bastard Child born of a Black Woman . . . cannot inherit any of the rights, privileges or immunities his reputed Father might have enjoyed under the Spanish Government." James D. Garvin, whose parents had been legally married, came before Phillips the same day. The next decision rendered was even more ominous. No free man of color, the magistrate fumed, was "entitled to the rights, privileges & immunities of a Free White citizen." According to the immigrant Phillips, "such a thing would have been inadmissable at the time of the Treaty with Spain and by the Laws of this Country, and of this State can never be tolerated." An appeal to the federal Superior Court apparently failed as the tax rolls for 1846–1860 reflect a defeat.[44]

Sensing that residence in St. Johns County no longer promised any hope of a prosperous future, most of the Clarke extended family, the county's most prestigious and important people of color, embarked on an exodus. In 1847, at least nine adult members, along with their children, lived on Key West. They no doubt saw it as an island of opportunity for employment linked to shipping, fishing, military activity, and related trades, as well as a place of relative racial tolerance. In October 1846, a powerful hurricane had pummeled the island, inundating the streets with five feet of water while damaging or destroying nearly every structure, including the lighthouse and fort. The aftermath of this devastation was a mushrooming population drawn by the jobs that federal repair money created. By 1850, it was the largest city in Florida, with, for the first time in its history, an appreciable black population, which numbered more than five hundred.[45]

The escape of Andrew Gué and his comrades reflected the accompanying sense of despair that the St. Augustine's enslaved felt for their freedom prospects, as well as their anger toward the new regime. Moreover, by the middle of the 1840s, the great majority of the leading family of color, the Clarkes, no longer resided in town, thus sapping the black community's strength. Those African Americans who remained in the Ancient City after Florida achieved statehood in 1845, somehow had to protect the liberties that they still enjoyed and keep hope for a happy future alive. They soon came to understand that the most potent weapon they could wield was Hispanic culture. Thus, they strove to preserve the benefits that this culture offered as best they could. Whites had not yet toppled four traditional pillars of black liberty in St. Augustine and its environs. Indeed, the remaining inhabitants of African descent would use blood ties with whites, manumission, military service, and landownership to stoke freedom's embers.

George J. F. Clarke: George J. F. Clarke was an influential Spanish colonial official and the patriarch of antebellum St. Augustine's most important free family of color. (Courtesy of the St. Augustine Historical Society Research Library)

Nelson Francis de Sales English: Part of a migration from St. Augustine to Key West in the 1840s, Nelson English became an outstanding community leader. (Courtesy of Monroe County Library Key West)

Frederick A. Clarke: A grandson of George J. F. Clarke and Flora Leslie, Frederick Clarke migrated to the Pacific Northwest and served as a territorial legislator and is one of the state of Washington's founders. (Courtesy of the Washington State Historical Society and Michael Cook)

William T. Garvin: A grandson of George J. F. Clarke and Flora Leslie, William Garvin left the Dominican Republic to serve in the Union Army during the Civil War. (Courtesy of James W. Curtis)

Edward Orval Gourdin: A grandson of William T. Garvin and a great-great grandson of George J. F. Clarke, he was an Olympic silver medalist, Harvard graduate, brigadier general, and judge. (Courtesy of James W. Curtis)

James W. Curtis: A great-great-great grandson of George J. F. Clarke and Flora Leslie, he holds a master's degree in physics and dedicated his career to the aerospace industry. He is pictured with his wife, Marjorie. (Courtesy of James W. Curtis)

Felicia Mary Garvin: A great-granddaughter of George J. F. Clarke and Flora Leslie, she was an ardent advocate for her family's rights and history. (Courtesy of James W. Curtis)

From left to right: Lianndra Davis, Sandra Fields, Jane Ball-Groom, Julia Groom, Amy Groom, and James Groom Jr., fifth and sixth generation descendants of Phoebe Dupont Shemetella and Theodore Shemetella. (Courtesy of E. Jane Ball-Groom)

Florida Garvin Lofton and Dr. Yvonne Payne Daniel, 1940, third and sixth generation descendants of Flora Leslie and George J. F. Clarke. (Courtesy of Orville Payne and Yvonne Payne Daniel)

6
Preserving Spanish Days: Marriage and Manumission

One Spanish-era legacy that persisted, although with muted or at least veiled advantages, was familial bonds with whites. Interracial relationships, however, occurred more surreptitiously and with less social pressure on white fathers to live up to their responsibilities. On 23 September 1847, Robert R. Reid informed George Burt that "Francis Forward was caught last night very quietly spending the evening with a molatto girl," thus attesting to the continuity, despite legal prohibitions, of a social pattern that stretched back to Spain's rule. The *St. Augustine News* noted the "many walking evidences" of these relationships in 1841, and visitors from the North often remarked on the number of racially mixed persons they encountered. William Cullen Bryant, who came in 1843, was impressed by the "agreeable, open, and gentle physiognomy" of the blacks he observed at Catholic Mass. The "Spanish race," he concluded, "blends more kindly with the African, than does the English, and produces handsomer men and women."[1] Bryant, then, was quick to recognize a distinguishing characteristic of the local black community.

The specifics of white-black conjugal ties, nevertheless, generally prove elusive. Compared to the Spanish period, Catholic baptismal records during the US antebellum regime offer very little data, but they sometimes hint of liaisons between prominent white men and African American women. David Levy Yulee, who served in the US Senate, and John Peck, a noted St. Augustine physician, were Protestants. This, along with antimiscegenation laws and the ridicule men faced in the press for race-mixing, makes it unlikely that Yulee and Peck would acknowledge their paternity if they sired biracial progeny. Yet, on 29 April 1839, a priest noted that "Gillermo," the son of "David Liby" and "Paty Mickler" was born. Eight years later, on 13 May 1847, "Francis Pecke[?]," a "colored boy" of "John Peke[?] and "Franc[e?]s Loid[?]"

entered the world. Thus, Senator Yulee and Dr. Peck possibly had children of color. Evidence is stronger for the planter Morris Sánchez (Joseph Simeon Sánchez's cousin), and Sheriff Rafael B. Canova, both Catholics. In late 1852, "Bridget Rebeca," the daughter of "Merris Sanchez" and the aforementioned "Patty Mickler," along with "Christina," born of "Harriet" and "Raphael B. Canova," were baptized.[2] These entries give evidence that some prestigious Hispanic whites remained willing to acknowledge their mixed-race offspring late into the antebellum period.

Secular records also point to possible blood ties between blacks and whites. George Center, a white St. Augustine merchant, Indian trader, and politician, at one time ran an ice house and grocery/liquor business with Martin Roddy. In the 1830s, Francis Roddy, whose wife was a free woman of color, owned a general store in town. Charlotte Erwin had lived with Felicia M. F. Garvin (George J. F. Clarke's mulatto daughter) and was a white planter's biracial child. On 9 May 1845, "George Center" and "Charlotte Irving" were blessed with a baby, "Ann Center." In 1850, "Charlotte Irwin," a mulatto in her midthirties, lived in the household of the mixed-race sexagenarian "George Santos." Still, neither she, nor her daughters, "Frances Irwin" and "Florida Irwin," bore the old man's surname. In his younger days, Santos would have been a good provider. During the 1830s, he had purchased his brother's freedom. Moreover, municipal officials had employed him to clean the marketplace and the city council's office. Five year-old "Anna Center" stayed with her Catholic godmother, the quadroon Honora Clarke, and the latter's white mother, Mary D. Clarke, in 1850. Ten years later, "Annie Center" resided with "Florida Center," "Frances Center," and "Charlotte Irvin." Interestingly, George Center was not Charlotte Erwin's white guardian in 1838 or 1858. Instead, he performed this duty for Fanny Fatio and Syke Saunders.[3] "Center" may have been a corruption of "Santos." On the other hand, in East Florida, free biracial women often became consorts of older whites who wielded economic or political power, and whites who had lived among the Seminoles frequently took wives of African descent.

Shifting black identities added to the uncertainty surrounding interracial relationships. In 1834, the free woman of color Amelia McQueen sued the United States for damages that its troops inflicted during the Patriot War. She filed her petition under the name of her deceased husband, Abraham McQueen. Judge Robert R. Reid ordered depositions taken "upon the application of Barsheba McQueen." One witness, Antonio Capo, stated that her husband had been "commonly called *Bashe* Abraham." Andreas Papy knew him as Abraham Bache, and his wife as Barsha McQueen. Her attorney, E. B. Gould, then explained that although she was "familiarly known as 'Mam Bash' or Barsheba as he supposes her name to be," she had informed him that her real name was Amelia. To resolve the problem, the court called on Charles Hill, "a free Blackman." He swore that the petitioner's name was Basha and that she usually was addressed as Aunt Bashy. Afterward, Hill muddied the waters, adding that he never heard the claimant referred to as Amelia. Rather, he deposed, Amelia was her daughter's name. Eight months later, in February 1842, "Aunt Bashy" filed another legal document as Amelia Nichols McQueen. Church records clarify the matter. On 17 April 1792, the biracial María del Carmen Nicoly was baptized. The priest listed her parents as the mulatto "Milla" and the black "Abraham." Both, he noted, had gained their liberty under Spain's sanctuary policy.[4]

In 1850, South Carolina native Amelia Nickols, a biracial woman eighty-five years of age, resided in St. Augustine with her daughter Tyra Nickols, aged fifty, and her fifteen-year-old grandson, Abraham Nickols. A decade later, Amelia Nickols was gone. Her daughter and grandson now carried the surname Lancaster. Joseph B. Lancaster, who the historian Canter Brown Jr. characterized as "one of Florida's most distinguished public servants," may have been Abraham Lancaster's father.[5] The relationship is not certain. Both Tyra Lancaster and her son were free-born. Hence, they were not identifying with a former owner. Many enslaved St. Augustinians kept unofficial surnames honoring male ancestors. The bondsman Antonio Fontané, for example, called himself Antonio Huertas (or Weltas), after his father, in Catholic liturgical celebrations.[6] Thus, Abraham Lancaster's father could have been one of Joseph B. Lancaster's bondsmen, or another owner's slave who used Lancaster as his first or last name. We may never know whether or not Joseph B. Lancaster was involved with Tyra Nickols, but once again, historical documents raise the possibility.

It is clear from post–Civil War sources that the free biracial Phoebe Dupont bore several children to a white man surnamed Shemetella (probably Theodore Shemytillo who fought in the Second Seminole War). The descendants of this family have inherited an oral history of their Afro-Jewish heritage. In 1850, her son called himself Moses Roberts after the white South Carolinian, James Roberts (possibly his grandfather), who in his 1814 will furnished Moses's mother with a small annuity and declared that she should be "as free." She and his younger siblings, however, in 1850 and 1860, used the surname of the wealthy St. Johns County planter, Abraham Dupont, who in 1835 followed the spirit of James Roberts's will by making the family completely independent. Once Yankee troops occupied St. Augustine, Phoebe Dupont became Phoebe Shemtala[?], and her son Julius Dupont served in the Union Army as Julius Shemetella. To be sure, free blacks in St. Johns County in the late antebellum period were overwhelmingly the products of black-white unions. According to the census of 1850, 79 of the 113 (70 percent) free persons of color in the county were biracial, as were 49 out of 82 (60 percent) of the free black community in 1860. In Florida as a whole, only around 10 percent of blacks were designated as biracial in both censuses.[7]

What these interracial relationships meant for the substance of black family life is speculative. It must have created tensions that some blacks capitalized on in countering the constrictions of a slave society. We know from one case that as late as 1860, blacks used their family connections to whites to preserve their liberty. John Gué had a white father, Francisco Gué, and a mixed-race mother, Harieta Fish. Like several of the biracial Clarkes, it appears that he served briefly in the Second Seminole War. Civil records render his racial status ambiguous, although Catholic registries denote him as a man of color. He owned slaves, in addition to real estate—assets that he most likely inherited from his father. In his family life, he followed the Spanish-era pattern of gaining respectability by marrying and baptizing his children within the Catholic Church. His fictive sacramental kinships provided his loved ones with additional security, because members of the Clarke clan and Minorcans sponsored his children between 1848 and 1858. The fact that the latter agreed to serve as godparents indicates the strength of his linkages to white relatives. During the 1850s, John Gué kept a tavern, purchased land from whites, lent money to them, and profited from real estate sales to them.[8]

Family ties apparently permitted Gué to enjoy an in-between status that helped him to circumvent racially based prohibitions. As a quadroon or octoroon, he bore predominantly European features, which may have masked his African ancestry, especially among his rural white neighbors. Gué's exceptional life attests to the survival of racial fluidity due to remnants of Spanish culture. Moreover, it demonstrates that free people of color could and did capitalize on blood connections and religious bonds with white patrons as they had under the Spaniards.

The enslaved, it may be assumed, likewise formed conjugal connections with whites and probably benefitted from them in ways that are not apparent from antebellum documents. One account, from an African American point of view, attests to the exploitive nature of many enslaved women's relationships with white men, and their slim prospects for freedom under the Americans. During the 1930s, Edward Lycurgus recounted a story that he had heard from his father, the antebellum free man of color George Lycurgus. Although documents do not completely support the details of the elder Lycurgus's tale, it nevertheless is a valuable piece of oral history. George Lycurgus told his son that around the time of the Civil War, he first spotted his future spouse, Julia Gray, on the auction block at St. Augustine's marketplace. Julia, he said, belonged to a "family where nobody ever was sold," but an estate division now occasioned an auction.[9] Here Lycurgus spoke to the vulnerability of enslaved families, even those who belonged to the most conscientious and benevolent owners.

Next, he addressed the dehumanization that this vulnerability entailed. Whites, Lycurgus reported, were "barter[ing] off po niggers lake dey was hogs." Consequently, "whole families sold together and some was split." Lycurgus also pointedly dealt with the issue of miscegenation, a practice that the American regime had criminalized, exposing the hypocrisy of Florida's plantocracy, even in supposedly easygoing St. Augustine. "An dey shore did git rid uf some pretty gals," he stressed, and "dey always looked so shame and pitiful upon dat stand wid all dem men standin dere lookin at em wid what dey had on dey minds shinin' in they eyes." Finally, Lycurgus turned paternalism upside down. Assuming the role of patriarchs such as Zephaniah Kingsley and George J. F. Clarke, he purchased Julia, his wife-to-be, for $950.[10] The implication is that white buyers would have manumitted neither the women that they acquired nor the biracial children that they would father.

Lycurgus's brief folk history indicates that the county's African Americans, enslaved and free, certainly understood the critical role of formal marriage and that they passed this knowledge down to their descendants. Whites also realized this and some patrons strove to make unions between the enslaved or between free blacks and slaves as official as possible. Slaves could not legally contract marriage, and unless they sired children by free women of color, their offspring inherited their status. Some biracial free men of color, including Clarkes, married slaves, solemnizing these relationships by a church wedding and/or civil procedures. Such marriages would have made a bondswoman's prospects for freedom brighter, because a free husband could earn wages with which he might purchase his family's liberty. In other cases, enslaved men married free women, who bore them free children. Under this circumstance, the bondsman's hopes of manumission grew.

No matter how well-connected a free spouse might be, if they married slaves, the resulting family lived under the threat of separation. In 1856, for example, upon suddenly learning that he was to be sold, the enslaved Prince Weedman, from Savannah, sent a letter to St. Augustine businessman George Burt, begging him to buy him so as not to separate him from his wife. "If you will try [to buy me] I will be very mutch oblidge to you," Weedman pleaded, "I wish you would as don't want to leave my wife." Regardless, some free blacks still gambled by taking slaves as their mates. Both Abraham Lancaster and Eulogius (Alex) Clarke, for example, in 1857 and 1862, respectively, wed bondswomen, although they took care to solemnize their nuptials in the Catholic Church. Lancaster even took the extraordinary step of obtaining a civil license. It is not known whether a lack of eligible, attractive free women accounted for the two men's choices of partners or simply the power of romantic love. Perhaps Lancaster and Clarke made some type of informal *coartación* arrangement with their wives' owners. The free quadroon George D. Clarke seems to have done so when he purchased his enslaved wife in 1844 and married her in the same year.[11]

Indeed, the sacrament of marriage was a Catholic practice many African Americans clung to in order to resist American attacks on their families. It actually grew in importance during antebellum times, for it defied Florida's proscription of legalized slave unions. Catholic nuptials were canonically valid, and believers violated them at the peril of their immortal souls. Spain's colonial government of East Florida had respected them, even in the face of powerful slave owners who wished to separate couples for profit or convenience. Prior to 1811, the Spaniards had even recognized common-law marriages among slaves, but after that date, and certainly subsequent to the American takeover in 1821, Jane Landers explained, "Anglo emphasis on property rights was beginning to supersede more traditional and flexible Spanish interpretations of 'family.'" Landers found only fifty-one church marriages between East Florida's persons of color from 1784 to1821. She surmised that the lack of access of rural slaves to priests accounted for this dearth. That some slave marriages were formalized, Landers concluded, was attributable to the conscientiousness of masters who felt obligated to comply with ecclesiastical precepts.[12]

From 1821 to 1862, St. Augustine's Catholic parish recognized eighty-four black unions. Forty-eight of them show up in marriage registries, and the other thirty-six appear in baptismal records. When one adds to these totals the twelve Protestant weddings and five civil ceremonies for which there are records, there is evidence of ninety-nine African American nuptials in St.

Johns County during the American period, approximately double the number recorded when Spain ruled from 1784 to 1821. The characteristics of black marriages in the two periods were similar. During the Spanish era, 29 percent of both partners were free, compared to 27 percent in the American period, whereas under the Spanish, 57 percent of the partners were both slaves as were 60 percent under the Americans. The remainder of the marriages—about one in every seven in both periods—united a slave and a free person of color.[13]

Applications for Civil War pensions made long after the fact suggest that the preceding figures understate the incidence of antebellum black Catholic marriages, though by how much will never be known. In 1898, for example, Sally Growles testified that while enslaved in 1850 and a few days after delivering her son, James Filomena Rogero, she had been married to the bondsman Handy Canova "in the Big Catholic church by the Priest," Father Edmond Aubril. Joshua Hagaman, antebellum St. Augustine's leading black Catholic godfather, along with William Natteel, attested that they had attended the wedding. Yet, no record of the ceremony existed in 1898. Growles conjectured that it had been destroyed by fire. The church registry does contain the baptism of her son, but the priest evidently did not recognize his birth as legitimate. Nor did the cleric name his father. There is no other entry for Sally Growles in surviving ecclesiastical records. Still, her claim is credible. The Rogeros, Canovas, and Solanas, who had owned Growles and her husband, had permitted other bond persons to marry in the church. The fact that Handy Canova witnessed a black wedding in 1858, and that the couple stood as godparents is evidence of their good standing as Catholics.[14]

Similarly during the 1890s, the ex-slave Peter Johnson claimed that Father Aubril officiated at his wedding to Amanda (Hermana) Canova, which seems to have taken place around the late 1830s, and which was blessed with ten children. A free man of color, Abraham Lancaster, supported Johnson's claim, as did John Williams, who recalled that he "used to go to their [the Johnsons'] house quite often" and knew that "they lived together and were known as husband and wife." Furthermore, the couple's son, John Mills, swore that his parents had been "lawfully married in slave time by Rev Father Obree" and attributed the absence of documentation either to a church fire or to the notion that "no records was kept of the marriage of slaves."[15]

The four children of the Johnsons who appear in Catholic baptismal records are not described as legitimate, nor is the father named, circumstances that challenge the claim of a sanctified union. On the other hand, the Johnsons between them sponsored seven godchildren, which suggests that they enjoyed the respect of the church and of their fellow black parishioners. Peter Johnson's owner, Susan Murphy, was Catholic and left a legacy of $100 to Father Aubril.[16] Thus, the Johnsons may well have been united in the church, despite the absence of marriage records.

The marriages of two other Solana family slaves, Peter and John, are documented in civil records in 1838–1839, though records of neither ceremony appear in extant Catholic registries. The fact that church records list the children of both men as legitimate indicates that the church had sanctified their unions. Evidence for another slave marriage missing from surviving registries appears for the year 1857, when the church acknowledged the legitimacy of a son born that year to José Pomar's bondwoman Manuela and that the parents had been together eight years, though no record exists of their marriage.[17]

Additional evidence of black Catholic nuptials may have perished in fires or natural disasters. Other weddings may have gone unrecorded because of irregular visits by the clergy during the 1820s to the late 1830s. The historian Ann Patton Malone, in her study of antebellum Louisiana, found that church records in general were kept "irregular[ly] at best." Moreover, bishops empowered priests in some Southern locales to conduct clandestine marriages in cases where masters refused permission for their slaves to wed. Also, in certain instances, when priests registered the names of both of an enslaved "natural" (as opposed to "legitimate") child's parents, they were in fact recognizing a marriage by inference.[18] Because Southern governments never legalized or recognized slave unions, enslaved couples who sought out Catholic clergy, either in the confessional or in private conversations, were engaging in subversive acts, as were the priests who were thus pressured to secretly sanction bond persons' relationships or who in fact encouraged slaves to approach them with their marital concerns.

Sacramental slave marriages could have a corrosive effect on the laws of bondage in a city that sported a majority Catholic population. For example, St. Johns County, contrary to state law, issued a marriage license to freeborn Abraham Lancaster and Jane Canova, a house slave, on 5 December 1857. Although county records confirm that Father Edmond Aubril "legally" married the couple on 6 January 1858, the marriage is not recorded in parish records. After the Civil War, however, Martin Dixon and Domingo Papy recalled the wedding taking place when they were boys. Thomas Williams, a former slave and Lancaster's childhood playmate, also recollected the marriage. Lancaster's niece, a girl about ten years old in 1858, could still visualize, decades later, the bridal wreath that Canova had worn. The niece also remembered that the ceremony had taken place in the "Cathedral," but she differentiated between this ceremony and the "wedding" that was held at her grandmother Tyra Lancaster's house on Charlotte Street. Thomas Richardson, a former slave, swore that it took place on a Saturday night. Finally, the baptismal records of 1860 list the Lancasters' son, John Vulter Canova, as "legitimate" rather than "natural."[19]

St. Johns County granted marriage licenses to two other enslaved Catholic couples in 1839 and to a free black–slave couple seventeen years later. In an ambience that featured intense competition for black converts, it followed that Protestant slaves also were issued county documents for their nuptials. Two enslaved Episcopalians, as well as two other bond persons belonging to that denomination who wed free partners, appear in civil records from 1843 to 1846. Moreover, county officials may have extended recognition to at least three additional Protestant slave unions. As the historian John Boles wrote, in the South, "strict uniformity in anything was the exception."[20] It is important to note, however, that Florida statutes did not acknowledge slave marriages as valid or respect their sanctity.

The spike in black Catholic antebellum marriages, as well as the surprising actions of St. Johns County's civil officials, occurred within the context of the fervent international debates of the 1840s regarding slavery, which, besides touching off a drive to evangelize bond persons impelled by an ideology that the scholar Blake Touchstone called "Christian paternalism," led to a professed concern, out of psychological, religious, reformist, and economic needs, for the protection of blacks' morals. The historian John W. Blassingame found that between 1830 and 1860, "at many times . . . more slaves were married in the Episcopal churches in some states than were whites." Blassingame noted that "many denominations required all slave members to take their marriage vows in the church." He concluded that historical sources support the notion that ministers attempted to put this ideal into practice. Thus, "thousands" of slaves wed in Christian ceremonies throughout the South in antebellum times. Yet, at the same time, Southern legislatures stubbornly balked at sanctioning slaves' connubial rights.[21] In short, the potent combination of Hispanic traditions, a reinvigorated Catholic clerical presence, and contemporary politics assisted St. Johns County's blacks in their efforts to defend their families.

Catholicism's institutional revival in St. Augustine formed part of what Randall Miller has described as an "ambitious extension of dioceses in the

South." At the same time, the American hierarchy pressed the clergy to "subject all parishioners to church discipline and to impose regular, uniform devotional practices." This ecclesiastical policy applied to the enslaved faithful as well, which melded with blacks' desires to utilize church weddings to better secure their families. Moreover, in areas of the antebellum South where priests maintained a strong presence, Catholic masters exercised a greater respect for the church's precepts regarding the sanctity of slave marriages. Indeed, as Miller asserted, a "vigorous priest could win converts and acceptance." In addition, by practicing Catholicism, the county's slaves identified themselves with the former Spanish regime, a government that had respected their right to marry legally.[22] Catholic canon law, practically speaking, represented the best available option.

Black Catholics, seizing the moment, rallied the shepherd of St. Augustine's newly created bishopric, Augustin Verot, to their cause after he arrived in 1858. Bishop Verot's pastoral concerns corroborate George Lycurgus's folk history. On 4 January 1861, to mark President James Buchanan's national day of prayer and fasting aimed at stemming civil war, Verot preached a sermon that would reverberate throughout the South. After justifying involuntary servitude using scripture and history, he proclaimed black inferiority to whites. Then, in unprecedentedly strong language, the churchman traced the gathering storm clouds of internecine bloodshed to God's anger at the sexual exploitation of black women. He emphasized the need for "holiness of life in masters." Unless white men desisted from sexually abusing their African American charges, they could not expect to triumph in war, for "the Almighty" might be using the "present disturbances" to destroy the "frequent occasions of immorality, which the subservient and degraded position of the slave offers to the lewd." Slave holders, he proclaimed, must encourage as well as respect slave marriages and black families. Verot also addressed the topic of free persons of color. He excoriated Florida legislators who "had before them" laws banishing them from the state or selling them into slavery. Instead of such laws, Verot insisted that the "rights of free colored persons" be "respected," and he exhorted whites not to "vex and molest them merely because they are colored."[23] They must, in effect, turn back the clock to Spanish days.

Verot sought both to protect blacks who already were free and implicitly, to encourage manumission, which, although it had slowed to a trickle in late antebellum years, still took place in St. Johns County. After Florida achieved statehood in 1845, laws against manumission activities were more vigorously enforced, and new restrictions were imposed on free blacks in 1848 and 1856.

By 1853, emancipations in northeastern Florida had become "exceedingly rare," and Anglo-American attitudes and practices "represented the new order and the general will." Statistics on emancipations in St. Johns County from 1821 to 1862 illustrate this pattern. The statistics, however, must be used with caution, for figures in the early years of this period represent freed persons in all of East Florida, an area that had splintered into several counties by 1862. Given this caveat, the numbers suggest that 1845 was a benchmark in the transition from the relatively easy attitudes and practices of the Spaniards concerning manumission, to the rigidity of those of the Anglo-Americans. Of 119 recorded emancipations between 1821 and 1862, only 21 took place in the 1840s. Of these, twelve occurred in 1844, the final year before statehood, when new restrictions loomed. From 1845 to 1862, merely eleven emancipations found their way into official record books.[24]

Notwithstanding the American crackdown, some manumissions in the 1840s included cases in which blacks were the emancipators. The case of Maria Anderson demonstrates that despite Jimmy Gibbs's defeat, his strategy of using the courts in cases involving one's liberty remained viable, although transmuted in form. On 3 July 1842, as Gibbs's dispute with Andrew Pow raged, Peter Sken Smith, a business partner of the deceased Dr. Andrew Anderson in the Southern Life Insurance & Trust Company, issued a "Certificate of Freedom" to Maria Anderson. Five years later, however, her freedom and that of her two small children, Henrietta and Dominga, faced a legal hurdle. It stemmed from provisions of Dr. Anderson's will, which listed Maria and her children among the property bequeathed to his widow, Clarissa Anderson. After hearing Maria's challenge to this bequest, the St. Johns County Circuit Court ruled that she had indeed been emancipated in 1842 and her three-year-old daughter Dominga, born after that date had inherited her free status. But her six-year-old, Henrietta, born enslaved, was not named in the "Certificate of Freedom." Consequently, the court ruled, Henrietta remained Clarissa Anderson's property. This situation may have been resolved by some form of *coartación*, for in1850, Henrietta was no longer enslaved, though no record of her manumission has survived.[25]

Other incidents show that free and enslaved St. Augustine blacks continued to purchase their freedom long after the American takeover, and that they could do so by installments. In 1842, María Sofía Hernández, born a slave in 1819, along with her infant son, were purchased at a marshal's sale by her father, Alexander Hernández, himself a bondsman. He made a down payment of $443.56 for his daughter and biracial grandson, but still owed

$171.44 for the "right title and interest" to them. He obviously had made some type of *coartación* arrangement with his owner, Joseph M. Hernández. In 1844, for the nominal fee of $5, "a man of Colour called Sampson" secured the freedom of his teenage son Cyrus from an army officer. Also in 1844, the free black Peter Ysnarde sent $1,060 from Cuba to John M. Fontané to buy the liberty of the latter's slaves Josepha and her two children. Circa 1844, the slave Willis told his mistress, Clarissa Anderson, that he wanted to buy his son William, whose mother was Ally, another Anderson slave. Mrs. Anderson agreed to the purchase. In 1846, William Dean, a free man of color, appeared on an insolvency list with a notation that he had "removed from the State." Nine years later, from California, he purchased a slave, Charles Bunch, from Antonio Canova in St. Augustine for $300, an indication that Dean had struck it rich on the west coast. Hence, St. Johns County's 1860 census lists a previously unnamed free man of color, Charles Dean, and describes him as a sixty-eight-year-old African native.[26]

A court case demonstrates that blacks, including the enslaved, had access to funds that could be used to buy their freedom or that of their loved ones. Tony Papy, "a man of industrious habits," had purchased his liberty for $450 in 1835. He subsequently freed his son with money that Tony Pow, a free black, advanced to him. There exists the intriguing possibility that Tony Pow may be the same man involved in the Jimmy Gibbs case. If so, another layer of complexity can be added to that sordid affair. Regardless, in 1844, Pow in turn wanted to borrow $150 from Papy, money Papy had been saving to buy the land on which he was living with his enslaved wife Katy. The couple occupied a "low one story house with a garret in the outskirts of St. Augustine." Perhaps in gratitude for Pow's earlier assistance, Papy lent Pow the money on the latter's assurance that he would repay it in time for Papy to buy the land that he wanted.[27]

Over the years, the bondswoman Mary-Ann, Papy's wife Katy's friend, had saved her money so that by the mid-1840s, she possessed $600 in silver. Mary-Ann's husband, who had moved to Cuba in the early 1820s, was the source of some of this silver, but the rest Mary-Ann had earned from the "opportunities she had had." When Mary-Ann's master called her into the country to work, she left her cache with Katy for safekeeping in a canvas-covered box. Hearing of the loan that Papy had made to Pow, Mary-Ann became alarmed. Papy's wife assured her that the silver was secure. After subsequently learning that her money had been stolen, Mary-Ann confronted her friend's husband, accusing him of theft. According to Papy's witnesses in the court case that resulted, Papy had arisen especially early on the day of the theft to go to St. Augustine for the purpose of fetching a pot to scald a hog that he was butchering for market. When Papy left the house, his wife was still sleeping. Two burglars then allegedly broke into the house. It was they, the witnesses swore, who made off with the coins. Despite this testimony, the jury found Papy guilty, fining him $600.[28]

The case could be argued in court because the defendant was a free black and his accuser likewise was a person of color. The jury appears to have implicitly recognized a slave's right to hold personal property, an underlying principle of *coartación*. Tony Papy appealed the decision, but no record exists of the outcome.[29] But the case demonstrates that at least some of St. Johns County's enslaved, during the mid-1840s, held property, took advantage of opportunities to earn cash, exercised a degree of autonomy in their lives, and maintained a financial support network among themselves and free African Americans. The case also reveals some of the pressures that the slave society exerted against black freedom. Tony Pow and Tony Papy were free men in financial straits. Mary-Ann was a slave whose savings of more than two decades disappeared and with them perhaps her hopes of self-purchase. Worse still, the case reveals the internal fissures that could disrupt black support networks.

As Mary-Ann's life indicates, connections with Cuba also functioned to keep *coartación* alive in St. Johns County long after the American takeover. To illustrate, Fernando Falany, a former East Florida resident originally from Italy, made a will in Cuba that was recorded, in Spanish, in St. Johns County in 1848. Falany's last wishes declared that four slaves who he still owned in the county remain *coartados* because of their good service to him. Three of them, Felipe, Francisca, and Catalina, he instructed, were to be sold by his executor for no more than 200 pesos each, and the fourth, María, for no more than 100 pesos.[30] Presumably, this was to ensure that they could more easily complete their self-purchases. Moreover, those who acquired them would do so with the understanding that they were acquiring partially free slaves. This recognition of Falany's wishes constituted yet another implicit official acknowledgment of the continued functioning of *coartación*. It is interesting to speculate on what might have happened in the courts had the buyers of Falany's slaves not honored the Cuban's wishes. The Jimmy Gibbs case indicates that the aggrieved bond persons would have had no legal recourse.

Manumission did become much more difficult as the Civil War loomed. Thus, in 1855, when Susan Murphy declared in her will that her slave Belinda should be freed, she was forced to make provisions for the fact that the state might nullify the manumission. In early 1858, Ventura Noda appears in Catholic records as a slave, but at the end of the year, St. Augustine authorities granted the now-free Noda an exemption "from a Certified permit during her short visit to the City." No emancipation deed for Noda has been discovered, but if she had indeed been freed in 1858 she might have had to leave Florida.[31]

Nevertheless, even as the grip of slavery tightened, a few St. Johns County blacks continued to be manumitted in ways that survived from Spanish times. Thus, George Papy obtained his freedom from Benjamin A. Putnam for $475 in 1855, and Lena Papy paid George Zehnbauer $410 for her liberty two years later. Neither left St. Augustine. Other slaves, though not officially free, were quasi-free. Jane Nattiel, her son recalled after the Civil War, "was a house girl and was permitted to do as she pleased, and was practically free." Such a situation may explain why two white neighbors of Lucy, a slave in the Rogero family, were uncertain about her freedom status in 1858.[32] The various degrees of freedom in antebellum St. Johns County reflected the degree to which many people of color thought and acted as though they owned themselves.

The manumission process, just as in Spanish days, could be onerous, even for slaves who had won their owners' affections through long, faithful service. For forty-four years, Tony Welters was a slave of the Fontané family, serving for much of that time as a "special servant and body guard" to patriarch John M. Fontané. In the mid-1850s, Fontané directed that Welters be manumitted upon his death. In an inventory of Fontané's estate made in 1855, Welters is listed as a slave valued at $700. Two of the deceased's heirs eventually relinquished their interest in the bondsman. A third, however, who lived in Georgia, refused to do so until he received $150 for what he considered his rightful legacy. During the three years it took to work this out, Welters lived in legal limbo.[33]

Indirect evidence suggests that the Fontané family made some type of *coartación* arrangement to enable Welters to pay the insistent Georgia heir. Welters does not appear in the 1860 census. If he owed the Fontané estate $150 at that time, he would have still been technically a slave and not enumerated by name. Shortly after the census, Welters must have obtained his freedom, for he enlisted in the town militia, the St. Augustine Blues. Since at least 1857, Welters had lived in his own residence, most likely with his enslaved wife. According to the 1850 census, there lived in St. Augustine one Felicia Fontané, a free black midwife. Her respected occupation earned her a general pass to visit her patients after curfew. Baptismal registries record Welter's mother as Felicia Fontané, but extant records specify no connection between the midwife and Tony Welters, nor are there manumission deeds for either person.[34]

Like Tony Welters, George Vanness lived in quasi freedom until manumitted in his master's will. Nehemiah Brush owned Vanness and his wife, Lugarda. They had lived autonomously as custodians of Brush's orange groves across the St. Johns River from Palatka. When Dr. Brush died in New York, he freed the couple on the condition that they spend a prescribed period of time demonstrating to Brush's heirs that they were "worthy" of manumission. This being done, Brush's executors pronounced them "free persons of color" in 1849, citing their "long and faithful services." Although they were emancipated in Putnam County, they are listed in the 1850 and 1860 censuses as inhabitants of rural St. Johns County and with the surname of Brush.[35] Their lives, like that of Tony Welters, demonstrate that the cultivation of white patrons was important for slaves wishing to obtain freedom.

Manumission and mixed-race families, although fiercely assaulted in the law books, remained viable though slim possibilities in late-antebellum St. Johns County. Culture and history assisted their persistence. Traditions of military service likewise survived. This survival reflects the black community's morale during the bleak years of racial oppression leading up to the Civil War. Moreover, it would prove fatal to Florida's slave society.

7
The Black Martial Heritage

The rise of a statewide romanticization of the Hispanic past starting in the late 1840s certainly worked in blacks' favor in their efforts to preserve Spanish days, as did the adjudication of the Patriot War claims.[1] These two factors were important for bolstering memories of the military traditions of St. Johns County's community of color. In fact, black veterans were able to publicly testify as to their heroics under the Spaniards. Whites assisted them in their efforts. The adjudication of the claims generated a rich historical record that documented the lives of black East Floridians under the Spanish regime on the eve of the Patriot War, as well as their service in the war itself.

The Patriot War experience was a controlling memory for those living in St. Johns County, whites as well as blacks. A white man, Lewis Fleming, declared in 1837 that the devastation of Francis P. Fatio's New Switzerland plantation was still "spoken of by inhabitants of this country with as much confidence as the Battle of Bunker Hill was in Massachusetts." Such memories were kept alive by searing experiences as that of María del Carmen Hill, the widow of Don Francisco Xavier Sánchez, who saw herself reduced from the matriarch of an estate "considered the most wealthy and valuable in the Province" to a mother who could not even afford to clothe her children, and who died in 1813 "of a broken heart." A similar experience drove George Long to an early grave in 1812, when this "moderately independent" rancher and farmer witnessed the destruction of his property. Twenty-five years later, Long's son, Matthew, bitterly complained that the US Treasury did not have enough money to repay his family "for a father's death, or for a life of poverty and blasted prosperity."[2]

Indeed, white East Floridians who survived the Patriot War remembered the conflict and its aftermath as a time of broken dreams. Sarah Acosta lamented that if not for the war, the region's "inhabitants would have become very rich." Abraham Daniels added similarly that East Florida "never did recover [from] the shock" of the war. "Such was the depression of Spirits and circumstances produced by the Revolution," James Arnowe recollected, "that few persons returned to their farms in 1813." Speaking in the midst of another such disruptive experience, the Second Seminole War, Mrs. Jane Redding opined that the "suffering of the poor People during the Revolution of 12 and 13 was far greater" than that of the Seminole War. Another witness, James Jones, recalled the "alarming and terrifying character" of the Patriot War as the cause of the "indelible" impressions it left on those who lived through it, impressions that "have been the subject of frequent discussions from that day up to the present."[3]

To be sure, the Patriot War claims hearings in the local federal court generated abundant proof of enduring memories of the war. Moreover, George J. F. Clarke's biracial heirs paved the way for free people of color to testify in the lawsuits, insisting that, "free negroes or mullatoes" played vital roles, and convincing Judge Isaac H. Bronson that "there was no law against [their] testimony." These hearings in St. Augustine's federal court thus tapped into a tradition of black petitions for redress of grievances that stretched back to the Spanish period. The black petitions and supporting testimony resembled those in antebellum Virginia, which historian Gregg D. Kimball has described as expressing "the ideals and aspirations of African Americans" and as offering insight into a "hidden transcript" of protest and resistance.[4]

The Clarkes' tenacity thus gave free men of color a voice in public, official proceedings, which they used to remind St. Johns County whites of past black achievements and, by implication, of their current potential as citizens and productive members of the community. Testimony in the Patriot War hearings recorded in writing the history of black valor and freshened it in the minds of all St. Johns County residents. It thus combated a hardening racial divide, while inspiring a younger generation of blacks. Memories of black experience during the Patriot War thus functioned as a psychological weapon at a time when public discourse and policies increasingly denigrated blacks.

The Patriot War claims cases also demonstrated and reinforced sincere bonds of friendship, or at least paternalism between the races, ties that softened St. Johns County's evolving slave society by reviving memories of associations forged in a Spanish society with slaves. The mostly Minorcan witnesses who testified on behalf of men of color remembered them positively, often fondly. Bartolo Solana, for instance, praised Felipe Edimboro as a "respectable man" who was "doing very well before the war." In 1827, while visiting Cuba, Domingo Cercopoly spoke with "many of the free negroes who had left [St. Augustine] previously" and learned that the black Domingo Davis had died. Andreas Pacetty and Michael Andreu recollected how they would often stop at Sancho Davis's place, where the black man would help them to obtain wood for fashioning canoes. In fact, Pacetty had spent "many a night" with Davis. Born about the time Prince Witten and his family reached East Florida as Georgia fugitives, Pacetty had known Witten "from childhood well." George Gianopoli routinely rested at Scipio Fleming's farm on his way to the Fatio family's New Switzerland plantation.[5]

Andrés Pacetty Sr., a Minorcan, remembered black soldiers as good customers for local vegetable farmers. Pacetty recollected "four companies of blacks from Havana one Company of mulattoes from Havana and one company of blacks raised in Florida under the Command of Capt: Prince." The first three of these companies had consisted of sixty men each, the last of eighty. Prince Witten's company, whites remembered, had relieved hunger in the besieged town by rounding up cattle in the surrounding hinterland. Many whites testified about the exploits of these blacks who supplied the town with beef, acknowledging the peril as well as the importance of the effort. Whites reserved their highest praise, however, for what Prince's Black Company achieved in the Twelve Mile Swamp on the evening of 11 September 1812. So successful was this ambush that the American invaders "immediately … fell back upon the St. Johns." Speaking more generally, Zephaniah Kingsley lauded the "about 50 coloured militia inhabitants of this then Province," who "saved by their Bravery and fidelity the City of St. Augustine from being taken & Plundered." In fact, so many whites extolled the merits of the black militia that Judge Isaac H. Bronson commented in 1847 on how often the phrase "Princes Black company" appeared in the record of the claims hearings. The whites who generated this record praised Prince and his men for many reasons: for their hard work and for their prosperity as civilians, as well as for their patriotism and contribution to the war effort.[6] In doing so, they found themselves, willy-nilly, helping blacks who were endeavoring to contradict contemporary images of the race that were increasingly negative in public and political discourse.

Even more remarkably, free blacks were able to officially record their versions of the history of the Patriot War and life under the Spanish regime. Juan Antonio Florencio, the son of Mariana Bisit, a fugitive from New York by way of Savannah, and a white father, was one of the men of color whose testimony resulted from the Clarkes' efforts. Florencio had been baptized a Catholic in 1789 when he was six years old and later attended an integrated boys' school in St. Augustine. After, in 1806, sacramentally marrying María Rosa Collins, the natural daughter of a biracial businessman, he had his own son, Francisco Bautista Agustín Florencio, baptized. During the Patriot War, Florencio had fought in Prince's Company, and in 1846, he recounted his experience:

> Myself & other Spanish soldiers used to go out into the Country during the war to get cattle & bring them in for the troops, & people in the city. The parties that went out were usually commanded by Prince Whilton & Tony Doctor, but sometimes a white sergeant went with us. Sometimes we got 40, Sometimes 50 & Sometimes 60 head of Cattle, just as we could find them. We went sometimes to Matanzas, Sometimes to Deep Creek & wherever we could find Cattle.

Describing another expedition in which he participated, Florencio reminded his listeners that blacks too had suffered heavy losses:

> During the war & while the patriots were in Camp out before St Augustine there was a party of 30 or 40 of us that went out into the Country up the North river, & went to Weedmans place & Princes place. Prince himself was one of the party, we found his place burned & destroyed, & all the places about in that part of the country had been burned. We went to Carlos Hills place & found that his house & property had been burned & destroyed also—we were after cattle that time & got 34 I think.[7]

Prince Witten's nearest rival as the greatest hero of the Patriot War was another man of color, Antonio Proctor, a slave who had earned his own freedom by adept use of his linguistic and diplomatic skills. Proctor was over ninety in 1841, when he testified on behalf of the claim of Felipe Edimboro. He had been employed as an interpreter by two trading companies, whose services the Spanish government used to maintain a precarious peace with the Indians, as well as by the American government. Modestly, and diplomatically, Proctor deposed that he had been freed for his "good conduct and services in behalf of the Spanish Government in East Florida" during the war.[8]

White deponents were quick to second Proctor's testimony and, with it, his role in the Patriot War. Thus, Stephen Arnow, a Minorcan, credited Proctor with persuading the Seminoles to "take sides with the Spaniards and act against the Patriots in 1812." Proctor "has always been considered a very honest and worthy man—as good as any Negro," Arnow added backhandedly, "and I believe him under oath as soon as I would any negro living." After Proctor gained his freedom, Arnow continued, he "went out very frequently on excursions after cattle with [Prince's] Company." On one such excursion with another free black man, Scipio Fleming, Proctor recalled that they were:

> Hunting cattle and [Fleming] had his horse— we stopped and turned the horse out to feed & he got away and went to the Patriot camp and they kept him. We tracked him up to the Camp but we dare not go near the Camp. In following the horse we not only tracked him, but we saw the horse before us, & followed him until we saw him go into the Patriot camp.[9]

Black deponents in the claims hearings sometimes contrasted white behavior during the war unfavorably with that of blacks. Thus, Tony Primus, a freeborn black who was nearly fifty when he testified in 1841, contrasted black heroism during the war with white inaction. "A party of us," Primus recalled, "(all coloured people for no whites would go) went out to get cattle." The Spaniards furnished the party with horses and supplies and promised to pay $4 for each head of cattle they brought into town. "We were at the time in the service of the Spanish Government, under command of Prince a Blackman," Primus boasted. Confidence in his good judgment, as well as concern for his freedom, guided Primus's conduct at the onset of the war. When he first learned of the Patriot incursion, he was cutting timber near Julington Creek "on wages" for George J. F. Clarke, whom he knew personally. William Garvin, the white who later married Clarke's mulatto daughter Felicia, was supervising the thirteen lumbermen. Knowing that the Patriots would sell him into slavery if they captured him, Primus told Garvin of his fears, only to have his supervisor dismiss them as a ruse to disrupt the timber harvest. However, when gunshots rang out in the distance, Garvin "could not keep us any longer," and the laborers fled.[10]

In addition to invoking memories of their courage in battle by testifying in court, blacks kept the Hispanic military past alive by participating in Catholic parish life. Antebellum St. Augustine remained overwhelmingly Catholic, in the words of the scholar Michael Gannon, "an island of Catholicism in a spreading sea of Protestantism."[11] This, combined with an atmosphere saturated with historical memories due to the ongoing Patriot War claims cases and the historical romanticism swirling about the state, imbued blacks' attendance at Mass or other church rituals with special meanings. Each time that people of color baptized their children, married, or fulfilled their Sunday obligation, it might remind them and their white coreligionists of Spanish days, when black Catholic warriors such as Jorge Biassou and Prince Witten cemented their bonds with comrades-in-arms inside the parish church's walls, and battled the faith's enemies outside of them. Just as the priest, when consecrating bread and wine, temporarily turned back time to Christ's crucifixion, so did black Catholics resurrect memories of their heroism under the Spaniards when they took part in liturgies.

Indeed, some black Catholics became noted for their spiritual heroism in the battle of earthly life. In antebellum St. Johns County, African Americans continued to act as Catholic soldiers of Christ, despite government policies that made war on their martial heritage. The case of Sprig Mosby is instructive. In 1825, he stood as godfather for George D. Clarke, one of the biracial heirs of the large and well-connected Clarke clan. When he did so, he was a married, property-owning businessman, but for some reason not altogether clear from surviving records, Mosby fell from the high social status associated with those circumstances to that of an impoverished drunkard. From 1842 to 1849, he vanished from the historical record, only to resurface in 1850, apparently having undergone a spiritual or at least social rebirth. After an absence of twenty-five years from the baptismal registries, he reappeared as the godfather for Rebecca, a child who belonged to Matthew Solana. Later that year, his name was entered into the sacramental volume twice more, once as godfather of an adult slave and then of an infant slave. His godchildren increased the following year, when he functioned in this capacity for three more enslaved children. When John and Fanny Mickler wed in September 1852, after themselves being baptized, Mosby as stood as their godfather and marriage witness.[12]

In 1858, two more people—a youngster and an adult "servant slave"—became Mosby's godchildren, as did another adult, John Canova, the following year. On the latter occasion, the priest recorded the godfather's name as John Sprig Mosby. Mosby's ties to John M. Fontané, the executor of George J. F. Clarke's will, can be gleaned from his sponsorships. Matthew Solana was Fontané's brother-in-law. After Fontané emancipated his trusty servant

Antonio, who then changed his name to Tony Welters, "John Sprig" witnessed Welters's marriage to Cydra Benet at a Catholic ceremony that also took place in 1858.[13]

The elderly Sprig Mosby was certainly a man of little wealth in these years of his godfatherhood, yet his stature among Catholics of color was quite high. When his material circumstances bottomed out in 1859, an alderman brought to the attention of the city council the "miserable and unfortunate condition of Moseby." The council in turn ordered the city treasurer to pay the black pauper $5 to relieve his destitution. Black Catholics had obviously selected Mosby as a godfather and marriage witness not because of his material resources but because of his sanctity and respectability. Mosby's white neighbors placed his virtue in writing, extolling the fact that over the course of the years, he had "extended daily the hand of charity to many of our poor population particularly widows." When in 1856 a mentally ill white man had "strayed" into town, a man city officials deemed a danger to society, Mosby sheltered him "on his premises." Soon, however, the officials appointed a committee to "call on Gov: Moseby & confer with him . . . to devise the best mode of removing [the deranged visitor] from the City."[14]

The support of whites for Mosby was unflagging. Among those who helped him were prominent Anglos and Minorcans, Protestants and Catholics. When the city proposed in 1860 to send the black pauper to "Mr John Ponce at the St. Johns Bar, who they understood purchased him some few years ago," Mosby's supporters would have none of it. Instead, they convinced the city to provide $3 a month for Mosby's maintenance, a sum soon increased to $4 due to his "continued present afflicted status." The money was to be entrusted to James B. Ponce or "some other suitable person who will take proper care of him." In the financial exigencies caused by the onset of the Civil War, the city, in early 1862, halted the payment of funds to all paupers "Excepting Spirigg Moseby."[15]

Whites had so marginalized Mosby that only their taxes kept him alive. Nevertheless, at a time when their treatment of persons of color was growing more repressive, their charity toward Mosby increased. The former slave had retained his sense of identity by becoming a Catholic role model. His life of poverty, religious activities in a white-controlled church, and his dedication to charitable works was an acceptable one to whites. It was unthreatening to the social and racial order and gave whites an opportunity to express their paternalism within the context of their conceptualization of the proper free-black social role. By funneling his energies into being a spiritual soldier,

Mosby, in his later life attained inner peace and esteem from his overlords. He also kept alive the example of black Catholic service to society under the former Spanish regime.

Another important way that blacks did this was by serving as godparents for black Catholic baptisms. Some 482 black Catholic godparents can be identified with some certainty in antebellum East Florida. Of these nearly five hundred people of color, approximately 40 percent were godfathers. Two-thirds of the godfathers and slightly more of the godmothers (seven in ten) had only one godchild, and most of the others in both categories had only two godchildren. These patterns tended to reinforce the personal nature of the godparent-godchild relationship. Yet a few individuals sponsored what can only be described as flocks of godchildren, the most prominent examples being the enslaved Joshua Dummett, who had twenty-three, and Betsy Benet and Mary Papy, bondswomen who had twenty-three and twenty-one, respectively. These leading godparents may have exercised leadership in some type of black Catholic organization, for on 6 June 1858, shortly after his arrival in St. Augustine, Bishop Augustin Verot's parishioners of color offered their prelate a pectoral cross.[16] Sponsors, particularly ones such as Dummett, Benet, and Papy, attained social prestige, not on the field of battle, but by battling sin through their holy lives.

Other blacks in town displayed their military potential on St. Augustine's streets, battling the city's curfew ordinances. In October 1843, the patrol arrested Jerry Mason, who was roving town at 10:00 p.m. without a pass, and confined him in a guard room. The next morning, Mason's captors discovered that he had escaped, the stock securing him having been cut. On the night of 20 August 1845, the slave Ben's quick wits caused an Army general and a young future Confederate general to come to blows over his arrest. Brigadier General William Worth had sent Ben, whom he rented from Gabriel W. Perpall's estate, to purchase ice and bread after the curfew bell had sounded. When civilian patrollers seized Ben for having no pass and confined him to the stocks, Ben took on a manner that Patrol Captain Albert A. Núñes characterized as "insolent" and "impertinent in the extreme." He cleverly taunted his captors with warnings that they would have to deal with General Worth.[17]

Soon enough, a livid Worth, whom a local newspaper had praised in 1842 for his "gentlemanly deportment and amiable manners," burst into the city council chambers where Ben was being held, demanding the slave's immediate release. The young William W. Loring, a future Confederate general and notorious hothead, refused to be intimidated by Worth's "imperious and dictatorial manner." He brashly walked into the guardroom and defiantly placed his foot on the stocks. Worth thereupon threatened to kill Loring, making motions at drawing a knife from his jacket. When Loring did not budge, Worth, a man in his late forties, grabbed a chair, and aimed "several deadly blows" at Loring's head. Loring, who was twenty years younger, struck back with a cane in a "severe struggle" that continued until a bystander broke it up. During the fight, Ben escaped, and Mayor E. B. Gould ordered the sheriff to arrest Worth. Eventually, cooler heads prevailed and the charges against the general were dropped. The outcome for Ben is unknown, but it is clear he was aware of the civilian-military conflicts that plagued St. Augustine and of the rivalry between the competing white officials involved in this incident. He skillfully played them against one another to his own advantage and to the local black community's delight.[18]

One August night in 1849, two patrollers spotted a "negro boy" on horseback at the city gates around 1:00 a.m. Alerted to the patrollers, the black "boy" wheeled his mount about, and headed into town over the bridge at María Sánchez Creek. The patrollers, on foot, moved to intercept the rider, but he "ran his horse through to St. George St. in the direction of North City." Despite a "brilliant" pursuit, the patrollers could not determine the horseman's identity. On 29 December 1849, when patrollers took up the slave Rip Van Winkle, his owners, the Watson family, paid the $1 fine for his release. James R. Sánchez, however, refused to do the same for his bondswoman Inez, whom patrollers had apprehended on the same evening, maintaining that Inez had been seized before the curfew hour.[19] Such disputes over the curfew frequently divided whites, giving leverage to slaves who roamed at night.

Earlier, in 1846, Robert R.[?] Reid gave his slave Peyton permission to attend a Saturday night ball, writing on a slip of paper, "Pass Peyton tonight July 25th 1846." Reid, however, then mistakenly handed Peyton another slip of paper. When the patrol officer refused to accept Reid's story to this effect, he was forced to pay "the constable $1. to save the boy from a whipping." His explanation, Reid complained, "would have been enough without the fine." According to one student of antebellum Florida, most whites, under normal circumstances, believed the state's slave laws were too strict, and such episodes as those just noted suggest that was indeed the case in St. Augustine and probably throughout East Florida.[20] It must be emphasized, however, that to a significant degree, the actions of blacks themselves were responsible for these white attitudes. By being soldiers who refused to submit to the restrictions imposed on them, African Americans circumscribed white freedom while at least to some degree protecting their own social space.

Some slaves used violence, rather than manipulation and wits to fight the American slave society. Like Andrew Gué before him, the slave Redmond personified the rage that many people of color in St. Johns County doubtlessly felt toward whites who deprived them of the liberties that they had enjoyed under the Spaniards. Hiring themselves out, a practice common since Spanish days, gave the enslaved considerable control over their own time, and when masters impinged on this practice, they had to deal with consequences that ranged from malingering to outright violence. In early 1850, Mrs. Incarnacio Hernández evidently had just this problem regarding Redmond, her thirty-year-old bondsman. Redmond objected so vehemently to Hernández leasing him to David Durrance, a farmer living along the rural Picolata Road, that she had him whipped. When Redmond arrived at the Durrance place, he was given a midday meal, permitted to rest, and then assigned to prepare potato beds with an elderly black man called Old George. On reaching the potato fields, and in the presence of the other laborers, Redmond announced that when he had left St. Augustine, he was "very cross" with his owner because of the whipping, yet for the remainder of the afternoon, he worked in a "rather jolly" manner.[21]

Nearly an hour before sunset, Durrance took his gun and proceeded to the woods to hunt. Shortly thereafter, Redmond shouted that he saw a "big Buck" and sent one of Durrance's young sons into the farmhouse to bring him a gun. When the boy returned empty-handed, Redmond seized an axe, saying that he was going to "knock the deer on the head with it." After briefly disappearing into a nearby hammock, Redmond threw his hat into a cart, placed the axe over his shoulder, and started off "over the branch," in the direction that Durrance had gone. When the latter returned home, he found his "considerably alarmed" wife and children standing in the doorway, fearful that Redmond had "intended to do mischief."[22]

A half hour after dark, Redmond appeared at the Durrance house "making all kinds of hallowing & noise." From the porch, Durrance ordered the black man Old George to calm the slave, who was standing fifteen feet away. When Durrance ventured to the gate of the yard, Redmond declared that he "had been over the branch and got converted and his sins pardoned," prompting the white man to order him back to St. Augustine. This order evidently triggered Redmond's anger over his recent whipping, for he repeatedly asked

Durrance if he was threatening to whip him. "Did you not know I was a Hell of a fellow?" Redmond shouted. "You do not know what sort of Man I am?" When Redmond reached for his knife, Durrance pointed his gun and ordered him to halt. As the slave drew nearer, Durrance shot him in the stomach at point-blank range. Within forty-five minutes, Redmond died.[23] He likely had been accustomed to hiring himself out, and he may have lived apart from his mistress, so that the job at Durrance's, besides depriving him of the freedom to choose his employment, required him to sleep away from his loved ones, for the practice of allowing slaves in St. Augustine to occupy residences away from their owner's home was widespread.

As the 1850s progressed and the 1860s dawned, more rage burst to the surface in St. Augustine. When sectional tensions mounted in the 1850s, St. Johns County slaves resisted the tightening slave society. In August 1857, four adolescent slaves received ten lashes each for "abusive language" in the streets of St. Augustine. Two months later, four other slaves suffered thirty lashes each for the same offense, and in late 1858, the mayor's court sentenced two young bondsmen to ten stripes each for playing the game of "shinney" on Sunday. More seriously, Sam, one of Venancio Sánchez's slaves who had been fined $10 for carrying a knife and club in August 1859, was convicted in May 1860 for fighting in public, for which he received twenty stripes. A fellow brawler, Powell, owned by Petronita López, received the same punishment. Five months later, Powell was in trouble again, this time being caught by the patrol near St. Francis Barracks without a pass. When captured, Powell laughed at his captors, who locked him up, only to have him escape by breaking the lock on the city jail. On 3 December 1860, Powell was again apprehended without a pass. For his repeated offenses, the mayor ordered the marshal to give him thirty-nine lashes. Four days earlier, authorities sentenced John Llambias to eighteen lashes for throwing stones.[24]

Indeed, the whip appeared to be a badge of honor for some St. Augustine slaves. In October 1860, Low, owned by Antonio Álvarez, received twenty-five stripes on the "bare back" for "provoking and insulting behavior." As 1861 opened, Venancio Sánchez's bondsman Lawrence endured thirty-nine lashes "well laid on" for disturbing the peace. In late February of that year, the patrol caught the slave Eleck on the streets after curfew, for which he suffered twenty lashes. Then, on 24 June, Sánchez's Lawrence again vented his rage, this time on Antonio Fontané, a recently freed black who had joined the local militia, the St. Augustine Blues. In the presence of several ladies, Lawrence used "provoking language to Tony Fontane the Fifer of the Blues whilst in line," and also "cursed and abused said Tony and disturbed the peace of the City." For this, the court meted out another thirty-nine lashes.[25]

Fontané's service as a musician in a white militia unit hearkened back to the early days of the Second Seminole War. At that time, as we have seen, terrorized whites, seeking to reassure themselves of the loyalty of those who history told them were formidable fighters, permitted blacks to play symbolic roles in the military. Moreover, the numerous whippings meted out indicate that the slave society in St. Johns County was unraveling as the Union dissolved and that slave discipline was diminishing. In October 1858, Mrs. Clarissa C. Anderson, wrote her son that her chicken coops were raided nightly. A few days previously, she reported, a neighbor found a black man hiding under his kitchen table. When he seized the intruder by the shirt, the man of color tore himself away, leaving the neighbor holding a sizable chunk of clothing. According to Mrs. Anderson, she and her friends were forced to ring bells at night, sometimes multiple times, to warn each other of noises that they feared were made by uninvited black visitors. In October 1860, the *St. Augustine Examiner* urged its readers to "take pains, each night before closing their houses to see that all their servants are at home" and to deliver to authorities "any servants of others . . . found at late hours in their yards." "There is too much remissness in regard to such matters," the paper editorialized, "and great evil is liable to result."[26]

In March 1861, Mayor R. B. Canova chastised the St. Augustine Blues for failing to halt the "many thefts" that "had been committed within the City, and at short intervals, within a short time." Canova, in disgust, ordered a return to customary civilian patrols, putting a halt to the recently instituted militia's handling of nighttime security. In mid-April, the patrols still had not apprehended the perpetrators of "the numerous thefts committed within the City of late and for some time past." As a result, the city council empowered Mayor Canova to do whatever was necessary to halt the crimes, including the use of "secret police to aid him in his Official duties." Ten days later, the thieves were captured. They turned out to be three slaves, Migales[?], Simon, and Eve, the first two of whom belonged to none other than the mayor's father, Antonio Canova. The court promptly convicted the trio of larceny, and ordered that they "be removed out of this County." The elder Canova had hoped to avoid the loss of valuable property, but decided to abide by the "voice of the people" in the matter.[27]

African Americans also harassed whites in rural East Florida and seem to have established a maroon community there. This must have evoked haunting memories of the Second Seminole War, along with horrifying portends of the future. In August 1860, the *Examiner* blamed the "outrageous murder" of Don Antonio Álvarez's slave Calistro on "runaway negroes, some of whom have been lurking in the neighborhood for sometime, with head quarters at Hurlburt's." Because the runaways recently had been spotted in town, the editor suggested that they survived by thievery. The "gang of out-laws and desperadoes," he thought, likely had allies within as well as without the gates. Fuming at "these renegades," the *Examiner* sought to rouse whites from their "indifference," an indifference that encouraged black defiance and "affect[s] unfavorably the negroes among us." "The bare fact, that negroes can run away, and remain out for months," the editor concluded, "operates injuriously upon every slave," making all slaves think "more of escape" as well as "disobedience and insolence," because they had "living evidence of its practicability and safety."[28]

On 13 March 1862, St. Augustine surrendered to Union forces. Up to that date, the city continued to punish slaves by whippings. Thus, George R. Fairbanks's slave March received twenty-five lashes in the public market on 14 February for "using abusive & threatening language" to a white man, and two weeks later, Antonio Álvarez's bondsman Low received thirty-nine lashes for carrying a pistol. In short, an increasingly defiant slave population hounded a white community desperately seeking to impose order. A good barometer of that situation on both sides of the racial divide was the frequent use of the whip.[29] Clearly then, whites had not stifled blacks' martial heritage.

During the Civil War, over one thousand Afro-East Floridians fought for the United States, compiling a "military record" that historian Daniel L. Schafer deemed "impressive." Given the martial heritage of blacks in this region, this record is not surprising. For example, George J. F. Clarke's son by the enslaved Hannah Benet, Eulogius "Ellick" (also known as Alexander) Clarke served. So did the elder Clarke's grandsons, George J. F. Garvin and William T. Garvin. In fact, the latter returned to the United States from Hispaniola to do so. William Williams, a son of the free man of color Sampson Williams, a member of the Clarke extended family, likewise joined, along with Abraham Lancaster, the grandson of Patriot War veteran Abraham McQueen. Julius Shemetella, whose white father performed militia duty during the Second Seminole War, also rushed to the federal ranks. His descendants have preserved a story of him helping slaves to escape before the Civil War. Edward Wanton, who seems to have been the white ex-Spanish loyalist Edward M. Wanton's grandson and a relative of the free black Wantons who fought for the Americans during the Second Seminole War, met his death while he was a member of the US Colored Infantry in South Carolina.[30] Although the military histories of the families of St. Johns County slaves who enlisted have not come to light, it is most probable that their fathers and grandfathers likewise had successively resisted the Patriot invaders, American soldiers combating the Seminoles, and municipal/county authorities attempting to enforce curfew laws.

But, as during the Second Seminole War, the Civil War divided St. Johns County's black community, as well as families within that community. Thus, the free blacks Isaac Pepino, Tony Fontané (also known as Huertas or Welters), and Emanuel Osborne, enlisted as musicians in the St. Augustine Blues, now a rebel unit under the commanded of John Lott Phillips, a St. Helena native who often had spoken with Napoleon Bonaparte while the latter lived on the island in exile. Samuel Osborn Sr., Samuel Osborn Jr., and John W. Welters, on the other hand, fought for the Union. After the war, Mary Perpall, who shortly before the conflict had married James Lang in an Episcopal ceremony and saw her husband join the Union forces, wed Manuel Osborne, presumably the same man of color who had joined the St. Augustine Blues.[31]

Recent historians have explored the impact of memories of military service on black aspirations for freedom. Mark M. Smith has argued that recollections of a sixteenth-century battle in Africa inspired the timing of the Stono Rebellion in South Carolina in 1739. Similarly, Gregg D. Kimball believes antebellum black Virginians found inspiration in "concentrated efforts of extended campaigning" by blacks during the American Revolution. Like Herbert Aptheker before him, Kimball posits a black "revolutionary heritage" that a "robust African American memory" kept alive through songs and folklore. Larry E. Rivers likewise attests to the importance of oral tradition among Florida blacks, surmising the tradition stretched at least as far back as the middle of the eighteenth century.[32]

In antebellum Florida, local, territorial, and then state laws concerning African Americans aimed to remind them constantly of their inferiority. This applied to laws governing free people of color as well as slaves. American territorialization and statehood were accompanied by an array of public policies intended to smother free blacks as a class by barring free black immigrants, constricting the rights of those in the territory and state, and eventually banning manumission. Among the most constraining measures enacted during the 1840s and 1850s were those that subjected every free black to a specified white guardian, thereby giving them a childlike standing. Collectively, these laws embodied the view of white Floridians that free blacks endangered their security, and were intended to convey to slaves the message that freedom had no real advantage.[33]

As we have seen, however, African Americans did not believe what the laws told them about themselves. Their oral traditions said otherwise. These traditions said that they were valiant soldiers who had saved East Florida from its enemies and rescued St. Augustine from starvation. In antebellum times, they used their military skills to make it inconvenient for whites to enforce demeaning laws and to remind them of their traditional role as defenders of the region. The awareness of having earned the distinction of "saviors" of the Spanish regime tremendously boosted what historian Steven Hahn has termed blacks' military "élan." This mentality had bolstered the resolve of St. Augustinians of color to protect the pillars of their liberty. A photograph that the black photographer Richard Aloysius Twine took during the 1920s captures this self-confidence, as well as African American efforts to preserve the memory of their battlefield valor in the Jim Crow era. It was a time in the city when the black Catholic congregation of St. Benedict the Moor parish was especially vibrant. It was a time when some black community elders continued to speak Spanish. Twine captured members of the black Catholic Order of the Knights of St. John, who were bearing swords and wearing military uniforms. Their steely miens silently shouted, as the slave Redmond had some seventy years earlier, "Did you not know I was a Hell of a fellow? . . . You do not know what sort of Man I am?"[34]

Traditions of landownership likewise survived and statistics on it constitute a good barometer for measuring St. Johns County's changing racial climate between 1821 and 1862. An examination of this pillar of liberty also casts light on the role of white patrons in assisting and exploiting the county's free people of color. In addition, it opens the door to an assessment of the impact of laws on the lives of this class. These are the subjects of the following chapter.

8
Land, Paternalism, and Laws

Free black landownership had badly eroded by the end of the antebellum period. In order to establish the context for an investigation of the US attack on this Spanish-era pillar of liberty, it is useful to survey St. Johns County's demography and economy. The number of free people of color in St. Augustine, the county seat and center for this population, dropped from 126 in 1830 to 67 in 1860. This constitutes a tumble from 7.4 percent of the city's inhabitants to 3.5 percent. During the same period, the city's enslaved population grew from 474 (27.8 percent) to 673 (35.1 percent). In 1830, 1,108 whites lived there. By 1860, this figure had reached 1,175, an increase of only 6 percent. The total population rose from 1,708 to 1,914 (12.1 percent).[1] To summarize, St. Augustine's demographic growth mainly came from its increasing number of enslaved residents. The number of whites remained relatively flat, while that of free persons of color dropped precipitously.

The county's population as a whole grew slowly because the economy was not generally robust. From 1830 to 1850, the number of inhabitants ranged from 2,500 to 2,700. Only after 1850 did it rise notably, increasing more than 20 percent in a decade. The proportion of the enslaved, which averaged about 38 percent from 1830 to 1850, fell to a third in 1860. This drop was due to the growth of the white population, because the actual number of bond persons was stable. Rural areas grew the most rapidly in the 1850s. Bearing in mind the unreliability of censuses and the county's changing dimensions, it appears that St. Johns County, in the thirty years before the Civil War, became increasingly rural, and the rural population increasingly white. These figures reflect the expansion of the white yeomanry in the countryside and a gradual urbanization of the enslaved. The county's free black population contracted in both absolute and relative terms, falling from 170 in 1830 to 82 in 1860, with the greatest proportional decrease occurring in the 1850s. From 7 percent of St. Johns County's inhabitants in 1830, the proportion of free persons of color declined to about 3 percent in 1860.[2]

At least 1,920 of the 3,695 acres (52 percent) in St. Johns County directly awarded by federal land commissioners to claimants of color at the dawn of American rule eventually ended up in whites' possession. In actuality, this figure certainly was much higher, for it does not include African American real estate that became part of other counties when St. Johns County was divided. The number of "voluntary" conveyances of real property that the county's blacks made was about fifteen in the 1820s, the same in the 1830s, and rose to twenty-one in the 1840s, due primarily to the emigration of the Clarke extended family. By the end of the 1840s, the acreage belonging to people of color was so small that only two transactions involving black landowners appear in the records from 1850 to 1861. All of these antebellum sales were ostensibly voluntary, but it is quite likely that economic, political, and social pressures stood behind many if not most of them. The numbers of court-ordered conveyances of land owned by blacks between 1820 and 1840 was five and involved three town lots and 325 rural acres. In the 1850s alone, there were fifteen court-ordered auctions of 5,441 acres and seven town lots.[3]

In 1850, the value of the real estate owned by free people of color in all of Florida was only $36,480, 70 percent of which was in Escambia County, the site of Pensacola, the former Spanish capital of West Florida. An additional 13.7 percent was located in Monroe County, where most of the Clarkes had moved. The St. Johns County portion stood at only $1,300 or 3.6 percent. The value of black-owned real estate in Florida grew marginally during the prosperous 1850s, but according to the 1860 census, no less than 58 percent of that value was accounted for by the holdings of a single individual, Martha Baxter, the biracial daughter of Zephaniah Kingsley, who lived in Duval County. In St. Johns County that year, African Americans owned a mere $1,400 worth of real property.[4] By the end of the antebellum period, in short, free blacks in the county had been reduced to an impoverished vestige of the class that had flourished under the Spanish flag.

Because free people of color had to conduct their real estate transactions through white guardians, they, to a much greater degree than their neighbors, were dependent on the honesty of lawyers, judges, and other officials. As in the case of Susan Murphy, it is difficult, especially from such a temporal distance, to judge the motives of these elites. Suffice it to say that they were in very advantageous positions when they conducted business for free blacks. Moreover, in hard times, the temptation to profit at the expense of their vulnerable charges loomed large. Though it is certainly true that white guardians rendered many invaluable services, either they or other whites often eventually ended up acquiring African American–owned land.

Discriminatory laws, as well as the social pressures that an increasingly racist society exerted on African Americans, frequently drove them to jettison their real property. In fact, whites' desire to rid blacks of their holdings must be viewed within the context of the Seminole Wars, whereby the government decided to strip these free people of color of their vast acreage by force of arms. The methods used against free blacks were more gradual and subtle. Rather than using guns, whites used the legal system as their weapon. However, what is legal often is neither moral nor just.

In 1838, love had placed the literate, landowning free man of color John N. Mackenzie in a bind. To avoid the breakup of his marriage to the enslaved biracial Harriet, Mackenzie had to buy her. On 18 May 1837, Robert R. Reid, Florida's future governor, had owed him $250 in wages. Reid met this obligation by contacting Joshua Joyner, who seven months earlier had sold a St. Augustine home on Charlotte Street to Charles Lawton "in trust" for the free woman of color Maria Darley. Reid purchased a house from Joyner on the same street in trust for Mackenzie. During the next several months, Mackenzie finished fencing the lot and constructed a second small house on it. Now, he needed Reid's assistance to mortgage it to the Southern Life and Trust Insurance Company. Accordingly, he signed a "deed of conveyance in trust" to Reid, who obtained a loan of $800 from the bank on 1 October 1838. Mackenzie had to repay this sum, with 10 percent interest, by 1 April 1839, or he lost Harriet as well as his home. He evidently did so, for in 1852, the property still belonged to him. Unfortunately, it was being advertised for a tax sale. Two years later, Mackenzie once again owed taxes on it. This time, on 4 June 1855, the well-connected white George R. Fairbanks bought it at auction for a paltry $21.77.[5]

Sometimes a free person of color's white agent could be a blood relative. Racism dictated that Joseph Sánchez could never be the man of affairs that his white "half brother," Joseph Simeon Sánchez, twenty-five years his junior, was. Both were sons of the prominent rancher, planter, and merchant Don Francisco Xavier Sánchez, but the quadroon Joseph Sánchez was a "natural" child. Although the patriarch left no will before his death in 1807, his widow and her ten "legitimate" white offspring agreed to the demands of their father's six children of color for an inheritance. Each natural child received one thirty-sixth of the grand estate. Joseph Sánchez's sisters sold their shares and migrated to Cuba, but he remained in St. Augustine after the American takeover. A carpenter by trade, he conducted business directly with whites, procuring a bay-front townhouse and four slaves from 1821 to 1823. Moreover, Joseph Simeon Sánchez sold him Capuaca, a 500-acre plantation three miles north of the city, for $2,000. It had been worth over $6,000 before the US invasion of 1812–1813.[6] These assets would allow Joseph Sánchez to lead a comfortable life in his few remaining years.

On 19 April 1826, when he made his will, his common-law wife was Susan Sánchez. Her father had purchased his freedom from Joseph Sánchez, and she had bought hers from his father's white widow, María del Carmen Hill. In 1812, Susan Sánchez's parents owned a small farm near Capuaca. Joseph Sánchez requested that he be "buried, in a stile suited to my situation, and circumstances in life." His executor, Joseph Simeon Sánchez, was to make the funeral arrangements. Because he had no children, the man of color in his midfifties bequeathed to Susan Sánchez his entire estate, which was to "rest in and remain for my wife during her natural life, that out of the profits thereof she may be supported." However, he emphasized that this bequest was merely "a life estate . . . and no more." After she died, it was "all to go to be divided equally amongst the children of Jose Simeon Sanchez." Less than two weeks later, on 1 May, Joseph Sánchez expired at his home on Marine Street, with at least one white man's family owing him money.[7]

Susan Sánchez survived for nearly thirty more years, passing away on 1 September 1854. Afterward, Capuaca, the Marine Street house, a vacant town lot, and an elderly slave, all worth $1,800, became the property of Joseph Simeon Sánchez's heirs, sparking an acrimonious court battle among them. The white Sánchezes were anticipating Susan Sánchez's demise as early as 1847, when one of the heirs, Mary V. Sánchez, who was about to be married, appointed George Center and Joseph B. Ferreira as managers of her share of the "Life Estate of Sue Sanchez, a black woman." In 1859, Capuaca, which had become "almost entirely unproductive and useless," was sold to Joseph R. Pacetty for $1,500 on behalf of seven of the heirs. But as the nineteenth century drew to a close, Joseph Sánchez was not forgotten. In 1893, the octogenarian John S. Masters remembered him, as did Sánchez's seventy-two-year-old white nephew, Francis M. Sánchez, who now resided in his uncle's former town house. It turned out that Joseph Sánchez had owned 210 acres in Volusia County, on the west bank of the Hillsborough River, south of New Smyrna. Joseph Simeon Sánchez's heirs now stood to inherit this tract, and they apparently did, after testifying, with no reference to color, that Joseph Sánchez was not the Joseph M. Sánchez who died in 1830.[8] Thus, the last of the "black Sánchez" property in East Florida vanished.

In other instances, as in the case of whites, courts might order the land of free people of color sold in the best interests of a minor family member. Here again, because persons of African descent were so disadvantaged, those who advised the court had to have spotless integrity, in addition to good judgment. Edward M. Wanton fathered at least ten quadroon children, but only three were alive by November 1851. His daughter Hannah recently had passed away, leaving her five-year-old son, Manuel López, in Savannah, Georgia. His father was "of Spanish extraction" and "in poor circumstances," so the child lived "nearly in a destitute situation." The lad was an heir to his white grandfather's estate, however, so funds could become available to alleviate his poverty.[9]

The Wanton estate, administered by the white James Edwards, held nearly 1,800 acres of East Florida land that could be sold and Manuel López's share of the proceeds could be invested, so that the interest might support him. López's uncle, Charles Wanton, recommended that George R. Fairbanks act as the child's guardian. As noted in a previous chapter, Fairbanks privately disdained biracial people. He also displayed a knack for acquiring free blacks' land at rock-bottom prices. The court appointed Peter B. Dumas as its special master to determine if it was in Manuel López's best interest for the estate to sell a 640-acre tract situated in Marion County, which had been part of the huge Spanish Arredondo Grant, and which Edward M. Wanton had purchased for his heirs. Moses Levy, who took care to inform the court that the Wantons were "colored persons," advised selling and investing. Benjamin Putnam agreed, stating that a price of $4 per acre was fair and adding that the little boy was "colored." Fairbanks also assented, as he thought that the acreage could not be rented for over $100 a year.[10]

As a result of these recommendations, Dumas, on 5 November 1851, reported that the sale would be to López's benefit. On 10 November, the court authorized the conveyance of the tract to John H. Cosby for $2,575. Fairbanks, who would be responsible for managing the child's share, noted that Charles Wanton had approved of this arrangement.[11] On paper, proper procedures had been followed with the appropriate safeguards. Yet, race was injected into the proceedings, which raises a red flag. Perhaps the expert witnesses merely were acknowledging how tough life would be for a person of color as he reached manhood. On the other hand, they may have signaled the court that what might not be good enough for a white child was sufficient for one of African descent. Moreover, Fairbanks's proclivities give fair cause to wonder how conscientiously he looked after López's interests in the long run.

Their unsuccessful class-action suit heightened the vulnerability of the Clarke clan's real estate. Increasing tax burdens, in addition to debts resulting from a gloomy economy, would make it more difficult for them to retain their lands, which were scattered throughout East Florida. In 1839, for example, Alachua County's tax collector announced that George J. F. Clarke's heirs were delinquent in the payment of county and territorial taxes on twenty thousand acres within his jurisdiction. In September 1839, Clarke's financially strapped daughter, Mrs. Felicia Garvin, sold the seven acres near St. Augustine's gates, which her father had conveyed to her nine years earlier as a hedge against hard times, to the prominent landholder Moses Levy for $750. Her brother, William R. Clarke, transferred his seven acres to Jacob Forman in April 1840 for $500. Four days later, Forman deeded it to Levy for $50 more. Three other brothers liquidated their seven-acre tracts about the same time. Thomas and Daniel Clarke, from Cuba, turned their acreage over to the wealthy Venancio Sánchez for a mere $70 each. Joseph Clarke garnered $460 from Forman. John D. Clarke's parcel went to Peter Sken Smith for $400. In 1842, James F. Clarke's heirs would lose their seven acres, along with the slave Maria, to Sánchez, who submitted the winning bid—$330—at a court-ordered public auction to satisfy a debt.[12]

At the same time, however, some of the Clarke extended family gained real land. George P. Clarke, another one of Felicia Garvin's brothers, bought two lots at Segui's Point, just across the María Sánchez Creek from St. Augustine, for $500 in 1840. In that same year, Jeremiah Henry Brown, a white soldier about to be transferred from St. Augustine, bequeathed to his "kind and beloved friends, William R. Clarke, George P. Clarke, and John D. Clarke . . . all free persons of color," fifty-six acres in the town of Hector, New York. Brown also directed that the Clarke brothers receive all of the money that one Horatio Palmer of Ovid, New York, was holding for him, as well as the debts that Palmer was required to collect for him. Finally, the soldier designated William R. Clarke as his "sole executor." Furthermore, some two years afterward, James F. Clarke's widow was poised to gain property from the estates of Philippa and Brigida Dulcet, who had died in Cuba and New Orleans, respectively. Also in 1842, the US Supreme Court confirmed title to the claim of George J. F. Clarke and George Atkinson to 15,000 acres.[13]

Then, on 10 November 1843, the George J. F. Clarke estate's lands were partitioned. Eight biracial heirs received two thousand rural acres. This amounted to less than half of the 33,950 nonurban acreage that the patriarch had bequeathed to them in 1834. Part of the latter was used to secure the settlement of claims against the estate. Clarke had designated a separate portion of his land to be used for raising funds to pay Mrs. Catalina Hernández Benet for the emancipation of his second biracial family (his mistress and their four children) and for their support. This manumission took place in 1844. Property on Amelia Island, as well as three lots in St. Augustine, came under the control of former Florida governor William P. Duval, whom the Clarkes appointed as their "lawful attorney." Duval was to work in their best interest by auctioning these common holdings and distributing the proceeds to the heirs of Clarke's first family.[14]

A squabble over a fourth St. Augustine lot proved particularly costly. In 1826, George J. F. Clarke had fictitiously mortgaged his valuable real estate on Charlotte Street to his daughter Felicia and his sons James and George. The cagey former surveyor general did so to protect it from creditors. His fears were not unfounded. Clarke ended up losing ten thousand acres to these creditors, Archibald Clarke and Remi Brunett, when a federal court ordered an auction to pay a judgment of $2,332. In 1837, Felicia Garvin mortgaged her portion of the Charlotte Street lot to obtain a loan of $294.40 from Gabriel W. Perpall. She must have repaid the loan, because in 1839, she mortgaged the same property to another white, Peter Sken Smith. Mrs. Garvin likewise apparently satisfied this second mortgage.[15]

Trouble ensued, however, when the Clarke heirs wanted $5,800 from their father's estate in 1843. The executor, John Fontané refused to release this sum, fearing that if he did, there would not be sufficient funds on hand to satisfy the estate's creditors. Therefore, the heirs used "certain lands devised to them," including the Charlotte Street lot, as security. Of the approximately $45,000 that George J. F. Clarke had claimed for Patriot War damages, the federal government paid about $22,000. Because Felicia Garvin's deceased husband had been a coclaimant, she received his share, around $4,700, separately from her siblings. The rest of the settlement, a little more than $15,000 was due to the estate, minus at least 10 percent for attorneys' fees.[16] Debts and administrative fees likely depleted this sum significantly.

Deeply indebted and needing cash for an upcoming move out of Florida with her beleaguered daughter Eliza, Felicia Garvin foreclosed on the fictitious, though official, Charlotte Street mortgage. In August 1844, she won a judgment of more than $2,800 against her father's estate. Accordingly, the court ordered the lot auctioned. Some three months later, Joseph M. Hernández obtained it for a bid of $235. Fontané, who now saw his personal assets vulnerable to Clarke's debtors, countersued in 1845. He initiated the suit as the executor of Dr. Richard Weightman, whose estate had claims for medical bills against the Clarke estate. E. B. Gould, another creditor, joined Fontané. They argued that because the mortgage had been fictitious, Garvin had no right to foreclose. Furthermore, they maintained that Garvin's portion of the lot, worth $600, had fetched only a third of its value. If this transaction stood, then the claims against the Clarke estate would be such that all of its available real estate would be "swept away." To testify regarding the mortgage's fictitious nature, Garvin's brothers had to be disinterested parties. Therefore, on 3 June 1845, George, John, and William Clarke, for $150 each, relinquished all of the lands to which they were entitled from their father's estate, to Pedro Benet.[17]

Felicia Garvin, on her part, sold other property, four hundred acres in Alachua County, to St. Augustine's prominent Peck family in 1846. Her cousins also were parting with their real estate. Charles W. Clarke's sons, George W. Clarke and Thomas W. Clarke, conveyed 150 acres on Moses Creek, south of St. Augustine, to Robert Martin for $200 in 1842. Two years later, they saw three hundred acres of their mother's land auctioned for debt. E. B. Gould secured this tract for $70, or $0.23 per acre. In 1846, George W. Clarke sold all of his inherited lands and other assets to Samuel Hill Williams for $700. The following year, Clarke's brother, Thomas, was so desperate that he conveyed his share of the Clarke-Wiggins estate to Williams for $175.[18]

A pattern developed. The threat of creditors' lawsuits, combined with the tax burdens accompanying landownership and being persons of African descent, moved the Clarkes to turn to white patrons for cash in desperate times. Their decision to unload their real estate was their only viable option. Otherwise, they ran the risk of having their holdings disappear at auction for a mere fraction of their worth. Hence, the Clarke family's fortunes, which were so tied to landownership, were fading rapidly by the mid-1840s. In 1845, the clan held seven St. Augustine lots, sixteen slaves, and seven thousand acres in rural St. Johns County. By 1855, its collective members possessed two town lots, three slaves, and slightly more than six hundred acres.[19]

According to the tax rolls, the wealthiest free person of color in St. Augustine in 1861 was Hagar Carr, who owned real estate assessed at $500. Carr was likely the "Haga" that Tomoka planter Frances Kerr manumitted by her will in 1820. The ex-slave's mother, "Old Lidy," had also received her freedom at that time, but her sister, Chapa, remained a bondswoman. Years later, "Old Lidy" married Dick Ferguson, a free black who owned a bay-front home that she inherited upon his death and eventually bequeathed to her daughter Hagar. The house had been passed from one owner of color to another from Spanish times to the end of the antebellum era, and Hagar Carr's sister, Chaper McCray, inherited it long after the Civil War. It still stands at 35 Marine Street.[20]

Tyra McQueen and Felicia Robio, two other females of color, also owned real estate in St. Augustine on the Civil War's eve, valued at $100 and $300, respectively. McQueen, as noted earlier, may have had an extended conjugal relationship with the prominent jurist and politician Joseph B. Lancaster. In any case, she inherited her home on Charlotte Street from her mother, Emilia Nichols, who died around 1856 at the age of ninety-one. Nichols had purchased the property in 1843 from John M. Fontané, Clarke's executor, for $450, a sum that she likely received from Washington's payment of her Patriot War claim in 1842. Felicia Robio was the wife of José de Regla, a free black tavern operator, who after nearly losing his home in a tax sale, willed his real estate to her and his son, José Luís Robio. The son sold his portion for $200 prior to leaving St. Augustine, but Felicia held onto her share, which at her death, around 1860, went to her daughter, Rosita Álvarez, who lived in Key West.[21]

The descendants of two Spanish-era biracial families hung on to at least part of their holdings in rural St. Johns County for much of the antebellum period. As late as 1850, Zephaniah Kingsley's heirs still owned at least 1,600 acres, although two years later, no Kingsley land appeared on the assessment rolls. Some of the lost acreage was auctioned for nonpayment of taxes. The remainder may have been sold at the direction of George R. Fairbanks, master in Chancery of the United States District Court, as a result of a lawsuit by one group of Kingsley legatees against another. The free-colored heirs of Edward M. Wanton's estate fared somewhat better than those of Kingsley's did, maintaining control of 970 acres in St. Johns County at the end of the antebellum era. In 1861, Wanton's quadroon son, Philip Wanton, owned taxable property assessed at $571, of which $435 was in land, and was the county's second wealthiest person of color. His property constituted 18 percent of the county's free black wealth.[22]

The wealthiest African American in the county at the end of the antebellum era was another Wanton heir, David Fleming, also known as David Gray, the father-in-law of George Lycurgus. The tax collector assessed Fleming's estate at $1,014, which amounted to almost a third of the county's black wealth. Between 1824 and 1829, Fleming had paid $500 to free his wife and children. The details of his life are obscure, but as they relate to landholding it is known that in 1844, the Wanton heirs sold him a twenty-five-acre tract in the county's northwest corner for $150. By 1850, Fleming's real estate was valued at $200 and his household consisted of six people besides himself. A decade later, he was cultivating twenty-five acres and, in addition to the requisite farm equipment, owned five horses and more than a hundred head of other livestock. In 1861, the assessment of his taxable property rose by $450 because of improvements.[23]

David Fleming, like Philip Wanton, acquired, maintained, and even augmented his real estate in rural late-antebellum St. Johns County. In the countryside, it may have been easier for African Americans to gain and hold property in the racially charged 1850s and early 1860s. To be sure, Fleming was a hard-working man of extraordinary energy linked to the quadroon Wantons and the white Fatios. An isolated location, hard work, and the favor of influential whites may account for Fleming's success where others failed. This success represents a trace of the economic mobility that some blacks had enjoyed in Spanish times.

Not surprisingly, prominent whites were the overwhelming beneficiaries of the free colored class's impoverishment. In May 1850, William R. Clarke, who did not migrate to Key West, desperately sought a buyer for his deceased mother's 461 acres ten miles west of town. Five months later, the tax collector advertised this tract. The Clarke family owed $4.75. Yet, they could not or would not pay this tax. On 3 February 1851, George R. Fairbanks bid $18.75 for the land, gaining possession of it for $0.03 to $0.04 per acre. Eight months later, Sheriff R. B. Canova announced that 3,850 acres and one city lot from the Clarke estate would be auctioned. On 7 April 1851, Thomas Holms bought the urban lot for $20. Holms also purchased 150 more acres located twenty miles south of the city. He paid $20.50 for it. The proceeds from this sale were used to repay the claims of E. B. Gould and Peter Dumas against the estate. The remaining 3,700 acres went to Judge Isaac H. Bronson for $580, which also was used to pay Gould and Dumas. Bronson later divided this acreage into equal shares with former sheriff John Beard and Fairbanks. The latter, over the years, acquired substantial black property—a slave, a town lot, and 1,732 rural acres for $357.50. Except for the slave, he bought all of this at tax auctions. His booty included 1,694 acres of Clarke land, for which he paid $0.12 an acre.[24]

Free persons of color, in rare cases, also benefitted from the forced sale of black-owned real estate. In 1835, Jack Forrester and his wife Fanny paid $600 for two lots, one on Charlotte Street and another on Marine Street. They soon mortgaged the properties to Venancio Sánchez for $250 and, after repaying the loan within a year, sold the Marine Street parcel. Mr. Forrester died in the mid-1840s. The county probate court, in 1851, ordered Venancio Sánchez, the administrator of his will, to auction the Charlotte Street home for debt payment. The property sold for $201, but was in turn conveyed to Hannah Sánchez, a free black, for $210.[25] Hannah's speedy acquisition of the property indicates a prior understanding with Venancio Sánchez. In the example of the Clarke acreage, one can argue that white purchasers merely were exercising their legal rights. Moreover, the woman of color Hannah Sánchez, with a white patron's assistance, had been able to do the same. But other cases involving the Clarke family cast a more ominous shadow over antebellum whites' acquisition of black land and convicts some prominent whites of outright chicanery.

The Clarke family's frequent disputes with their physicians regarding medical bills exemplify some of the financial pressures that caused blacks' real estate to be transferred to whites. Both Patty Wiggins and John D. Clarke were involved in lawsuits over medical bills. The shifting racial climate of St. Johns County is perhaps reflected in the outcomes of these disputes. In 1825, Wiggins won her case due to a legal technicality, whereas two decades later, Clarke lost his, as well as an appeal that both his cousin and his nephew supported financially. In the mid-1840s, two other physicians sued George J. F. Clarke's estate. That the Clarkes frequently sought medical assistance is clear from the account books of Dr. Seth Peck and his son John Peck. When judges ruled against them in their clashes with physicians, the victors either sought land as compensation, or the Clarkes sold land in order to pay court-ordered sums.[26]

Their bitter fight with Dr. John Peck over land in what is now Alachua County likely originated in an unpaid medical bill. The Spaniards had granted a thousand acres at Youngblood Hammock to the white William Garvin as a reward for his services during the Patriot War. The United States confirmed this grant in 1828, and Garvin's widow, the biracial Felicia M. F. Garvin, apparently deeded two hundred acres to the Presbyterian Church and used the remaining eight hundred acres to obtain credit for merchandise and the purchase of a home in St. Augustine during the 1830s. The financial arrangements regarding the home were complex and seem to have involved unwritten understandings with Mrs. Garvin's white attorney, Peter Skenandoah

Smith, as well as with Dr. Andrew Anderson and the Pecks, all members of St. Augustine's Presbyterian congregation. On the eve of her migration from Florida in 1842, Mrs. Garvin evidently still held title to four hundred acres in Youngblood Hammock.[27]

The widow appointed her son, James D. Garvin, as her agent, instructing Smith that he was to secure his approval before selling any of her real estate. Mrs. Garvin also insisted that none of her land be conveyed for under $1.25 per acre. Contrary to her instructions, however, Smith sold the remaining four hundred Youngblood Hammock acres to the Peck family for a dollar per acre. "Generall Smithes sails," Mrs. Garvin's daughter, Mrs. Eliza Whitwell, later complained, "was only a money making affair." "No sail by G. Smith," Whitwell contended, "Can Stand for he had no power to sell."[28]

Smith had burst on the St. Augustine scene from upstate New York in late 1834 as part of a contingent of winter residents. Before coming to Florida, he had risen to the rank of major general in his state's militia. By 1837, he had inherited $46,000 from his father, along with an annuity of $800. He invested his fortune in a number of St. Augustine development schemes, paid half of the Presbyterian minister's salary, established a law office, and built the grandest residence in town. In 1838, he lost his bid to enter the political arena because his opponents used the abolitionism of his brother, Gerrit Smith, against him. Hard times in St. Johns County drove him to Philadelphia in the 1840s, but not before he watched his property disappear at tax sales and saw himself subjected to arrest and criminal investigation. Mrs. Garvin owed money to Smith, and as 1840 began, she found her business affairs strongly intertwined with those of a man whose fortunes were on the brink of collapse.[29]

According to Mrs. Whitwell, "on account of the [dis?]advantages which surrouded us in those days [Peter Sken Smith] did not consider it wourth his notice & those persons who bought of him considered [consulting the Garvins] unnecessary." When James Garvin found out about Smith's unsanctioned conveyance, he successfully pressed the Pecks for $100 more, so that the purchase price would be $1.25 per acre. Dr. Seth Peck's account books suggest that the sale was linked to Smith's private arrangements for the payment of Mrs. Garvin's medical bills, as well as her son James Garvin's efforts to settle his own accounts. Deed books display seemingly irrefutable evidence that the Garvins had transferred ownership to the Pecks. Developments after the Civil War, however, support the black family's contention that during the late 1830s and early 1840s, the various white parties associated with the Youngblood Hammock tract had engaged in some type of fraud. Stunningly, in 1907, during the bleak days of Jim Crow segregation, the United States issued to the Garvins a patent for William Garvin's entire thousand-acre Spanish grant, despite the outrage of the Pecks, who claimed that they had held clear title to six hundred acres of the grant since 1840.[30]

The negligence or dishonesty of whites also resulted in Mrs. Felicia Garvin losing the home that she had purchased from Dr. Andrew Anderson. Eliza Whitwell claimed that her mother made a down payment of $1,000 shortly before migrating from Florida and instructed Peter Sken Smith to pay the balance out of the Patriot War settlement that she expected to reach St. Augustine momentarily. Eight days after Garvin's departure in 1842, this money arrived, and from a distance, the widow felt that her home had been secured. Several years later, unfortunately, the attorney O. M. Dorman informed her that Smith never paid the Andersons. Consequently, Mrs. Garvin lost her down payment, for Dr. Anderson's widow kept it. Although Mrs. Anderson was entitled to this down payment, Christian charity might have made her reflect on the notion that what is legal is not necessarily just. However, she faced financial pressures of her own in a town hit hard by tough economic times. She neither could pay her debts nor collect from those indebted to her, because money was tight from 1842 to 1844. This made it easier to assert her right to Mrs. Garvin's mortgaged home, as well as to the down payment.[31] Once again, the financially distressed Smith had not followed the instructions of the woman of color whose interests he was bound to protect. As Mrs. Garvin's white agent, the sum from the Treasury Department was in his hands, and these funds surely tempted him.

The undependability of white patrons also is indicated by the controversy surrounding the Garvins' claim to their grandfather George J. F. Clarke's eight thousand acres at White Springs, now Green Cove Springs, in Clay County. Clarke apparently mortgaged this land to General Duncan L. Clinch and when the mortgage was repaid, he deeded it back to Clarke. After Clarke's death, however, his biracial children for some reason were not able to assert their ownership. Thus, Clinch's heirs took possession. As in the case of the disputed Youngblood Hammock tract, however, the federal government recognized that some injustice had been committed in antebellum times. In 1902, the Garvins received a patent for the eight thousand acres.[32]

The Garvins certainly recognized that unscrupulous whites took advantage of the restrictions that a slave society placed on persons of color, in order to take away their land. In 1842, Felicia Garvin accused her father's executor,

John M. Fontané, of treating her "more like a slave than a adopted Daughter." Her daughter blamed "bad management" by the "two Grand Villains," Fontané and Peter Sken Smith, for allowing others rather than the Garvins to benefit from the George J. F. Clarke estate. Fontané, the Garvins maintained, used the estate's assets "as he thought proper" rather than for what was in the best interest of the Clarke family. They also charged Smith and Mrs. Clarissa Anderson with defrauding her mother. George W. Rossignol, the son of Susan Clarke and the white L. H. Rossignol, alleged that the United States in 1848 had confiscated a hundred acres of Clarke land on Amelia Island without the Clarkes ever having "received a cent of it." Records of the US General Land Office lend credence to these assertions, for after the Civil War, this agency issued twenty-one patents for a total of 25,679.96 acres to the Clarkes, of which at least 898.63 acres were located in St. Johns County.[33] Until these patents were issued, whites were in possession of much of this land.

Members of the extended Clarke family were not the only African Americans to level post–Civil War charges of theft against distinguished white antebellum families. Jane Sánchez was the slave of the powerful Don Francisco Xavier Sánchez. Born in 1800, she originally belonged to Sánchez's white wife, María del Carmen Hill. When Hill's daughter wed Phillip Dewees, Jane Sánchez was given as a house servant to the couple. Jane had "legally married" Charles Fatio, another Sánchez slave, with a justice of the peace presiding at the ceremony. By the time of Fatio's death in 1858, Sánchez had borne seventeen children, nine of whom were alive.[34] The large size of this family indicates a stable domestic life.

When Jane Sánchez was twenty-two, she delivered a son, Adam, in St. Augustine, with her young mistress, Doña María del Carmen Sánchez y Dewees, assisting at the birth. Adam lived with the Dewees family in St. Augustine and accompanied it, along with his parents, to Jacksonville. The Deweeses protected Adam, never hiring him out "for any length of time." Nevertheless, despite the fact that Adam was a "large and fleshy" man, "very clumsy & not active," with poor eyesight, they eventually sold him to a Key West physician in 1849.[35] There were limits, then, to paternalism, even that of an old Spanish family, especially when whites' finances were at stake.

Adam Fatio clearly missed his family and strove to maintain his connections to them from afar, a sentiment consistent with the statements issued by married slaves who had been separated by their masters. In Key West, Fatio worked as a common laborer, sometimes shoveling in a coal yard, but mostly doing lighter work because he was not very "robust." He was permitted to keep a portion of his wages, for when he heard of his father's passing, he sent his mother $9, along with three dresses, promising to do all that he could to assist her. Relaying such sums was no small sacrifice for Fatio, "a Man of good Moral habbitts" who, rather than "go . . . in some frolic," would tell his friends that "he could not afford to spend his money in that way— as he had an old mother that depended upon him." He faithfully continued to write to the Dewees family, expressing a strong attachment to all of them, particularly his mother. Fatio always ended his letters with the sentence, "I am glad to say I am well & I hope you all are the same."[36]

After the Civil War, Frances Dewees insisted that Adam Fatio had furnished cash to his enslaved mother in amounts ranging from $5 to $15. Jane Sánchez disagreed. Although she acknowledged that her son was "very kind," she swore that money from him passed into her hands only once—shortly after her husband's demise. Her former owners characterized her in 1883 as "a good faithful Servant" whom the Deweeses continued to support and "esteem . . . highly." Likewise, a federal official wrote that Sánchez "one of the best old colored women I have ever known." Her sterling reputation, combined with her public disagreement with the whites that fed and clothed her at a time when she was "old & helpless," adds weight to her accusations.[37] During her enslavement, both Sánchez and her owners experienced financial distress, with the result being the disruption of the black woman's family life and the worsening of her material circumstances. To be sure, other African Americans in St. Johns County faced similar situations.

Marriages between slaves, even those contracted within the Catholic Church and recognized by community consensus, stood on shaky ground. Peter Johnson and his wife Amanda Canova saw their domestic lives deteriorate as Susan Murphy, Johnson's owner, lingered on her deathbed in 1855–1856. Johnson was conveyed in trust to George R. Fairbanks when Murphy was organizing her affairs in preparation for her death. For a time, it seemed that Venancio Sánchez would buy Johnson, but this deal never materialized. Instead, US Senator David L. Yulee, one of Mrs. Murphy's legatees, sent Johnson north to Fernandina, away from wife and family. "I was compelled to come," Johnson bitterly reminded federal officials in 1893, "I was separated from my wife by my owner." Abraham Lancaster concurred, recalling that the Johnsons "were separated by the white people."[38]

Indeed, according to the law, slave marriages existed at whites' pleasure. Historians point to East Florida as the portion of the state where owners acted most conscientiously to maintain their slaves' family units, citing the area's Spanish heritage as a major explanatory factor.[39] Nonetheless, an examination of approximately one hundred Civil War pension files of black East Floridians impressed on the author the widespread emotional devastation caused by forced separations. Thus, at the most fundamental level of human existence, the vast majority of St. Johns County blacks faced insecure lives in which the bonds of parental, familial, and conjugal love could be shattered in an instant, no matter how much they strove to curry their owners' favor and buttress their domestic lives with Hispanic institutions or customs. Bishop Augustin Verot's famous sermon attests to this shameful state of affairs.

On the other hand, blacks in late antebellum St. Johns County sometimes could manipulate paternalism. Things did not go well for William R. Clarke after most of his family left St. Augustine. Toward the end of 1849, the night patrol seized him, his cousin Thomas Clarke, and Joseph M. Hernández's slave William, for violating curfew. On 11 June 1850, a jury convicted William R. Clarke of retailing liquor without a license. He was fined $30 plus court costs and ordered to be incarcerated until he paid. Not more than a month later, Florida's governor, Thomas Brown, much to the chagrin of St. Johns County's authorities, used his executive clemency to remit the fine because he considered Clarke's a "hard case." In early January 1851, in accordance with an 1848 state requirement, Clarke saw himself forced to select a white guardian. He chose Joseph Simeon Sánchez. Later in 1851, Clarke was convicted of "keeping a Common ill-governed & disorderly House," jailed for a day, and charged court costs.[40]

William R. Clarke's poverty burdened him heavily. It is of little wonder, then, that by June 1854, his health had deteriorated. On 27 May 1855, he begged the mayor and councilmen to exempt him from the $3 municipal tax on his African ancestry. He reminded the authorities that "he [was] not an able bodied man & has not been so for more than a year." His plea gained the council's sympathy. In 1856, he was excused from paying the tax once again. By 1857, he had regained his ability to work. But, three years later, Clarke, who was in his early fifties, snapped. On one mid-June night, the patrol picked him up drunk in the street, using "improper language," which he admitted was "highly disrespectful" to Mayor Paul Arnau. Subsequently, as he and Sampson Williams had done more than twenty years earlier, he composed an apology letter for his "bad conduct." He stated that he wished to "beg forgiveness of his Honor the Mayor and Council, and also at the same time humbly beg[ged] his sentence may be commuted," due to "his sickly and diseased body, as well as his old age." The council records indicate that his strategy succeeded.[41]

Clarke's father had been an influential colonial official. His other white relatives likewise had prospered. A white aunt lived in England with her husband, a medical professor and hospital inspector. Another white aunt resided in Cuba with her prominent husband, Don Antonio Matanza, who, like George J. F. Clarke, had been a leading member of Spanish East Florida's government establishment. A white uncle, Thomas Clarke, served as a military officer in Britain, and another white uncle, James Clarke, captained an Irish regiment in Spain. A third white uncle, Charles W. Clarke, also had held responsible civilian and military positions under the Spaniards. Perhaps this elite background, because the biracial Clarkes no longer posed a threat to local society, accounts for the mercy that whites extended to him. For toward the century's end, his niece, Mrs. Eliza M. Whitwell, similarly became a historical curiosity for condescending whites.[42]

The sorry condition of William R. Clarke and free blacks generally in late antebellum St. Johns County contrasts starkly with the situation in neighboring Putnam County. A small group of Clarkes migrated just across the St. Johns River, to the town of Palatka. Here, Spanish-era patterns of blood ties with whites and landownership continued. Susan Clarke, who either was a daughter from the mixed-race marriage of James F. Clarke and Mary Dulcet, or a child of the biracial couple John D. Clarke and Elizabeth Fish, entered into a permanent relationship with a white lumber merchant from Georgia, L. H. Rossignol, around 1847. In the 1850s, she acquired property in Palatka, as well as an eighty-seven-acre farm outside of town. Her neighbors included her young uncles Philip and Alex Clarke, her grandfather's sons by the slave Hannah Benet, and Amelia Anderson Clarke, her absent cousin's (or brother's) wife. In 1860, she shared a household with Rossignol, seven biracial children, and her young uncle Alex Clarke. Through her efforts, the latter acquired Palatka real estate. Thirty free blacks resided at the river port in 1860, including Amelia Anderson Clarke, Hannah Benet, and Ramona Fernández, another mixed-race woman linked to the Clarkes. Susan Clarke functioned as the matriarch of this small free black community, which had tripled in size since 1850.[43]

Her pedigree, ancestral ties to the Palatka locale, property ownership, and business skills helped to make her a leader. In addition, her alliances with local whites bolstered her position. Rossignol, at times described as her "agent" or "guardian," lived with her until at least 1870. Susan Clarke's young uncles boarded for a time in the household of the prominent white Robert R. Reid. She and Rossignol borrowed funds from Reid and his business partner, Henry R. Teasdale, both of whom were tied by marriage to the Benet family, the former owners of Hannah Benet, the mother of George J. F. Clarke's second biracial family.[44] White paternalism functioned much more benignly in late-antebellum Palatka than it did in St. Augustine.

Rural Duval County also was more hospitable to free people of color. There, Zephaniah Kingsley's biracial daughters, who had married white men prior to 1837, had been able to live with their husbands unmolested on their plantations after shipboard weddings that evaded the territorial ban on interracial marriages. A year later, however, Kingsley's wife, Anna Madgigine Jai, along with her son John Maxwell Kingsley, fled to Haiti, where the patriarch had purchased vast acreage. But, in 1846, three years after her husband's passing, Jai returned to Florida to lead a court battle against the patriarch's white relatives who were disputing his will. She won because she had been a free Spanish subject in Florida prior to 1821. The federal judge ruled that the Adams-Onís Treaty protected her rights. Afterward, asserted historian Daniel Schafer, she, like Susan Clarke in Palatka, "helped found a unique free black community on the eastern shore of the St, Johns River, across from Jacksonville," which "flourished in the 1840s and 1850s, despite the racist hysteria that accompanied the drive for secession from the Union." Schafer noted that this community depended on the cooperation of "sympathetic court officials," who refused to enforce Florida law.[45]

On the other side of the state, free black families in Pensacola did not emigrate until a decade after the Clarke extended family left St. Augustine for Key West in 1847. Indeed, their white neighbors regarded them so highly in that year, that they petitioned Florida's legislature to eliminate racially based taxes. Perhaps cultural influences emanating from New Orleans had preserved their social standing. The scholars Ruth B. Barr and Modeste Hargis concluded that the law that drove the West Florida city's creoles of color away was an act in 1856 that strictly enforced a guardianship statute, essentially marking them with the "stigma of slavery." Even though some Pensacola whites offered to "become their guardians merely as a legal formality," the creoles' "pride revolted at even this nominal mark of servitude," causing them to migrate to Tampico, Mexico.[46]

In effect, Florida law subjected free blacks to the paternalistic vagaries of the communities in which they lived. Thus, from one perspective, they increasingly had become "slaves" of their white neighbors, who might or might not decide to use racist statutes against them. Moreover, even when whites practiced forbearance, they still held free persons of color in their debt. As the examples of antebellum Palatka, rural Duval County, and Pensacola demonstrate, it is difficult to generalize about the impact of anti-black legislation, even in regions that shared the same Hispanic past. But, it is clear that everywhere they were enacted, such legislation increased whites' power over people of African descent.

One might argue that the Clarkes left St. Augustine primarily to pursue economic opportunities. Family correspondence, however, suggests that racist laws were the greater culprits. In a letter to Dr. John Peck in 1868, Mrs. Eliza Whitwell testified to the importance of discriminatory legislation. "I am pleased to say," the widow jabbed, "that the bad laws are . . . dead those laws that drove us away from our homes." Mrs. Whitwell's cousin, Frederick A. Clarke, who had gone west to seek his fortune in California's gold rush, had expressed similar sentiments fourteen years earlier. Writing from Washington Territory in 1854 to his brother James Washington Clarke, who was living in Key West, Frederick addressed the subject of the slave Peter. He instructed his brother that he could either retain Peter or allow him to purchase his liberty. Regarding the latter option, Frederick Clarke was adamant about one condition. "Butt when you give him his Freedom he must leve the country and Stay a way from it," he insisted, "or I wont agree for him to be free." His reason for this condition reflected his own feelings about being a free man of color in Florida. "For if you leve him there," he solemnly reflected, "he will allwers be a slave."[47]

Frederick A. Clarke, on his part, erected four pillars of Spanish-era liberty in the Pacific northwest. He first manumitted himself from living in Florida's slave society. Then he married a white woman, served in the militia, and, in the words of a descendant, Michael Cook, he "wasted little time in following . . . a family tradition of acquiring, or controlling land." He also ran several businesses and engaged in politics. In 1852, he was one of thirteen men who petitioned Congress to establish Washington as a separate entity from Oregon. After the Civil War, Clarke served in Washington's Territorial Assembly, Territorial Council, and as commissioner of Pierce County, where he died in 1878. The names of his daughters, Mary and Florida, honored his white mother, Mary Dulcet Clarke, as well as his birthplace. A Washington state highway marker commemorates his early settlement at Cowlitz Landing and lauds him as one of the state's founders. According to Cook, his brother, George D. Clarke, eventually migrated to British Columbia, where he remarried, died, and was buried in Port Alberni's Catholic cemetery.[48]

The Freedman's Society of St. Augustine celebrated the collapse of the slave society by organizing a "grand barbeque on the plaza" on New Year's Day 1864. This celebration, as well as the numerous enlistments of St. Johns County blacks in the Union forces poignantly contradicted the statements by whites and some blacks that the city was an antebellum paradise for people of color. "I have never," the journalist C. F. Woolson wrote in 1875, "been able to make [St. Augustine blacks] confess that they were more comfortable in [slavery] days, no matter how poor and destitute they [now] may be."[49] That is, although African Americans had exerted decades of pressure in a variety of ways to ease the constrictions of the slave society, the resulting "heaven" was, in the eyes of blacks, no substitute for freedom. And, attaining freedom, as well as living as a free person of color, had become much more difficult under the Americans than under the Spaniards.

That the policies of Florida's slave society, as implemented by whites in St. Johns County, squandered the community's human resources is apparent from the achievements of the descendants of those who antebellum law sought to marginalize. Jeanne E. English, a great-granddaughter of James D. English (who would serve on the Monroe County Commission from 1868 to 1877) and Mary Fish, could point with pride to the accomplishments of her grandfather, Nelson Francis de Sales English. Born in St. Augustine in 1848, he became one of Key West's outstanding citizens, raising five children who distinguished themselves in adulthood. As a government official and cofounder of the Welters' Cornet Band, he enriched island life. Ms. English's father, Leo Victor English, also a talented musician, obtained his medical degree from Northwestern University. Her uncle, James N. F. English, garnered a PhD in mathematics from the University of Chicago.[50]

Edward Orval Gourdin, a great-grandson of Felicia M. F. Clarke and William Garvin, won a silver medal in the 1924 Olympics, earned a law degree from Harvard, attained the rank of brigadier general, and was the first African American justice to serve on Massachusetts's Superior Court. James W. Curtis, a great-great-great-grandson of Clarke and Garvin, who holds a master's degree in physics, has traced the descendants of George J. F. Clarke and Flora Leslie in detail. The biographical sketches contained in his genealogical history speak of optimism and love: family men, mothers, and good citizens who exercised their talents as government officials, entrepreneurs, attorneys, judges, musicians, professors, writers, physicians, engineers, military officers, librarians, teachers, dancers, journalists, athletes, dentists, and artists. They migrated abroad from Florida to the Bahamas, Jamaica, the Dominican Republic, Cuba, Canada, and Iceland, or within the United States to New Mexico, California, Pennsylvania, Washington state, New York, Massachusetts, Ohio, and Washington, DC.[51] Our nation and our world would be much poorer today if two eighteenth-century young people "in trouble," the enslaved Flora Leslie and George J. F. Clarke, a white apprentice of her owner, had not allowed their unplanned child Felicia to live.

A great-great-great-granddaughter of Flora Leslie and George J. F. Clarke, Mrs. Orville Payne, remembered how her family valued real estate. "When you owned property," she asserted, "you had respect." Indeed, landownership was deemed so important to maintaining her family's esteem at a time of segregation and lynching that the tax bills on their holdings were settled before the children's school bills. When her father died in 1975, he left his heirs a number of lots in St. Johns County. During the 1920s, the Clarke descendants held some 30,000 acres of Florida tracts. They recognized that in Jim Crow Florida, as in antebellum and Spanish days, and, as had been the case on the seventeenth-century eastern shore of English Virginia, "the possibility to acquire property [was] the basis of genuine freedom."[52]

Paradoxically, antebellum Florida, by promulgating anti–free black legislation as a means to address its security concerns, sowed the seeds for the destruction of its slave society. Lawmakers regarded free people of color in a similar manner as they did the Indians. In the words of historian Jon Meacham, free blacks, like the Seminoles, were viewed as people "to be manipulated and managed in the context of what most benefited . . . white America." In St. Johns County, as in the United States as a whole regarding Indian removal, "enough white people had a stake" in oppressing free persons of African descent, "or sympathized with it," that the county's "institutions . . . allowed it to go forward." In several other Florida locales, this political will was not as strong. Therefore, free blacks in Pensacola, Palatka, Key West, and rural Duval County enjoyed more liberty. St. Johns County's white paternalists did not see themselves as evil, for as Meacham noted, "evil can appear perfectly normal to even the best men and women of a given time." Instead, they probably felt that they were "practical" humanitarians looking out for the best interests of their charges.[53]

The scholar James R. Colburn has characterized St. Augustine as a "historic community" whose inhabitants continue to be "influenced by the traditions of the past." He also described a certain "smugness" regarding the city's "unique heritage" and the notion that "blacks had been well treated."[54] This study, however, argues that by taking into account the treatment of free people of color in certain other Florida communities, white antebellum St. Augustinians could have done much better. From our point of view, it was not "heaven" for blacks. Compared to many regions of Florida, especially Middle Florida's plantation belt, nevertheless, it indeed would have been a paradise of sorts. It must be kept in mind, however, that the city's African American community worked diligently to craft the freedoms that it did enjoy. Thus, post–Civil War black allusions to a heavenly Ancient City can be interpreted as proud statements of the skills of its antebellum African American "soldiers" in waging war against a slave society.

Ironically, the free blacks who abandoned St. Augustine for Cuba in 1821 may have made a major mistake. Cuba severely persecuted its free people of color in the early 1840s, causing many to leave the island.[55] Moreover, slavery persisted there some two decades after the US Civil War. To be sure, the traditional foe of the Spaniards and the Americans, Great Britain, emerged as the champion of black liberty. Thus, in retrospect, the best decision of East Florida's free blacks may have been to migrate to one of the British West Indies in 1821. Cuba now appears to have been the worst choice.

Although they did not succeed in preventing blood ties between themselves and blacks, antebellum whites diminished the benefits of these connections for people of color. St. Johns County had much greater success in curbing manumission and limiting black landownership, but even here, Spanish-era customs survived in residual forms. Whites failed miserably, however, in quashing what they regarded as a major security threat—the black martial tradition. This shortcoming was a thorn in the side of the slave society and played an important part in its eventual downfall. Hispanic culture and history, in short, became tools that African Americans manipulated to keep this critical tradition alive and well. Their reward was their liberty.

When the United States acquired Florida in 1821, the oppression of free people of color in St. Augustine was not inevitable. A series of poor decisions in Washington, Tallahassee, and in the Ancient City itself resulted in self-inflicted tragedy for blacks and whites. After the Civil War, St. Augustinians enjoyed new opportunities to forge race relations based on mutual respect. Unfortunately, another chain of short-sightedness caused the African American activist Andrew Young, in the 1960s, to describe the former Spanish capital as an "intractably racist town."[56] Some seeds of this racism, as we have seen, were present under the Spaniards. Others were sown during antebellum American rule.

Nevertheless, we must keep in mind that despite the slavery, racism, and chicanery, some African Americans and whites in pre–Civil War St. Augustine had cared deeply for one another, loving to the best of their abilities. The free people of color who remained in East Florida after the Spaniards departed had faith in themselves and their future. African Americans facing the twentieth century after the Civil War surely felt the same way. The ugliness of the Ancient City in the 1960s was not inevitable. Love's capacity to cross racial divides and to conquer history should inspire hope in us, as should the lives of the antebellum blacks of St. Johns County and their many wonderful descendants. Perhaps our choices will be the right ones.

Notes

Introduction

1. Gregg D. Kimball, "African, American, and Virginian: The Shaping of Black Memory in Antebellum Virginia, 1790–1860," and W. Fitzhugh Brundage, "No Deed but Memory," both in *Where These Memories Grow: History, Memory, and Southern Identity*, ed. W. Fitzhugh Brundage (Chapel Hill: University of North Carolina Press, 2000), 58, 22; Lee H. Warner, *Free Men of Color in An Age of Servitude: Three Generations of a Black Family* (Lexington: University of Press of Kentucky, 1992), 1.

2. For examples see: William W. Dewhurst, *The History of St. Augustine, Florida* (1885; reprint, Rutland, Vermont: Academy Books, 1968), 149; David Y. Thomas, "The Free Negro in Florida before 1865," *South Atlantic Quarterly* 10 (October 1911): 336; Thomas Graham, *The Awakening of St. Augustine: The Anderson Family and the Oldest City, 1821–1924* (St. Augustine, FL: St. Augustine Historical Society, 1978): 19–21; David R. Colburn, *Racial Change and Community Crisis: St. Augustine, Florida, 1877–1980* (New York: Columbia University Press, 1985), 17–18; Daniel L. Schafer, " 'A Class of People Neither Freemen nor Slaves': From Spanish to American Race Relations in Florida, 1821–1861," *Journal of Social History* 26 (Spring 1993): 587–609; Larry Eugene Rivers, *Slavery in Florida: Territorial Days to Emancipation* (Gainesville: University Press of Florida, 2000), 1–2, 15, 68–70.

3. Ira Berlin, *Many Thousands Gone: The First Two Centuries of Slavery in North America* (Cambridge: Harvard University Press, 1998), 8, 12, 17, 306; Jane G. Landers, "Introduction," in *Colonial Plantations and Economy in Florida*, ed. Jane G. Landers (Gainesville: University Press of Florida, 2000), 6.

4. Jane L. Landers, "Traditions of African American Freedom and Commu-

nity in Spanish Colonial Florida," in *The African American Heritage of Florida*, eds. David R. Colburn and Jane L. Landers (Gainesville: University Press of Florida, 1995), 34–35; Jane Landers, *Black Society in Spanish Florida* (Urbana: University of Illinois Press, 1999), 23–60.

5. Landers, *Black Society in Spanish Florida*, 22, 24–25, 33; Mark M. Smith, "Remembering Mary, Shaping Revolt: Reconsidering the Stono Rebellion," *Journal of Southern History* 67 (August 2001): 517, 534.

6. Landers, *Black Society*, 24–30, 59, 69, 204, 231–237, 244–246; Patricia C. Griffin, "The Spanish Return: The People-Mix Period 1784–1821," in *The Oldest City: St. Augustine Saga of Survival*, ed. Jean Parker Waterbury (St. Augustine, FL: St. Augustine Historical Society, 1983), 131–133, 148; Rivers, *Slavery in Florida*, 191–192.

7. Griffin, "The Spanish Return," 130; Graham, *The Awakening of St. Augustine*, 13–14, 24; Patricia C. Griffin, "Mullet on the Beach: The Minorcans of Florida, 1768–1788," special issue, *El Escribano: The St. Augustine Journal of History* 27 (1990): 1, 3–4.

8. Graham, *The Awakening of St. Augustine*, 14–16, 18; Griffin, "Mullet on the Beach," 16, 32, 64, 66, 144, 151, 154, 156–157, 169, 179–180; E. P. Panagopoulos, *New Smyrna: An Eighteenth Century Greek Odyssey* (Gainesville: University of Florida Press, 1966), 90; Griffin, "The Spanish Return," 138–139.

9. "Sitiki, 'The Story of Uncle Jack' Draft 2," Buckingham Smith Papers, Manuscript Division, New York Historical Society, New York City; Graham, *The Awakening of St. Augustine*, 37; Griffin, "Spanish Return," 138–139.

10. Graham, *The Awakening of St. Augustine,* 14–16; Griffin, "Mullet on the Beach," 16, 32, 64, 66, 151, 154; Landers, *Black Society*, 121.

11. Pablo Tornero Tinajero, *Relaciones de Dependencia Entre Florida Y Estados Unidos (1783–1820)* (Madrid: Ministerio de Asuntos Exteriores, 1979); 21–22, 51, 127–128; Rufus Kay Wyllys, "The East Florida Revolution of 1812–1814," *Hispanic American Historical Review* 9 (November 1929): 415, 445; William Earl Weeks, *John Quincy Adams and American Global Empire* (Lexington: University Press of Kentucky, 1992), 27–28; David J. Weber, *The Spanish Frontier in North America* (New Haven, CT: Yale University Press, 1992), 274–275, 285, 297; Rembert W. Patrick, *Florida Fiasco: Rampant Rebels on the Georgia-Florida Border, 1784–1790* (Athens: University of Georgia Press, 1954), 3–4.

12. Susan R. Parker, "Men Without God or King: Rural Settlers of East Florida, 1784–1790," *Florida Historical Quarterly* 69 (October 1990): 135–136, 140–141, 148–149, 152–153, 155; Tornero, *Relaciones de Dependencia*, 52, 57, 59, 61; Weber, *The Spanish Frontier*, 280–281; Patrick, *Florida Fiasco*, 48.

13. Patrick, *Florida Fiasco*, 49–50, 56–57, 65–67.

14. Ibid., 68–69, 75, 83–100.

15. Kenneth Wiggins Porter, "Negroes and the East Florida Annexation Plot, 1811–1813," *Journal of Negro History* 30 (January 1945): 11–17, 20.

16. Ibid., 20, 29; Patrick, *Florida Fiasco*, 191–194; Weber, *The Spanish Frontier*, 298.

17. Weber, *The Spanish Frontier*, 278; Charlton W. Tebeau, *A History of Florida* (Coral Gables. FL: University of Miami Press, 1971), 119, 122; Joseph Nathan Kane, *The American Counties*, 3rd ed. (Metuchen, NJ: Scarecrow Press, 1972), 493–524.

18. Graham, *The Awakening of St. Augustine*, 3, 27, 32–34, 64; George E. Buker, "The Americanization of St. Augustine," in *The Oldest City: St. Augustine Saga of Survival*, ed. Jean Parker Waterbury (St. Augustine: St. Augustine Historical Society, 1983), 152.

19. Graham, *The Awakening of St. Augustine*, 14–16, 18; Griffin, "Mullet on the Beach," 16, 32, 64, 66, 151, 154; Panagopoulos, *New Smyrna*, 90; Weber, *The Spanish Frontier*, 337.

20. Buker, "The Americanization of St. Augustine," 155; Graham, *The Awakening of St. Augustine*, 19.

21. *St. Augustine Florida Herald & Southern Democrat*, 13 March 1843; *St. Augustine Ancient City*, 5 January 1850; *St. Augustine Examiner* (hereafter cited as SAE), 29 October 1859, 7 April, 21 April, 18 August, 25 August, 1860.

22. SAE, 9 March 1861; Buker, "The Americanization of St. Augustine," 175; Graham, *The Awakening of St. Augustine*, 84–88.

23. Rivers, *Slavery in Florida*, 8–9; Matthew Frye Jacobson, *Whiteness of a Different Color: European Immigrants and the Alchemy of Race* (Cambridge, MA: Harvard University Press, 1998), 22–30, 37–38.

24. Rivers, *Slavery in Florida*, 65–84; Graham, *The Awakening of St. Augustine*, 19–21; Landers, *Black Society*, 139–140.

25. Rivers, *Slavery in Florida*, 1–2, 15, 68–70; Graham, *The Awakening of St. Augustine*, 19–21; Colburn, *Racial Change*, 17–18; Schafer, "'A Class of People Neither Freemen nor Slaves,'" 587–609.

26. Patricia C. Griffin and Diana S. Edwards, "Richard Aloysius Twine: Photographer of Lincolnville, 1922–1927" (unpublished manuscript), 39, St. Augustine Historical Society Research Library, St. Augustine, Florida; William Cullen Bryant, *Letters of a Traveller; or, Notes of Things Seen in Europe and America,* 3rd ed. (New York: George P. Putnam, 1851), 110–111; Arthur W. Thompson, *Jacksonian Democracy on the Florida Frontier* (Gainesville: University of Florida Press, 1961), 49.

27. Colburn, "Introduction," in *African American Heritage of Florida*, 2–5.

Chapter 1

1. Eliza M. Whitwell to Dr. John Peck, 30 May 1868, Peck Papers, St. Augustine Historical Research Library (hereafter cited as SAHL), St. Augustine, Florida.

2. Jane Landers, *Black Society in Spanish Florida* (Urbana: University of Illinois Press, 1999), 150–152, 336n52, 128–129.

3. Ibid., 151–152, 129, 336n52; Deed Book A, 12–16, St. Johns County Courthouse, St. Augustine, Florida; entry 35, Colored Marriages, 1784–1882, and entry 161, Colored Deaths, both in Records of the Cathedral Parish, SAHL; Joseph Sanchez Will, St. Johns County Court, Papers, box 158, file 51, SAHL; Susannah Sanchez, Patriot War Claims, SAHL.

4. Herbert S. Klein, *Slavery in the Americas: A Comparative Study of Virginia and Cuba* (Chicago: University of Chicago Press, 1966), 196–199.

5. Landers, *Black Society*, 88, 147, 151, 164; Landers, "Black Society in Spanish St. Augustine, 1784–1821" (PhD diss., University of Florida, 1988), 149–158.

6. Landers, *Black Society*, 121–122, 264–265, [268].

7. Ibid., 196–197.

8. Ibid., 23–39.

9. Ibid., 37–45, 76–77, 81, 101, 119, 122, 127–128, 209–217.

10. Ibid., 88, 94, 97, 145–146; Account No. 98273, Prince Whilton, Settled Miscellaneous Treasury Accounts, September 6, 1790–September 29, 1894, Office of the First Auditor, Records of the Accounting Officers of the Department of the Treasury, Record Group 217, National Archives, College Park, Maryland (hereafter cited as RG 217).

11. J. H. Alexander, "The Ambush of Captain John Williams, U.S.M.C.: Failure of the East Florida Invasion 1812–1813," *Florida Historical Quarterly* 56 (January 1978): 280, 293–295; Alexander, "Swamp Ambush in Florida," *Military History* 14 (March 1998): 40, 44; Captain John Williams to Lieutenant Colonel Franklin Wharton, 15 September 1812, vol. 16, Letters Received, 1798–1817, Office of the Commandant, Headquarters, US Marine Corps, Record Group 127, National Archives, Washington, DC; Account Nos.: 73350, Francisco D. and Peter Pons; 81963, John Ponce; 86844, Philip Edinborough, RG 217.

12. James G. Cusick, *The Other War of 1812: The Patriot War and the American Invasion of Spanish East Florida* (Gainesville: University Press of Florida, 2003), 4, 8; Robert Raymond Reid to the Secretary of the Treasury, 31 August 1836, Records of Letters Sent, Florida Claims 1834–1842, Correspondence, General Records of the Department of the Treasury, Record Group 56, National Archives, College Park, Maryland.

13. Account No. 99008, Scipio Fleming, RG 217.

14. Account Nos.: 98273, Prince Whilton; 73347, Francisco D. and Peter Pons; 86225, Henry Yonge, RG 217.

15. Account Nos.: 97990, Charles Hill; 98272, Sancho Davis; 98271, Domingo Davis; 89445, John Howley; 99162, Abraham Rocho; 85048, Abraham McQueen, RG 217.

16. Account Nos.: 94419, Isaac Bacchus; 94421, John Morrell; 98270, George Clarke; 74759, Toby Herreira; 83177, George J. F. Clarke; 94415, Charles Witter Clarke, RG 217.

17. Landers, *Black Society*, 104; Account No. 86844, Philip Edinborough, RG 217; Benjamin Wiggins, Patriot War Claims, SAHL.

18. Depositions of Dr. P. B. Mauran, Dr. John Peck, W. D. Mosley, Mary A. Streschka, and Dr. Francis Weems, "Contested Will," 4 June 1856; George R. Fairbanks[?] to David L. Yulee[?], 18 June 1856; all in "In Case of the Estate of Susan Murphy," Treaty of 1819 (Florida Claims), Spain, International Claims, Records of Boundary and Claims Commissions and Arbitrations, Record Group 76, National Archives, College Park, Maryland (hereafter cited as RG 76); "The Susan Murphy Will Case, Testimony at Trial," Eastern Circuit of Florida in the Circuit for St. Johns County, Spring Term, 1858, *In the matter of the Contested Will of Susan Murphy decd. Francis Bridier Exct. Propounder ats David L. Yulee Caveator*, and, In Supreme Court, Florida, February Term, 1860, *D. L. Yulee Appellee, caveator. Ads. Francis Bridier, Executor, Brief of G. R. Fairbanks, Counsel of Appellee* (Jacksonville, FL: Columbus Drew, 1860), RG 76; John Mills, Soldier's Certificate No. 490204, Civil War and Later Pension Files, Records of the Veteran's Administration, Record Group 15, National Archives, Washington, DC (hereafter cited as RG 15).

19. Landers, *Black Society*, 192, 349; Mark M. Smith, *Debating Slavery: Economy and Society in the Antebellum American South* (Cambridge: Cambridge University Press, 1998), 18, 91; Account Nos.: 89536, James Cashen; 82290, James Cashen; 89535, James Cashen, RG 217.

20. Landers, *Black Society*, 176; Account Nos.: 98273, Prince Whilton; 73347, Francisco D. and Peter Pons; 86225, Henry Yonge, RG 217.

21. For more detail on the background to the Patriot War, see: Cusick, *The Other War of 1812;* J. C. A. Stagg, "George Mathews and John McKee: Revolutionizing East Florida, Mobile, and Pensacola in 1812," *Florida Historical Quarterly* 85 (Winter 2007): 269–296; Pablo Tornero Tinajero, *Relaciones de Dependencia Entre Florida Y Estados Unidos (1783–1820)* (Madrid: Ministerio de Asuntos Exteriores, 1979); "Reminiscences of S. Murphy," RG 76.

22. Cusick, *The Other War of 1812,* 103–125; Rembert W. Patrick, *Florida Fi-*

asco: Rampant Rebels on the Georgia-Florida Border, 1784–1790 (Athens: University of Georgia Press, 1954), 68–69, 75, 83–100; Account Nos.: 82290, James Cashen; 89535, James Cashen, RG 217; "Reminiscences of S. Murphy," RG 76.

23. "Reminiscences of S. Murphy," RG 76.

24. Ibid.

25. Ibid; Testimonies of Dr. Joseph Gantt, Jane Gantt, Francis P. Fatio, George Atkinson, RG 76.

26. Account No. 89535, James Cashen, RG 217; "Spanish Treaty Claims (Cashen) Information relating thereto," RG 76; Testimonies of John Percival, "Negro man Kent," Jim Edinboro, Richard Leake, Salley Wallen, "Letters Received from Owners of Slaves," General Jesup, Generals Papers & Books, Office of the Adjutant General, Record Group 94, National Archives, Washington, DC.

27. Testimony of William A. Forward and Mary A. Streschka, RG 76.

28. "Spanish Treaty Claims (Cashen) Information Relating Thereto," *In Supreme Court, Florida, February Term, 1860, D. L. Yulee Appellee Caveator. Ads. Francis Bridier, Executor, Brief of G. R. Fairbanks, Counsel of Appellee*, Fairbanks[?] to Yulee[?], 18 June 1856, Susan Linde for Hire of Slave Ansell," Fairbanks to Yulee, 10 June 1856, Fairbanks to Yulee, 13 March 1858, RG 76.

29. "Will of March 14th, 1855," testimony of William A. Forward and Dr. Francis Weems, all in RG 76.

30. "Codicil of August 30th, 1855," RG 76.

31. Peck to Yulee, 28 June 1855, Fairbanks Brief, testimony of Peck, all in RG 76.

32. Testimony of Mauran, Fairbanks to Yulee, 15 June 1856, all in RG 76.

33. Fairbanks to Yulee, 8 August 1856, and Fairbanks Brief, both in RG 76; See: Ira Berlin, *Slaves without Masters: The Free Negro in the Antebellum South* (New York: Pantheon, 1975), 108–110; Landers, *Black Society,* 118–119; Colored Baptisms, vols. 1–3, Records of the Cathedral Parish, SAHL.

34. Fairbanks to Yulee, 15 June 1856, Yulee to Daniel Kerr, 23 January 1857, RG 76; Supreme Court of Florida, *Francis Bridier, Ex'r of Susan Murphy, Deceased, Appellant, v. David L. Yulee, Caveator, Appellee, 1861*, in John B. Galbraith, reporter, *Reports of Cases Argued and Adjudged in the Supreme Court of Florida, at Terms Held in 1860-'1*, vol. 9 (Tallahassee: Office of the Floridian and Journal, 1861), 481–488, http://books.google.com/books?id=DXYDAAAAQAAJ&dq=Florida+Supreme+Court+Cases+1861+Francis+Bridier&source=gbs_navlinks_s (accessed 17 June 2012); "Estate of Mrs. Susan Murphy or Linde to Dr. Jno. E. Peck," 25 July 1873, Fairbanks to Yulee, 6 August 1857, testimony of Venancio Sanchez, all in RG 76; Indictments of Andre Gué and companions, SEN 28A-E3, Records of the US Senate, Record Group 46, National Archives, Washington, DC; John Mills, Soldier's Certificate No. 490204, RG 15.

35. Landers, *Black Society*, 125–127.

36. Ibid., 248, 252.

37. T. H. Breen and Stephen Innes, *"Myne Owne Ground": Race & Freedom on Virginia's Eastern Shore, 1640–1676* (New York: Oxford University Press, 1980), 6, 112–113.

Chapter 2

1. Jane Landers, *Black Society in Spanish Florida* (Urbana: University of Illinois Press, 1999), 247.

2. Deed Book H, 303 (hereafter cited, for example, as DB-H, 303) and DB-B&L, 3, St. Johns County Courthouse, St. Augustine, Florida (hereafter cited as CCH).

3. *St. Augustine East Florida Gazette*, 4 August 1821; *St. Augustine Florida Herald* (hereafter cited as FH), 1 March 1823; *St. Augustine East Florida Herald* (hereafter cited as EFH), 31 May 1825.

4. Patricia C. Griffin, "The Halifax-Mosquitoes Plantation Corridor: An Overview," *The Florida Anthropologist* 52 (March–June 1999): 15–16; DB-D, 5–6; St. Johns County Court, Records (hereafter cited as CCR), box 123, file 20 (hereafter cited, for example, CCR, 123-20), St. Augustine Historical Society Research Library, St. Augustine, Florida (hereafter cited as SAHL); Colored Baptisms (hereafter cited as CB), vol. 3, entry 572, SAHL; Fifth Census of the United States, 1830, Florida Territory, St. Johns County.

5. Landers, *Black Society*, 167–169, 170n37.

6. Account numbers: 83177, George J. F. Clarke; 94415, Charles Witter Clarke; 84941, Tony Primus, Settled Miscellaneous Treasury Accounts, September 6, 1790–September 29, 1894, Office of the First Auditor, Records of the Accounting Officers of the Department of the Treasury, Record Group 217, National Archives, College Park, Maryland (hereafter cited as RG 217); DB-E, 372–373; CCR, 157-48.

7. CCR, 147-37.

8. Ibid.; Return Book, 1835, Tax Rolls, St. Johns County, 1829–1835, Florida State Archives, Tallahassee, Florida (hereafter cited as FSA).

9. Frederick P. Bowser, "Colonial Spanish America," in *Neither Slave Nor Free: The Freedman of African Descent in the Slave Societies of the New World*, ed. David W. Cohen and Jack P. Greene (Baltimore, MD: Johns Hopkins University Press, 1972), 22–31.

10. *Escrituras* (Notarized Instruments), 1784–1821, East Florida Papers, bundle 365, *Quadernos* 6, 7, 8, microfilm reel 55-A, pp. 258–260, 339–342, 348-351, SAHL; DB-D, 11–14; DB-F, 234–235; DB-H, 152, 288, 293.

11. Frank Tannenbaum, *Slave and Citizen* (Boston: Beacon Press, 1992), 57, 63; Landers, *Black Society*, 121; CB, vol. 3, entry 468; DB-AA, 97–98.

12. DB-H, 318–319.

13. DB-D, 37–40; DB-M, 193; DB-E, 105, 422; Landers, *Black Society,* 241.

14. DB-D, 3–5; DB-E, 338–339; DB-F, 122–123; DB-N, 53.

15. Entry for 15 May 1835, Receipts: 1832–1837, City of St. Augustine, Papers (hereafter cited as City Papers), SAHL; Entries for 30 March 1826 and 2 October 1826, Receipts: 1823–1829, City Papers; *Escrituras,* 1784–1821, East Florida Papers, bundle 365, *Quadernos* 2, 9, microfilm reel 55-A, pp. 50–53, 408–410, SAHL; DB-I&J, 311–313; DB-G, 191; CB, vol. 2, entry 786; DB-E, 105.

16. DB-D, 10–11; DB-E, 149, 401–402, 451; DB-B&L(front), 161.

17. George J. F. Clarke v. Waters Smith, 12 January 1831, Territorial Court of Appeals, Case Files, 1825–1846, Series 73, Record Group 1110, FSA.

18. Ibid.; DB-F, 108–109; CCR, 164-48.

19. Clarke v. Smith; CCR, 164-48; Order Book A, 5, CCH; Eighth Census of the United States, 1850, State of Florida, Clay County.

20. DB-E, 343–344; DB-F, 108–109; Account No. 83177, George J. F. Clarke, RG 217; Book No. 2, Box No. 6, Index Claims Florida War, "List of Claims Growing Out of the Florida War and Paid by Disbursing Officers," in State Claims Relating to the Florida Indian Wars, November 1836 to August 1856, Land, Files, and Miscellaneous Division, State Claims, Records of the Accounting Officers of the Department of the Treasury, Record Group 217, National Archives, College Park, MD.

21. EFH, 31 January 1826; DB-G, 221; DB-B&L, 63; DB-M, 136–137, 176–177, 314–317; Return of Persons Defaulted in Payment of City Taxes, for 1833, 1834, and 1835, and Who Have Paid Me Their Arrears, 19 July 1837, Taxes: 1821–1837, City Papers; Return Book, 1835, Tax Rolls, St. Johns County, 1829–1835, FSA; Account Book, Ledger C [Dr. Seth Peck], 62, Peck Papers, SAHL; Petition of Jack Forrester, 24 December 1830, Liquor: 1825–1836, City Papers; Fanny Forrester, Charlotte S., 13 March 1838, Licenses: Liquor 1831–1839, City Papers; No. 5 Jack Forrester $22, Receipts: 1838–1839, City Papers; CCR, 352-58; DB-H, 314; DB-I&J, 14; DB-N, 386–387; Judgment Record A, 7-8, CCH; DB-G, 220–221; DB-M, 176–177.

22. Landers, *Black Society,* 259–260; Spanish Land Grants (hereafter cited as SLG), Confirmed, microfilm reels 50-I, entry G-4, 51-B, entry L-10, 51-G, entry W-24, P. K. Yonge Library of Florida History, University of Florida, Gainesville, Florida (hereafter cited as PKY).

23. Landers, *Black Society,* 237–242, 244–246; US Congress, *American State Papers: Documents of the Congress of the United States in Relation to Public Lands,*

from the First Session of the Twenty-First to the First Session of the Twenty-Third Congress, Commencing December 1, 1828, and Ending April 11, 1834, ed. Asbury Dickins and John W. Forney (Washington, DC: Gales & Seaton, 1860), 78, 113 (hereafter cited as ASP-PL); Joe Knetsch, "The Development of Amelia Island in the Second Spanish Period: The Impact of George J. F. Clarke" (lecture presented to the Amelia Island Museum of History, Fernandina Beach, FL, 26 March 1999).

24. ASP-PL, vol. 4, 596–597; SLG, Confirmed, microfilm reel 50-G, entry E-4, and SLG, Unconfirmed, microfilm reel 51-J, entry C-11, PKY; Charlton W. Tebeau, *A History of Florida* (Coral Gables, FL: University of Miami Press, 1971), 122–123.

25. DB-A, 12–16, 68, 77–81; DB-AA, 118–120; DB-H, 33; DB-Q, 214–216; Order Book A, 85–89, CCH; Landers, *Black Society,* 151–152; Account no. 74969, Francis X. Sanchez, RG 217; Book or Register of City Lots, SAHL; CCR, 158-51, 166-28.

26. Clara Talley Kingston, "Sarah Warner Fish," *El Escribano: The St. Augustine Journal of History* 24 (1987): 74–82.

27. DB-F, 160–163; DB-H, 80–81, 201–202.

28. CCR, 174-54.

29. DB-E, 372–373; DB-E, 132–133; See Frank Marotti Jr., "Edward M. Wanton and the Settling of Micanopy," *Florida Historical Quarterly* 73 (April 1995): 456–477; DB-H, 146; Tom W. Shick, *Emigrants to Liberia, 1820 to 1843: An Alphabetical Listing* (Newark: University of Delaware Press, 1971), 89–91; Shearjashub B. Townsend to R. R. Gurley, 25 January 1832, American Colonization Society Records, series 1, vol. 37, reel 13, Library of Congress, Washington, DC.

30. CCR, 117-14; Seventh and Eighth Censuses of the United States, 1840, 1850, Florida, St. Johns County; CB, vol. 3, entries 540–542, vol. 2, pp. 68–69, 198; DB-F, 160–162; DB-P, 317–318; Judgment Record A, 20, CCH; DB-E, 202–203; DB-G, 31–36; CCR, 116-19; EFH, 8 August 1826; "Union Army Census of Northeast Florida, 1864 and 1865," Department of the South, Census of the District of Florida, Charles E. Coolidge, Seventh US Infantry, Provost Marshal, SAHL; "Taxes: 1821–1837," City Papers; Tebeau, *A History of Florida*, 135–136; Lee H. Warner, *Free Men of Color in an Age of Servitude: Three Generations of a Black Family* (Lexington: University Press of Kentucky, 1992), 27.

31. DB-E, 202–203; DB-F, 160–161; DB-G, 31–36, 74; CCR, 116-19; "Taxes: 1821–1837," City Papers.

32. Return Books, 1829–1835, 1845–1846, 1848–1850, 1852–1856, 1859–1861, Tax Rolls, St. Johns County, FSA; "Receipts: 1830–1831," and "Blacks: 1824–

1855," City Papers; "Printed Matter, Newspaper Clippings," Joseph Simeon Sanchez Papers, SAHL; EFH, 27 December 1832; CCR, 98-45; Minute Book B, 16, 20, 27, 195, 205–206, City Papers.

33. FH, 2 December 1829.

34. Daniel L. Schafer, "'A Class of People Neither Freemen nor Slaves': From Spanish to American Race Relations in Florida, 1821–1861," *Journal of Social History* 26 (Spring 1993): 591.

35. EFH, 23 October 1824; *Escrituras*, 1784–1821, East Florida Papers, bundle 365, *Quaderno* 9, Library of Congress microfilm reel 168, pp. 2857–2859, *Quaderno* 10 ("Isaac Wickes grants liberty to the mulatta Rosa") and ("Antonio Rivas to Isaac Wickes"), SAHL; George Vanness Jr., Soldier's Certificate no. 258248, Civil War and Later Pension Files, Records of the Veteran's Administration, Record Group 15, National Archives, Washington, DC (hereafter cited as RG 15); *Escrituras* (Notarized Instruments), 1784–1821, East Florida Papers, bundle 365, *Quaderno* 10, microfilm reel 55-A, pp. 445–450, SAHL; DB-E, 338–339, 422; Deed Book A, 75, Putnam County Clerk of the Court, Palatka, Florida; CCR, 215-91.

36. EFH, 23 October 1824; See "An Ordinance Relating to Free Persons of Colour," Ordinance no. 29, 19 July 1824, Florida Historical Records Survey, *Ordinances of the City of St. Augustine*, vol. 1, 1821–1827 (Jacksonville: Florida Historical Records Survey, 1941), 53–54.

37. EFH, 23 October 1824.

38. EFH, 6 November, 29 November, 1824, 10 January 1826; Louise Biles Hill, "George J. F. Clarke, 1774–1836," *Florida Historical Quarterly* 21 (January 1943): 198, 209–212; CCR, 150-11.

39. EFH, 26 July 1825. Unfortunately, the *Herald*'s next issue is not extant.

40. Michael Gannon, *The Cross in the Sand: The Catholic Church in Florida, 1513–1870* (Gainesville: University of Florida Press, 1965), 119, 121, 128; CB, vol. 3, entry 515.

41. CB, vol. 3, entries 540–542, 578; "Clarke, George F. Last Will and Testament," Clarke Papers, SAHL; DB-E, 202–203; DB-F, 162. James Clarke's uncle, Charles W. Clarke, had a biracial son, Thomas Clarke, who, along with another son, Jorge Juan Clarke, Jane Landers did not note in her list of Charles W. Clarke's children. This Thomas Clarke probably would have been too young to have served as Susana Clarke's godfather. See Landers, *Black Society,* 366n43; DB-M, 305, 307–309; DB-O, 262–263, 307–309, 490–491, 502–503, and CB, vol. 3, entry 536.

42. "Sitiki, 'The Story of Uncle Jack' Draft 2," Buckingham Smith Papers, Manuscript Division, New York Historical Society, New York, New York; Janet Duitsman Cornelius, *Slave Missions and the Black Church in the Antebellum South*

(Columbia: University of South Carolina Press, 1999), 128; Cooper C. Kirk, "A History of the Southern Presbyterian Church in Florida, 1821–1891" (PhD diss., Florida State University, 1966), 52–53.

43. Sixth Census of the United States, 1830, Territory of Florida, St. Johns County; Shick, 89–91; Shearjashub B. Townsend to R. R. Gurley, 25 January 1832, American Colonization Society Records, series 1, vol. 37, reel 13, Library of Congress; H. S. Pratt to E. B. Gould, 1 January 1828, Records of the Presbyterian Church, SAHL; E.[?] Hazard Snowden to Benjamin Brand, 17 December 1831, American Colonization Society Records, series 1, vol. 36, reel 13, Library of Congress; FH, 25 October 1832; DB-E, 91, 202–203; DB-G, 31–36; DB-H, 146, 402–403; DB-M, 327–328; DB- I&J, 128–131, 139–141, 397–398; DB-K, 31–33.

44. Council Meetings, 27 August 1821–29 December 1828, 237–238, 248, 251, 255, 258, City Papers; Tabb Smith to Mayor and Aldermen, St. Augustine, 27 December 1827, "Leases: 1823–1869," City Papers; "Finances: 1814, 1821–1829," "Receipts: 1832–1837," Licenses: Billiard tables and others, 1825–1881," City Papers; Return Books, 1829–1831, 1833, Tax Rolls, St. Johns County, FSA; "Taxes: 1821–1837," "Taxes, Collectors Report: 1827–1830," City Papers; W. Smith Rect $42.62, "Financial Reports: 1830–1839," Joseph Simeon Sanchez Papers, SAHL; *Ordinances of the City of St. Augustine*, vol. 1, 97–98; CCR, 169-68.

45. CCR, 169-68; Julie Ann Lisenby, "The Free Negro in Antebellum Florida, 1821–1861" (master's thesis, Florida State University, 1967), 17–18; Russell Garvin, "The Free Negro in Florida Before the Civil War," *Florida Historical Quarterly* 46 (July 1967): 16.

46. For an excellent general discussion of this issue, see Melvin Patrick Ely, *Israel on the Appomattox: A Southern Experiment in Black Freedom from the 1790s through the Civil War* (New York: Alfred A. Knopf, 2004), 455–468; for Florida, see Canter Brown Jr., "Race Relations in Territorial Florida, 1821–1845," *Florida Historical Quarterly* 73 (January 1995): 287–307; James M. Denham, *"A Rogue's Paradise": Crime and Punishment in Antebellum Florida, 1821–1861* (Tuscaloosa: The University of Alabama Press, 1997), 130–131; Daniel W. Stowell, ed. and annot., *Balancing Evils Judiciously: The Proslavery Writings of Zephaniah Kingsley* (Gainesville: University Press of Florida, 2000), 5, 7.

47. Stowell, *Balancing Evils*, 6–10.

48. "Letter to the Editor of the *East Florida Herald* (1826)," and "Address to the Legislative Council of Florida on the Subject of Its Colored population by Z. Kingsley, a Planter of That Territory," in Stowell, *Balancing Evils*, 26–38; Ibid., 3–5, 36n1.

49. Zephaniah Kingsley, "A Treatise on the Patriarchal, or Co-operative System of Society," in Stowell, *Balancing Evils,* 40–63, 69.

50. CCR, 215-91; Kingsley, "Treatise," in Stowell, *Balancing Evils,* 66–67, 73.

51. FH, 2 September 1829.

52. Daniel L. Schafer, *Anna Madgigine Jai Kingsley: African Princess, Florida Slave, Plantation Slaveowner* (Gainesville: University Press of Florida, 2003), 37–38.

53. Ibid., 38.

Chapter 3

1. Thomas Graham, *The Awakening of St. Augustine: The Anderson Family and the Oldest City, 1821–1924* (St. Augustine: St. Augustine Historical Society, 1978), 8, 10, 33, 37–51; David Nolan, *Fifty Feet in Paradise* (New York: Harcourt Brace Jovanovich, 1984), 21–26, 31, 34, 44–52; Whittington B. Johnson, *Race Relations in the Bahamas, 1784–1834: The Nonviolent Transformation from a Slave to a Free Society* (Fayetteville: University of Arkansas Press, 2000), 158, 161–164.

2. See Daniel L. Schafer, "'A Class of People Neither Freemen nor Slaves': From Spanish to American Race Relations in Florida, 1821–1861," *Journal of Social History* 26 (Spring 1993): 587–610; St. Johns County Deed Books, Order Book A, Wills and Letters of Administration I, all in the St. Johns County Courthouse, St. Augustine, Florida (hereafter cited as CCH).

3. Louise Biles Hill, "George J. F. Clarke, 1774–1836," *Florida Historical Quarterly* 21 (January 1943), 200, 207–208; Deed Book I&J, 25–26 (hereafter cited, for example, as DB-I&J, 25–26); DB-M, 472, CCH; Seventh Census of the United States, 1850, Florida, Monroe County; St. Mary's Star of the Sea, Catholic Church, Baptisms, vol. 1, 7–32, Monroe County Public Library, Key West, Florida; DB-N, 421.

4. DB-H, 327–329, DB-M, 86.

5. St. Johns County Court, Records (hereafter cited as CCR), box 91, file 2 (hereafter cited, for example, as CCR, 91-2), St. Augustine Historical Society Research Library, St. Augustine, Florida (hereafter cited as SAHL); DB-N, 386; Jane Landers, *Black Society in Spanish Florida* (Urbana: University of Illinois Press, 1999), 149–157, 171 (n15).

6. Order Book A, 4, CCH; DB-M, 300–301; CCR, 102-56; *St. Augustine Florida Herald* (hereafter cited as FH), 26 May 1837.

7. Colored Baptisms (hereafter cited as CB), vol. 3, entry 554, Records of the Cathedral Parish, SAHL; Account no. 85048, Abraham McQueen, Settled Miscellaneous Treasury Accounts, September 6, 1790–September 29, 1894, Office of the First Auditor, Records of the Accounting Officers of the Department of the Treasury, Record Group 217, National Archives, College Park, Maryland (hereafter cited as RG 217); Fifth United States Census, 1830, Florida, St. Johns

County; "Southern Life Insurance: 1836–1838," Joseph Simeon Sanchez Papers, SAHL; Inventories, "Old" Book 3: 1840–1861, pp. 154–155, St. Johns County, County Judge, Probate Records, 1784–1933, Florida State Archives, Tallahassee (hereafter cited as FSA); Account Book, Ledger B, Dr. Seth S. Peck, 10 May 1837–15 May 1841, p. 138, Peck Papers, SAHL; Copy of the Proceedings versus Stepney Bulow Caesar for a breach of the City Ordinance passed 13 March 1838, "Carriages: 1838–1887," City of St. Augustine, Papers (hereafter cited as City Papers), SAHL; *St. Augustine News* (hereafter cited as SAN), 22 December 1838.

8. Passes 1838, "Blacks: 1824–1855," City Papers; Tax Rolls, St. Johns County, 1829–1835, FSA; Sixth Census of the United States, 1840, Florida, St. Johns County; CB, vol. 3, entry for 7 November 1842; Inventories, "Old" Book 3: 1840–1861, pp. 65–66, St. Johns County, County Judge, Probate Records, 1784–1933, FSA; Deed Book D, 13, Monroe County Courthouse, Key West, Florida; Monroe County Tax Rolls, 1847, FSA.

9. *St. Augustine Florida Herald & Southern Democrat* (hereafter cited as FHSD), 5 July 1839.

10. Patrol Report, 16 May 1837, Patrols—1836–1837, City Papers.

11. *St. Augustine East Florida Herald* (hereafter cited as EFH), 29 November 1824, 25 July 1825; CCR, 150-11, and 98-25.

12. Return Books, 1829–1832, Tax Rolls, St. Johns County, FSA; CCR, 98-25 and 100-33; FH, 14 June 1832, 27 November 1833.

13. CCR, 100-33; FH, 14 June 1832, 27 November 1833; DB-O, 153–156, 162, 184.

14. Spanish Land Grants (hereafter cited as SLG), Confirmed, microfilm reel 50-E, entry C-52, microfilm reel 50-F, entries C-63, C-68, microfilm reel 50-I entry G-4, P. K. Yonge Library of Florida History, University of Florida, Gainesville, Florida (hereafter cited as PKY); CCR, 117-14; DB-F, 242–247; DB-G, 87–93; DB-H, 306–307, 495–497; DB-I&J, 26–28, 30–31, 33–34, 39–43, 120–121, 250–251, 459–461; "Clarke, George F. Last Will and Testament," 28 August 1834, Clarke Papers, SAHL.

15. Introduction to "Venancio Sanchez Letterbook," Venancio Sanchez Papers, SAHL; Marjorie G. Meyer, "Venancio Sanchez: Nineteenth Century St. Augustine Citizen" (master's thesis, Arkansas State Teacher's College, 1959), 1, 3–4; Last Will and Testament of Christina Hill Sanchez, CCR, 164-20; "Information from Mrs. E. Brewer 1988, Genealogy of Sanchez Family in Alachua County," Joseph Simeon Sanchez Papers, SAHL; Jane L. Landers, "Black Society in Spanish St. Augustine, 1784–1821" (PhD diss., University of Florida, 1988), 126; Kim Hazouri, "From Jose Mariano Hernandez to Joseph Martin Hernandez: 1788–1856," 9–13, in Joseph Hernandez Biographical File, SAHL;

Samuel Williams Biographical File, SAHL; Ianthe Bond Hebel, "The Samuel Williams Family: Early Residents On the Halifax," *Journal of the Halifax Historical Society* 2 (no. 1) [n.d.], 25–28; Claim of Abner Williams, Patriot War Papers, SAHL; Account no. 84638, John Bunch; Account no. 89050, Robert McHardy; Account no. 108178, James and Emanuel Ormond, all in RG 217; Will of Don Guillermo Williams, 21 November 1807, Testamentary Proceedings, 1784–1821, East Florida Papers, microfilm reel 140, Library of Congress, Washington, DC; Site 8SJ577, Historical Structures Form, Master Site File, SAHL; Clara Talley Kingston, "Sarah Warner Fish," *El Escribano: The St. Augustine Journal of History* 24 (1987): 64, 75, 79; DB-F, 162; DB-M, 80–82.

16. Fifth Census of the United States, Florida, 1830, St. Johns County, Mosquito County; CCR, 169-60; CB, vol. 3, entries 575–578, and pp. 313–314, 317; Kingston, "Sarah Warner Fish," 64, 74–78; DB-F, 160–163; DB-H, 80–81, 201–202, 288; DB-M, 270–272, 444–446; DB-B&L, 117–118; CCR, 174-54, and 105-11; St. Johns County Marriage Licenses, 1830–1840, 26 September 1827, 11 February 1840, SAHL; Petition of Dolores English, Patriot War Papers, SAHL.

17. DB-B&L, 117–118; DB-M, 71–72, 80–82, 270–272; DB-O, 118–120; DB-P, 253, 317–318.

18. DB-H, 33, 146; DB-E, 202–203; DB-F, 160–161; DB-I&J, 42–43, 120–121, 128–131, 139–141, 250–251, 456–457, 459–461; DB-K, 104–106; DB-B&L, 63, 117–118; DB-M, 270–272, 417–418, 444–446; DB-O, 108, 117, 187, 569–570; Aggregate statistics are derived from the deed books at the CCH.

19. "Treaty of Amity, Settlement and Limits between Spain and the United States, Signed at Washington, 22 February 1821," in *The Consolidated Treaty Series*, vol. 70, ed. Clive Parry (Dobbs Ferry, NY: Oceana, 1969), 11; "An Act to Carry into Effect the Ninth Article of the Treaty Concluded between the United States and Spain, the Twenty-Second Day of February, One Thousand Eight Hundred and Nineteen," *Statutes at Large* 3, sec. 1–2, 768 (1825); "An Act for the Relief of Certain Inhabitants of East Florida," *Statutes at Large* 6, sec. 1–2, 569 (1834); Rembert W. Patrick, *Florida Fiasco: Rampant Rebels on the Georgia–Florida Border, 1784–1790* (Athens: University of Georgia Press, 1954), 302; Account no. 50118, George J. F. Clarke and George J. F. Clarke Surviving Partner of Clarke & Garvin; Account no. 83177, George J. F. Clarke; Account no. 83763, George J. F. Clarke surviving partner of Clarke & Garvin, all in RG 217. The summary figures were derived from the Patriot War claims in RG 217. For the formula for monetary values, see Daniel L. Schafer, "'A Swamp of an Investment'?: Richard Oswald's British East Florida Plantation Experiment," in *Colonial Plantations and Economy in Florida*, ed. Jane G. Landers (Gainesville: University Press of Florida, 2000), 33n18.

20. "Petition of S. Williams & Clark relative to a summons," [c.1835–1836], and "Petition of Sampson Williams," 5 December 1835, and Certificate of Sampson Williams's Moral Character, 2 November[?] 1836, Licenses: Liquor—1825–1836 and "Tax Collectors Return 1837," Taxes, 1836–1845 and Shop License, William Clarke, 18 March 1830, Taxes, Collectors Report—1827–1830, all in City Papers; CCR, 170-6; Return Books, 1830, 1835, Tax Rolls, St. Johns County, FSA; Mrs. Sanchez to Louisa Clarke, 5 May 1836, "Report of Committee of Management to Court Ball, 1834," Financial Reports and Statements 1830–1839, Joseph Simeon Sanchez Papers, SAHL; SAN, 10 April 1840; Graham, *The Awakening of St. Augustine*, 57–63.

21. CCR, 117-14; Estate of James Erwin, Patriot War Claims, SAHL; DB-D, 11–14; Sixth and Seventh Censuses of the United States, Florida, 1840, 1850, St. Johns County; CB, vol. 4, entry 3; H. S. Pratt to E. B. Gould, 1 January 1828, Records of the Presbyterian Church, SAHL; Shearjashub B. Townsend to R. R. Gurley, 25 January 1832, American Colonization Society Records (hereafter cited as ACS), series 1, vol. 37, microfilm reel 13, Library of Congress; E.[?] Hazard Snowden to Benjamin Brand, 17 December 1831, ACS, series 1, vol. 36, microfilm reel 13, Library of Congress; FH, 25 October 1832; FHSD, 17 July 1840; CCR, 117-14; David Y. Thomas, "The Free Negro in Florida before 1865," *South Atlantic Quarterly* 10 (October 1911): 344; CB, vol. 3, entry 540.

22. "Receipts: 1840–1889," City Papers; FHSD, 21 February 1839; SAN, 2 August 1845; *Jacksonville News*, 19 December 1845.

23. Melvin Patrick Ely, *Israel on the Appomattox: A Southern Experiment in Black Freedom from the 1790s through the Civil War* (New York: Alfred A. Knopf, 2004), 87–89, 351–354.

24. "Tax Collectors Report: 1827–1830," City Papers; "Patrols: 1836–1837," City Papers; Tax Rolls, St. Johns County, FSA; "Blacks: 1824–1855," City Papers; Sixth Census of the United States, Florida, 1840, St. Johns County; FHSD, 14 November 1839; CCR, 131-7; CCR, 140-28; CCR, 141-44; CCR, 103-18.

25. CCR, 117-14; David J. Weber, *The Spanish Frontier in North America* (New Haven, CT: Yale University Press, 1992), 276, 328.

26. DB-C, 83–84; "Liquor: 1825–1836," City Papers; Estimate of Taxes on Stores & Billiard Tables for 1827, Clerks Report of Debts Due the Corporation March 31st 1827, "Finance: 1814, 1821–1829," City Papers; St. Johns County Tax Rolls, 1830, 1839, 1845, FSA; FH, 9 January 1834; Petitions of: Sampson Williams, 5 December 1835, Jack Forrester, 24 December 1830, "Licenses: Liquor, 1825–1836," City Papers; Petition of William Clarke, 23 December 1836, Petition of Wm Clark for retail license, 23 September 1837, "Licenses: Liquor, 1831–1839," City Papers; FH, 5 April 1837.

27. CCR, 170-6.

28. Return Book, 1835, Tax Rolls, St. Johns County, FSA; "Petition of Sampson Williams," 5 December 1835, Licenses: Liquor—1825–1826, City Papers; "Clarke, George F. Last Will and Testament," Clarke Papers, SAHL

29. Petition of S. Williams & Clarke relative to a Summons," n.d., Licenses: Liquor—1825–1836, City Papers.

30. Petition of Sampson Williams, 5 December 1835, Licenses: Liquor—1825–1836, City Papers; "Petition of William Clarke," 23 December 1836, "Petition of Wm Clark for Retail License," 23 September 1837, Licenses: Liquor—1831–1839, City Papers; FH, 5 April 1837; Nolan, 46, 50–51; Receipts—1840–1859, City Papers; Finances—1840–1889, City Papers.

31. Landers, *Black Society*, 118–119, 150.

32. CB, vols. 1–3.

33. FH, 15 March, 7 July, 1832; "Florida—Inhabitants of, Memorial to Congress Complaining of Certain Acts of the Legislative Councils—28 January 1833," Petitions, Various Subjects, Committee on Territories, HR 22AG23.1, Records of the US House of Representatives, Record Group 233, National Archives, Washington, DC.

34. "Florida—Inhabitants of, Memorial to Congress Complaining of Certain Acts of the Legislative Councils—28 January 1833."

35. Daniel L. Schafer, *Anna Madgigine Jai Kingsley: African Princess, Florida Slave, Plantation Slaveowner* (Gainesville: University Press of Florida, 2003), 81; Schafer, "U.S. Territory and State," in *The New History of Florida*, ed. Michael Gannon (Gainesville: University Press of Florida, 1996), 213–214; Michael Gannon, *The Cross in the Sand: The Catholic Church in Florida, 1513–1870* (Gainesville: University of Florida Press, 1965), 121, 152; CB, vols. 1–4.

36. CB, vols. 1–4.

37. Julie Ann Lisenby, "The Free Negro in Antebellum Florida, 1821–1861," (master's thesis, Florida State University, 1967), 11; Russell Garvin, "The Free Negro in Florida before the Civil War," *Florida Historical Quarterly* 46 (July 1967): 13; Snowden to Brand, 17 December 1831, ACS, series 1, vol. 36, reel 13, Library of Congress; Townsend to Gurley, 25 January 1832, ACS, series 1, vol. 37, reel 13; DB-I&J, 204; DB-K, 27–29, 31–33, 59–60, 68–72; Emigration Register—Ship *Hercules*, ACS, series 6, vol. 17, reel 314; Tom W. Shick, *Emigrants to Liberia, 1820 to 1843: An Alphabetical Listing* (Newark: University of Delaware Press, 1971), 88–91; "Printed Matter: Newspaper Clippings," Joseph Simeon Sanchez Papers, SAHL; FH, 27 December 1832; Hill, "George J. F. Clarke," 244–245. For Charles W. Clarke, see: DB-M, 307–309; DB-N, 422–423; DB-O, 120–121, 262–263.

38. Gannon, *The Cross in the Sand*, 132, 150–152, 157–158, 162.

Chapter 4

1. Compiled Service Records of Volunteer Soldiers Who Served in Organizations from the State of Florida during the Florida Indian Wars, 1835–1858 (hereafter cited as CSR), Microcopy 1086, microfilm rolls 10, 14, 25–26, 39–41, Record of the Adjutant General's Office, Record Group 94, National Archives, Washington, DC; Militia and Troop Lists (hereafter cited as MTL), and Index, Claims, Florida War, Both in State Claims Relating to the Florida Indian Wars, State Claims, Land Files, and Miscellaneous Division, Records of the Accounting Officers of the Department of the Treasury, Record Group 217, National Archives, College Park, Maryland.

2. Kenneth W. Porter, "Negro Guides and Interpreters in the Early Stages of the Seminole War, Dec. 28, 1835–March 6, 1837," *Journal of Negro History* 35 (April 1950): 179–180; Deposition of Benjamin Wiggins, 10 July 1836, in US Congress, House, Document 283, 27th Cong., 2nd sess., 1841–1842, p. 119; Guard Report, 12th Aug. 1837, "Patrols, 1836–1837," City of St. Augustine, Papers (hereafter cited as City Papers), St. Augustine Historical Society Research Library, St. Augustine, Florida (hereafter cited as SAHL); CSR, Microcopy 1086, microfilm rolls 26, 40–41.

3. Jane Landers, *Black Society in Spanish Florida*, (Urbana: University of Illinois Press, 1999), 91, 99, 104, 225; US Congress, House of Representatives, 27th Cong., 2nd sess., 1841–1842, H. Doc. 283, pp. 4, 33.

4. Porter, "Negro Guides," 179–180; Frederick P. Bowser, "Colonial Spanish America," in *Neither Slave nor Free: The Freedman of African Descent in the Slave Societies of the New World*, ed. David W. Cohen and Jack P. Greene (Baltimore, MD: Johns Hopkins University Press, 1972), 53–58; "Job Wiggins," St. Augustine, 26 January 1797, Testamentary Proceedings, 1784–1821, East Florida Papers, microfilm roll 137, P. K. Yonge Library of Florida History, University of Florida (hereafter cited as PKY).

5. CSR, microfilm rolls 10, 14, 25–26, 39–41, 48; MTL and Index; St. Johns County Marriage Licenses, 1830–1840, 26 September 1827, 11 February 1840, SAHL; Will of Don Guillermo Williams, 21 November 1807, Testamentary Proceedings, 1784–1821, East Florida Papers, microfilm reel 140, Library of Congress, Washington, DC; Colored Baptisms (hereafter cited as CB), vol. 3, pp. 313–314, Records of the Cathedral Parish, SAHL; Infant Deaths (white), 1784–1826, entry 27, Records of the Cathedral Parish, SAHL; Colored Marriages (hereafter cited as CM), entry 49, Records of the Cathedral Parish, SAHL; Deed Book D, 10–11 (hereafter cited, for example, as DB-D, 10–11), DB-G, 220, St. Johns County Courthouse, St. Augustine, Florida (hereafter cited as CCH); Jane L. Landers, "Black Society in Spanish St. Augustine, 1784–1821" (PhD diss., Uni-

versity of Florida, 1988), 134–135; Louise Biles Hill, "George J. F. Clarke, 1774–1836," *Florida Historical Quarterly* 21 (January 1943): 197, 205–208, 216–221, 225, 228–229, 234; "Clarke, George F. Last Will and Testament," Clarke Papers, SAHL.

6. Landers, "Black Society in Spanish St. Augustine," 30–31, 203; Gregg D. Kimball, "African, American, and Virginian: The Shaping of Black Memory in Antebellum Virginia, 1790-1860," in *Where These Memories Grow: History, Memory, and Southern Identity*, ed. W. Fitzhugh Brundage (Chapel Hill: University of North Carolina Press, 2000), 63; Russell Garvin, "The Free Negro in Florida before the Civil War," *Florida Historical Quarterly* 46 (July 1967): 13–14; Thelma Bates, "The Legal Status of the Negro in Florida," *Florida Historical Quarterly* 6 (January 1928): 163; *St. Augustine Florida Herald* (hereafter cited as FH), 31 August 1836; *St. Augustine News* (hereafter cited as SAN), 20 December 1839; Passes, "Blacks: 1824–1855," City Papers.

7. Frank Marotti Jr., "Edward M. Wanton and the Settling of Micanopy," *Florida Historical Quarterly* 73 (April 1995): 457–458; Account no. 80361, Edward M. Wanton, Settled Miscellaneous Treasury Accounts, September 6, 1790–September 29, 1894, Office of the First Auditor, Records of the Accounting Officers of the Department of the Treasury, Record Group 217, National Archives, College Park, Maryland (hereafter cited as RG 217); Robert Franklin Crider, "The Borderland Floridas, 1815–1821: Spanish Sovereignty under Siege" (PhD diss., Florida State University, 1979), 129; Kenneth W. Porter, *The Negro on the American Frontier* (New York: Arno Press, 1971), 267; Index to Compiled Service Records of Volunteers Who Served during the Indian Wars and Disturbances, 1815–1858, Microcopy 629, microfilm roll 39, Records of the Adjutant General's Office, Record Group 94, National Archives, Washington, DC; CSR, microfilm rolls 15, 18, 40, 47, 55–56; Index, Claims, Florida War, State Claims Relating to the Florida Indian Wars, November 1835–August 1856, State Claims, Land Files and Miscellaneous Division, Records of the Accounting Officers of the Department of the Treasury, Record Group 217, National Archives, College Park, Maryland.

8. CB, vol. 2, entry 573; Susan R. Parker, "Success through Diversification: Francis Philip Fatio's New Switzerland Plantation," in *Colonial Plantations and Economy in Florida*, ed. Jane G. Landers (Gainesville: University Press of Florida, 2000), 69; Account nos. 76455, Francis P. Fatio Sr. and 94405, Francis P. Fatio Jr., RG 217; Kenneth W. Porter, "The Early Life of Luis Pacheco *Ne* Fatio," *Negro History Bulletin* 7 (December 1943): 52; Porter, "Three Fighters for Freedom," *Journal of Negro History* (January 1943): 66.

9. Account no. 94405, Francis P. Fatio Jr.; Account no. 76455, Francis P. Fa-

tio Sr.; Account no. 89602, Francis P. Fatio Sr., all in RG 217; Porter, "Luis Pacheco," 52, 54; Canter Brown Jr., *Tampa before the Civil War* (Tampa: University of Tampa Press, 1999), 25.

10. Porter, "Luis Pacheco," 54; Brown, *Tampa*, 25, 50; Frank Laumer, *Massacre!* (Gainesville: University of Florida Press, 1968), 36–37, 39, 111; John K. Mahon, *History of the Second Seminole War* (Gainesville: University of Florida Press, 1967), 106; Porter, "Three Fighters for Freedom," 67–70; Porter, "Florida Slaves and Free Negroes in the Seminole War, 1835–1842," *Journal of Negro History* 28 (October 1943): 393.

11. Porter, "Three Fighters for Freedom," 66, 68; Mahon, *History of the Second Seminole War*, 106; Brown, *Tampa*, 25; Laumer, *Massacre!*, 170; Porter, "Luis Pacheco," 62, 64.

12. Porter, "Florida Slaves and Free Negroes," 393–395; Account no. 84638, John Bunch; Account no. 108178, James Ormond, RG 217; David Bushnell, "The Florida Republic: An Overview," and L. David Norris, "Failure Unfolds: The Loss of Amelia Island," in *La Republica de las Floridas: Texts and Documents*, comp. David Bushnell (Mexico City: Pan American Institute of Geography and History, 1986), 7–10, 24–25; "Petition to Congress by Inhabitants of St. Augustine," March 1836, in *The Territorial Papers of the United States*, vol. 25, ed. Clarence Edwin Carter (Washington, DC: National Archives, 1962), 265.

13. Porter, *The Negro on the American Frontier*, 266, 268–269, 341; George E. Buker, "The Americanization of St. Augustine," in *The Oldest City: St. Augustine Saga of Survival*, ed. Jean Parker Waterbury (St. Augustine: St. Augustine Historical Society, 1983), 164–165; Duncan L. Clinch to Brevet Brigadier General A. Jones, Adjutant, Fort King, Florida, 22 January 1835, and Clinch to Jones, St. Augustine, 9 October 1835, Duncan Clinch Letterbook, 1834–1836 and Slave List 1859, Camden County, Georgia, Records of the Ante-Bellum Southern Plantations from the Revolution through the Civil War, Series C, Selections from Holdings of the Library of Congress, Part 2, Alabama, Georgia, and South Carolina, microfilm reel 1, Library of Congress, Washington, DC; B. A. Putnam to R. K. Call, 26 July 1836, and Putnam to Lewis Cass, 31 July 1836, "Letterbook & Accounts for B. A. Putnam, 1836–1844," Calhoun Putnam Papers, SAHL.

14. FH, 17 August 1836, 22 September 1836, 24 November 1836, 26 January 1837; Porter, *The Negro on the American Frontier*, 266, 268–269.

15. FH, 17 August to 1 December, 1836; Porter, *The Negro on the American Frontier*, 269–271; Canter Brown Jr., "Race Relations in Territorial Florida," *Florida Historical Quarterly* 73 (January 1995): 304; Putnam to Cass, 31 July 1836, Calhoun Putnam Papers.

16. Porter, *The Negro on the American Frontier*, 34, 273–275, 400–401; State-

ment of Randall Irving and "Examination of Stephen Merritt. Alias Stephen Wright," St Augustine, 4 February 1837, The United States vs. Randall Irving & Stephen Merritt, Free Persons of Color, Letters Received Petitions from Citizens, General Jesup, Generals Papers and Books, Office of the Adjutant General, Record Group 94, National Archives, Washington, DC (hereafter cited as Jesup Papers).

17. Porter, *The Negro on the American Frontier*, 34, 273–275, 400–401; FH, 19 January 1837, 26 January 1837, 21 March 1837; *St. Augustine Florida Herald & Southern Democrat* (hereafter cited as FHSD), 7 August 1843; SAN, 16 March 1839, 23 March 1839, 30 March 1839; Petition of the inhabitants of the City of St. Augustine, 14 September 1838, "Blacks: 1824–1855," City Papers.

18. Porter, *The Negro on the American Frontier*, 265–266; DB-D, 11–14; Spanish Land Grants (hereafter cited as SLG), Confirmed, microfilm reel 50-G, entry E-10, PKY; Claim of James Erwin, Patriot War Papers, SAHL; St. Johns County Court, Records, box 117, file 14 (hereafter cited, for example, as CCR, 117-14), SAHL; SAN, 17 November 1838; FHSD, 11 July 1839; Seventh and Eighth Censuses of the United States, 1850 and 1860, Florida, St. Johns County; CB, vol. 3, entry for 1 February 1840, vol. 4, entry 3; Wills and Letters of Administration I, 422, 436-438, CCH; Guardian list for 1838, "Blacks: 1824–1855," and "Receipts: 1832–1837," City Papers; DB-M, 86.

19. FH, 19 January 1837, 29 March 1837; CB, vol. 1, entries 258, 259, vol. 2, entries 139, 496, 616, vol. 3, entries 298, 362, 421; Landers, *Black Society*, 220, 260; SLG, Confirmed, microfilm reel 50-C, entry B-58, and Unconfirmed, microfilm reel 52-C, entry W-28, PKY; US Congress, *American State Papers: Documents of the Congress of the United States in Relation to Public Lands, from the First Session of the Twenty-First to the First Session of the Twenty-Third Congress, Commencing December 1, 1828, and Ending April 11, 1834*, ed. Asbury Dickins and John W. Forney (Washington, DC: Gales & Seaton, 1860), 113.

20. See baptismal records: CB, vol. 1, entries 258, 259, vol. 2, entries 139, 496, 616, vol.3, entries 298, 362, 421; and CM, entries 17, 51; Account no. 74759, Toby Herreira, RG 217; SAN, 30 March 1839; "Examination of Stephen Merritt. Alias Stephen Wright," St Augustine, 4 February 1837, The United States vs. Randall Irving & Stephen Merritt, Free Persons of Color, Letters Received Petitions from Citizens, Jesup Papers.

21. John M. Fontane to Joseph Simeon Sanchez, 8 March 1839, in "Correspondence 1839-41, Letters from Fontane, J. M., Business, Politics, etc.," Jose Simeon Sanchez Papers, SAHL; James M. Denham, *"A Rogue's Paradise": Crime and Punishment in Antebellum Florida, 1821–1861* (Tuscaloosa: University of Alabama Press, 1997), 122, 130, 132.

22. Statements of Randall Irving and John Clarke, St. Augustine, 4 February

1837, The United States vs. Randall Irving & Stephen Merritt, Free Persons of Color, Letters Received Petitions from Citizens, Jesup Papers.

23. "Examination of Stephen Merritt. Alias Stephen Wright," Jesup Papers.

24. "Testimony of Jim Edinburg, a Free Colored Man," St. Augustine, 30 January 1837, and abstract of "Antonio Pellicer's Testimony," The United States vs. Randall Irving & Stephen Merritt, Free Persons of Color, Letters Received Petitions from Citizens, Jesup Papers.

25. Petition of the inhabitants of the City of St. Augustine, 14 September 1838, "Blacks: 1824–1855," City Papers; FH, 19 January, 26 January, 21 March, 1837; SAN, 16 March, 23 March, 30 March, 1839, 13 September 1839, 4 October 1845; FHSD, 7 August 1843; Jose Antonio Puig Ortiz, *Emigración de Libertos Norteamericanos A Puerto Plata En La Primera Mitad Del Siglo XIX: La Iglesia Metodista Wesleyana* (Santo Domingo: Editora "Alfa y Omega,"1978), 84, 99; Daniel L. Schafer, *Anna Madgigine Jai Kingsley: African Princess, Florida Slave, Plantation Slaveowner* (Gainesville: University Press of Florida, 2003), 2; DB-O, 578.

26. Benjamin A. Putnam to Richard K. Call, 26 July 1836, Letterbook and Accounts for B.A. Putnam, 1836–1844, Calhoun Putnam Papers; John K. Mahon and Brent R. Weisman, "Florida's Seminole and Miccosukee Peoples," in *The New History of Florida*, ed. Michael Gannon (Gainesville: University Press of Florida, 1996), 184; FH, 21 March 1837; *New-Hampshire Sentinel*, 6 April 1837; Gil Wilson, "An African American Fight for Freedom," *The Ancient City Genealogist* 3, no. 1 (1992): 16; Porter, *The Negro on the American Frontier*, 34, 265–266, 273–275, 347, 349, 400–401.

27. Denham, 130–131; Ordinance relating to Patrols, 1836, "Patrols, 1836–1837," City Papers; Morning Report of the Patrol for the City of St. Augustine, 15 May 1837, "Patrols, 1836–1837," City Papers.

28. Patrol Reports, 29 May; 11, 22, 24, 25 June; 29 July; 13 August 1837 and Ordinance relating to Patrols, 1836, in "Patrols, 1836–1837," City Papers; Patrol Report, 9 April 1840, "Patrols, 1838–1867," City Papers.

29. Patrol Report for 6th June 1837, Guard Report, 12th Aug. 1837, "Patrols, 1836–1837," City Papers.

30. Aguiar's Statement, Testimony of Francis Andreu, 2 May 1837, "Blacks: 1824–1855," City Papers.

31. Aguiar's Statement, Testimonies of Emanuel Garrido, Betsy, Jim, 2 May 1837, "Blacks: 1824–1855," City Papers.

32. Thomas Graham, *The Awakening of St. Augustine: The Anderson Family and the Oldest City, 1821–1924* (St. Augustine: St. Augustine Historical Society, 1978), 31, 63–64; SAN, 17 August 1839; Patricia C. Griffin, "The Spanish Return: The People-Mix Period 1784–1821," in *The Oldest City: St. Augustine Saga*

of Survival, ed. Jean Parker Waterbury (St. Augustine: St. Augustine Historical Society, 1983), 145; George E. Buker, "The Americanization of St. Augustine," in Waterbury, ed., *The Oldest City*, 152; Patricia C. Griffin and Diana Edwards, "Richard Aloysius Twine: Photographer of Lincolnville, 1922–1927" (unpublished manuscript, 1991), 46, SAHL; Fifth and Sixth Censuses of the United States, Florida, 1830, 1840, St. Johns County.

33. FHSD, 7 February, 17 August, 14 November, 15 December, 1839, 26 June 1840; SAN, 13 July, 20 July, 13 December, 20 December, 1839, 30 January, 28 February, 5 June, 31July, 1840; SAN, 20 December 1839.

34. Graham, *The Awakening of St. Augustine*, 49–51; John T. McLaughlin to the Secretary of the Navy, US schooner *Flirt*, Key Biscayne, 11 August 1840, and Governor Reid to the Secretary of War, 22 August 1840, and Secretary of War to George L. Phillips, 3 October 1840, and Memorial to Congress by Citizens of St. Johns County [referred 16 February 1841], all in *The Territorial Papers of the United States*, vol. 26, ed. Clarence Edwin Carter (Washington, DC: National Archives, 1962), 194, 202, 216–217, 266.

35. Porter, *The Negro on the American Frontier*, 34, 265–266, 273–275, 347, 349, 400–401; SAN, 30 October 1840, 6 November 1840, 27 November 1840; St. Johns County Court, Minute Book, 13 September 1827–12 July 1845, 133, SAHL.

36. Porter, *The Negro on the American Frontier*, 355–356; Porter, "Slaves and Free Negroes in the Seminole War," 417–419; Larry Eugene Rivers, *Slavery in Florida: Territorial Days to Emancipation* (Gainesville: University Press of Florida, 2000), 205–207.

37. Larry Eugene Rivers, *Slavery in Florida*, 13, 149, 219; Porter, *The Negro on the American Frontier*, 238.

38. SAN, 22 November 1839.

Chapter 5

1. See Daniel L. Schafer, "'A Class of People Neither Freemen nor Slaves': From Spanish to American Race Relations in Florida, 1821–1861," *Journal of Social History* 26 (Spring 1993): 587–610; Schafer, *Anna Kingsley*, revised and expanded ed. (St. Augustine, Florida: St. Augustine Historical Society, 1997), 37; Zephaniah Kingsley, *A Treatise on the Patriarchal or Cooperative System of Society as it Exists in Some Governments and Colonies in America, and in the United States, under the Name of Slavery, With Its Necessity and Advantages*, 2nd ed. (1829; reprint: Freeport, NY: Books for Libraries, 1970), 7.

2. Deed Book H, 314 (hereafter cited, for example, as DB-H, 314) St. Johns

County Courthouse, St. Augustine, Florida (hereafter cited as CCH); DB-I&J, 14; DB-K, 104–106; Colored Baptisms (hereafter cited as CB), vol. 1, entries 285, 461, 527, Records of the Cathedral Parish, St. Augustine Historical Society Research Library, St. Augustine, Florida (hereafter cited as SAHL).

3. St. Johns County Court, Records, box 91, file 2 (hereafter cited, for example, as CCR 91-2), SAHL. Another source states that Jimmy Gibbs belonged to the Methodist church in 1837. See "Examination of Emanuel Aguiar Statement Relative to Charges of Insurrection among the Negroes," Blacks 1824–1855, City of St. Augustine, Papers (hereafter cited as City Papers), SAHL.

4. CCR, 91-2.

5. Ibid.; Marriage Licenses, Volume A, 6, Judgment Record A, 7–8, CCH; DB-O, 518.

6. CCR, 91-2; Judgment Record A, 7, CCH; DB-O, 518; Order Book A, 3, CCH; "Examination of Emanuel Aguiar," Blacks: 1824–1855, City Papers; Entry D49, 7 December 1858, entry D45, 7 December 1858, Negro Passes and Permits, City Papers.

7. Tax Rolls, St. Johns County, 1847–1848, 1850, 1853, Florida State Archives, Tallahassee, Florida (hereafter cited as FSA); Inventories, "Old" Book 3: 1840–1861, p. 178, St. Johns County, County Judge, Probate Records, 1784–1933, FSA; Seventh Census of the United States, 1850, Florida, St. Johns County; CB, vol. 4, entry 37.

8. CCR, 91-2.

9. *St. Augustine Florida Herald & Southern Democrat* (hereafter cited as FHSD), 9 July 1841; *St. Augustine News* (hereafter cited as SAN), 19 November 1842; FHSD, 30 September 1843.

10. There is some uncertainty regarding this date. St. Augustine's rival newspapers, FHSD and SAN report different dates in different issues. SAN on Saturday, 29 July 1843 states that the escape occurred on "Monday night last" or 24 July. FHSD on Monday, 31 July 1843 uses the phrase "On Tuesday morning last" for when the escape was discovered, which would be 25 July. However, FHSD on 7 August 1843 and SAN on 12 August 1843 both report that it happened a week earlier, on 18 July 1843. Yet, SAN on 22 July and FHSD on 24 July made no mention of the shocking event. A letter from Joseph S. Sánchez to his son written on 14 August 1842 assigns a date in July beginning with "2" although the second numeral is illegible. (See "Correspondence 1843 Taxes, Accounts etc.," Jose Simeon Sanchez Papers, SAHL.)

11. FHSD, 31 July 1843; Sánchez to Son, 14 August 1842; SAN 29 July 1843; SAN 30 September 1843.

12. FHSD, 31 July 1843; FHSD, 7 August 1843; SAN, 22 November 1839.

13. Item no. 9, "Receipts, 1838–1839," City Papers; CB, vol. 3, p. 319; FHSD, 9 July 1841; FHSD, 31 July 1843; Sixth and Seventh Censuses of the United States, 1840, 1850, Florida, St. Johns County; CCR, 95-17.

14. Sánchez to Son, 14 August 1843, Jose Simeon Sanchez Papers.

15. FHSD, 31 July 1843; Sánchez to Son, 14 August 1843, Jose Simeon Sanchez Papers; "Mayor and Council of St. Augustine to the Secretary of the Treasury," 14 August 1843 in *The Territory of Florida, 1839–1845*, ed. Clarence Edwin Carter, vol. 26 of *The Territorial Papers of the United States* (Washington, DC: National Archives, 1962), 722–724.

16. SAN, 30 September 1843; FHSD, 31 July 1843.

17. SAN 29 July 1843; Sánchez to Son, 14 August 1843, Jose Simeon Sanchez Papers; FHSD, 7 August 1843; SAN, 12 August 1843.

18. SAN, 12 August 1843.

19. Fergus M. Bordewich, *Bound for Canaan: The Epic Story of the Underground Railroad, America's First Civil Rights Movement* (New York: HarperCollins, 2005), 271–274, 283–287.

20. *New-York Daily Tribune*, 20 September 1843, (image 2), in Library of Congress and National Endowment for the Humanities, Chronicling America: Historic American Newspapers, http://chroniclingamerica.loc.gov (accessed 17 June 2012).

21. Ibid.

22. Marvin Dunn, *Black Miami in the Twentieth Century* (Gainesville: University Press of Florida, 2002), 7–14; 164; George Klos, "Blacks and the Seminole Removal Debate, 1821–1835," in *The African American Heritage of Florida*, ed. David R. Colburn and Jane L. Landers (Gainesville: University Press of Florida, 1995), 133; SAN 7 October 1843; FHSD, 10 October 1843.

23. This date is uncertain. The indictments of the fugitives issued on 13 November 1843 state 1 September (see indictments of Andrew Gué and Companions, Messages Transmitting Reports and Communications from the Secretary of State, February 9, 1844 to February 21, 1844, SEN 28A-E3, Records of the US Senate, Record Group 46, National Archives, Washington, DC); FHSD, 31 October 1843, speculated that it occurred between 18 and 22 September.

24. Indictments, SEN 28A-E3; SAN, 7 October 1843; FHSD, 31 October 1843.

25. FHSD, 31 October 1843.

26. Ibid.; SAN, 4 November 1843.

27. FHSD, 31 October 1843; SAN, 4 November 1843; Indictments, SEN 28A-E3; Joseph B. Browne to Sir Francis Cockburn, 26 December 1843, in US Congress, House of Representatives, 28th Cong., 1st sess., 1844, H. Exec. Doc. 160, pp. 6, 19.

28. *British And Foreign Anti-Slavery Reporter*, 10 January 1844, 2.

29. Account no. 76042, Samuel Williams, Settled Miscellaneous Treasury Accounts, September 6, 1790–September 29, 1894, Office of the First Auditor, Records of the Accounting Officers of the Department of the Treasury, Record Group 217, National Archives, College Park, Maryland (hereafter cited as RG 217); CB, vol. 3, p. 323.

30. Account no. 76042, Samuel Williams, RG 217; Spanish Land Grants, Confirmed, microfilm reel 51-I, entry W-29, P. K. Yonge Library of Florida History, University of Florida, Gainesville, Florida; Ianthe Bond Hebel, "The Samuel Williams Family: Early Residents on the Halifax," *Journal of the Halifax Historical Society* 2 (no. 1), 25; Alan Gregor Cobley, "That Turbulent Soil: Seafarers, the 'Black Atlantic,' and Afro-Caribbean Identity," in *Seascapes: Maritime Histories, Littoral Cultures, and Transoceanic Exchanges*, eds. Jerry H. Bentley, Renate Bridenthal, and Kären Wigen (Honolulu: University of Hawai'i Press, 2007), 164.

31. Indictments, SEN 28A-E3; Abel P. Upshur to Henry S. Fox, 20 November 1843, Fox to Upshur, Washington, DC, 21 November 1843, in US Congress, House of Representatives, 28th Cong., 1st sess., 1844, H. Exec. Doc. 160, pp. 2–3; Browne to Upshur, 17 December 1843, SEN 28A-E3; Cockburn to Lord Stanley, 1 January 1844, Governor 2/25, Duplicate Governor's Despatches, 18 January 1843–30 December 1846, Department of Archives, Nassau, Bahamas (hereafter cited as Gov 2/25); W. Fletcher Turtle to Daniel Webster, 17 May 1843, Despatches from US Consuls in Nassau, West Indies, 1821–1906, Records of the Department of State, Record Group 59, National Archives, College Park, Maryland.

32. Robert J. Morgan, *A Whig Embattled: The Presidency under John Tyler* (Lincoln: University of Nebraska Press, 1954), 129–131; Claude H. Hall, *Abel Parker Upshur: Conservative Virginian, 1790–1844* (Madison: State Historical Society of Wisconsin, 1964), 192–194; Edward B. Rugemer, "Robert Monroe Harrison, British Abolition, Southern Anglophobia and Texas Annexation," *Slavery and Abolition*, 28 (August 2007), 174, 178–180.

33. Edward D. Jervey and C. Harold Huber, "The Creole Affair," *Journal of Negro History*, 65 (Summer 1980): 204–205, 207; Cockburn to Stanley, 11 December 1843, 30 December 1843, Gov 2/25; Michael Craton and Gail Saunders, *Islanders in the Stream: A History of the Bahamian People*, vol. 2 (Athens: University of Georgia Press, 1998), 11; Phillip Troutman, "Grapevine in the Slave Market: African American Geopolitical Literacy and the 1841 *Creole* Revolt," in *The Chattel Principle: Internal Slave Trades in the Americas*, ed. Walter Johnson (New Haven, CT: Yale University Press, 2004), 216.

34. Susan Wyly-Jones, "The 1835 Anti-Abolition Meetings in the South: A New Look at the Controversy over the Abolition Postal Campaign," *Civil War History* 47 (December 2001): 290; Janet Duitsman Cornelius, *Slave Missions and*

the Black Church in the Antebellum South (Columbia: University of South Carolina Press, 1999), 127–128; Annie Heloise Abel and Frank J. Klingberg, eds., *A Side-Light on Anglo-American Relations, 1839–1858: Furnished by the Correspondence of Lewis Tappan and Others with the British and Foreign Anti-Slavery Society* (Lancaster, PA: Association for the Study of Negro Life, 1927) 3, 24; Joshua Leavitt to John Beaumont, 15 November 1843, J. H. Hinton to Earl of Aberdeen, 6 December 1843, Hinton to Henry Capern, 14 December 1843, in *A Side-Light on Anglo-American Relations*, 122n94,149, 153–156n119; *British And Foreign Anti-Slavery Reporter* (hereafter cited as BFASR), 10 January 1844, 2, 21 February 1844, 25.

35. BFASR, 10 January 1844, 2, and 21 February 1844, 25; David M. Turley, "'Free Air' and Fugitive Slaves: British Abolitionists versus Government over American Fugitives, 1834–1861," in *Anti-slavery, Religion and Reform: Essays in Memory of Roger Anstey*, eds. Roger Anstey and Christine Bolt (Folkestone, England: Wm. Dawson & Son, 1980), 171, 173; Thomas Clarkson to Aberdeen, 13 February 1843, Leavitt to Beaumont, 15 November 1843, Clarkson to Aberdeen, 11 October 1843, Hinton to Aberdeen, 6 December 1843, Hinton to Capern, 14 December 1843, in *A Side-Light on Anglo-American Relations*, 122–124n94, 149–157n119; Donald V. Macdougall, "Habeas Corpus, Extradition and a Fugitive Slave in Canada," *Slavery & Abolition* 7 (September 1986): 120.

36. BFASR, 17 April 1844, 63; Cockburn to Timothy Darling, 25 December 1843, John C. Lees to Cockburn, 30 December 1843, Browne to Cockburn, Nassau, 30 December 1843, Gov 2/25; US Congress, House of Representatives, 28th Cong., 2nd sess., 1845, H. Exec. Doc. 114; Cockburn to Stanley, Nassau, 1 January 1844, Gov 2/25; *British And Foreign Anti-Slavery Reporter*, 21 February 1844, 25; Sandra Riley, *Homeward Bound: A History of the Bahama Islands to 1850 with a Definitive Study of Abaco in the American Loyalist Plantation Period* (Miami: Island Research, 1983), 226.

37. Hinton to Aberdeen, 6 December 1843, in *A Side-Light on Anglo-American Relations*,153n119.

38. John Lewis Gaddis, *Surprise, Security, and the American Experience* (Cambridge, MA: Harvard University Press, 2004), 16–18, 21; Richard Kluger, *Seizing Destiny: How America Grew from Sea to Shining Sea* (New York: Alfred A. Knopf, 2007), 305, 333–334, 336; Bordewich, *Bound for Canaan*, 291; "Governor Duval to the Secretary of War," 23 September 1823, in *The Territory of Florida, 1821–1824*, ed. Clarence Edwin Carter, vol. 22 of *The Territorial Papers of the United States* (Washington, DC: National Archives, 1960), 744–745; Webster to Ashburton, 1 August 1842, Great Britain Foreign and Commonwealth Office. *British and Foreign State Papers: 1841–1842*, vol. 30 (1858), 182–183; FHSD, 27 June 1839, 31 July 1843; SAN, 22 November 1839; SAN, 29 January 1841; SAN,

30 September 1843; Rosalyn Howard, *Black Seminoles in the Bahamas* (Gainesville: University Press of Florida, 2002), 31–32; Howard Johnson, *The Bahamas in Slavery and Freedom* (Kingston, Jamaica: Ian Randle, 1991), 32, 35.

39. FHSD, 6 August 1844.

40. FHSD, 30 July, 6 August, 13 August, 22 October 1844.

41. FHSD, 8 October 1841; FHSD, 17 December 1841; FHSD, 23 January 1843.

42. Schafer, "'A Class of People Neither Freemen nor Slaves,'" 593; CCR, 117-14; *St. Augustine Tatler*, 27 January 1894, SAHL; *St. Augustine Record*, clipping [Spring 1890s?], William Whitwell Dewhurst Papers, SAHL; J. P. Whitwell to J. R. Poinsett, 12 January 1840, Letters Received by the Adjutant General's Office, 1822–1860, Microfilm Publication M567, microfilm roll 220, 1840, V221–W193, #0287, #0288, Records of the Adjutant General's Office, Record Group 94, National Archives, Washington, DC; Registers of Enlistment in the US Army, 1798–1914, Microfilm Publication M233, microfilm roll 20, vol. 41, 1835–1837, p. 231, Record Group 94; DB-O, 449, 624; Schafer, *Anna Kingsley*, 41–42, 61n54; David Y. Thomas, "The Free Negro in Florida before 1865," *South Atlantic Quarterly* 10 (October 1911): 335–345; James W. Curtis, *The Descendants of Flora Leslie and George John Frederick Clarke* (Riverside, California: James W. Curtis, c. 2004), 19–20.

43. CCR, 122-5; CCR, 98-58; DB-M, 304–305; SAN, 24 June 1843; SAN, 9 April 1842, SAN, 9 August 1845; FHSD, 18 February 1842.

44. CCR, 122-5; Return Books, 1846–1860, Tax Rolls, St. Johns County, FSA.

45. Return Books, 1846, 1848, Tax Rolls, St. Johns County, FSA; Sheriff's Report of Insolvencies on Assessment return of 1847, "Accounts of Jose S. Sanchez as Tax Collector & Papers Relating Thereto 1839–1848," Joseph Simeon Sanchez Papers; Tax Rolls, 1847, Monroe County, Florida, FSA; SAN, 19 August 1843; Canter Brown, Jr., *Ossian Bingley Hart, Florida's Loyalist Reconstruction Governor* (Baton Rouge: Louisiana State University Press, 1997), 67–71; Jefferson B. Browne, *Key West: The Old and the New, A Facsimile Reproduction of the 1912 Edition* (Gainesville: University of Florida Press, 1973), 171.

Chapter 6

1. *St. Augustine News* (hereafter cited as SAN), 25 December 1841; Robert Reid to George Burt, 23 September 1847, Burt Papers, St. Augustine Historical Society Research Library, St. Augustine, Florida (hereafter cited as SAHL); William Cullen Bryant, *Letters of a Traveller; or, Notes of Things Seen in Europe and America,* 3rd ed. (New York: George P. Putnam, 1851), 111.

2. Colored Baptisms (hereafter cited as CB), vol. 3, pp. 320–321, 337, Rec-

ords of the Cathedral Parish, SAHL; CB, vol. 4, pp. 33–34; Deed Book P (hereafter cited, for example, DB-P), 230–231, St. Johns County Courthouse, St. Augustine, Florida (hereafter cited as CCH); "Some Descendants of Jose Sanchez de Ortigosa y de Giles and Juana Theodora Perez y de Lansarote," http://www.rootsweb.ancestry.com/~flsags/josesanchez.htm (accessed 10 November 2011); Sandra Willis, transcriber, "1850 Census of St. Johns County, FL," http://www.rootsweb.ancestry.com~flstjohn/resources/1850Census/218B.HTM (accessed 17 June 2012); Sandra L. Willis, transcriber, "Putnam, FL 1860 Federal Census," http://files.usgwarchives.net/fl/putnam/census/1860 (accessed 10 November 2011).

3. SAN, 17 November 1838; SAN, 21 May 1842; *St. Augustine Florida Herald & Southern Democrat* (hereafter cited as FHSD), 29 May 1841; FHSD, 24 June 1841; FHSD, 10 December 1841; *St Augustine Ancient City* (hereafter cited as AC), 15 November 1851; St. Johns County Court, Records, box 157, file 16 (hereafter cited, for example, as CCR, 157-16), SAHL; CCR, 157-5; Return Book—1832, Tax Rolls, St. Johns County, 1829–1835, Florida State Archives, Tallahassee, Florida (hereafter cited as FSA); Claim of James Erwin, Patriot War Papers, SAHL; CCR, 122-9; CB, vol. 4, p. 1; Seventh Census of the United States, 1850, Florida, St. Johns County; DB-M, 86; "Receipts:1832–1837," City of St. Augustine, Papers (hereafter cited as City Papers), SAHL; Eighth Census of the United States, 1860, Florida, St. Johns County; Guardian List for 1838, "Blacks: 1824–1855," City Papers; Wills & Letters of Administration, vol. 1, 422, 436–438, CCH.

4. Account no. 85048, Abraham McQueen, Settled Miscellaneous Treasury Accounts, September 6, 1790–September 29, 1894, Office of the First Auditor, Records of the Accounting Officers of the Department of the Treasury, Record Group 217, National Archives, College Park, Maryland (hereafter cited as RG 217); CB, vol. 1, entry 262. Jane Landers, in *Atlantic Creoles of Color in the Age of Revolutions* (Cambridge, MA: Harvard University Press, 2010), 248, reports that Abraham McQueen also was known as Abraham Hannahan and that his owner, Zephaniah Kingsley, freed him. Later, Landers wrote, he left East Florida for Cuba in 1821, leaving his wife Basha behind in St. Augustine. The Patriot War claim for Abraham McQueen does not mention these events. Two Minorcan witnesses suggest that he died in Florida. The free black Charles Hill testified that he died after the US invasion but prior to the change of flags. Also, Catholic records imply that McQueen gained his freedom by running away to Florida. Hence, even modern historians can disagree about black identities in this period.

5. Seventh and Eighth Censuses of the United States, 1850, 1860, Florida, St. Johns County; Abraham Lancaster, Soldier's Certificate no. 671600, Civil

War and Later Pension Files, Records of the Veteran's Administration, Record Group 15, National Archives, Washington, DC (hereafter cited as RG 15); Canter Brown Jr. *Tampa before the Civil War* (Tampa: University of Tampa Press, 1999), 129–130.

6. CB, vol. 2, entry 243; Colored Marriages, 1785–1882 (hereafter cited as CM), pp. 56, 61–62, Records of the Cathedral Parish, SAHL; Testimony of Antonio Huertas, 10 February 1893, letter 162, Segui-Dallum Papers, SAHL.

7. Theodore Shemytillo, Churchill's Escort, Florida Mounted Militia, Compiled Service Records of Volunteer Soldiers Who Served in Organizations from the State of Florida during the Florida Indian Wars, 1835–1858 microfilm roll 39, Record Group 94, Records of the Adjutant General's Office, National Archives, Washington, DC; Julius Shemetella, Soldier's Certificate nos. 522752 and 174818, RG 15; Jane Ball-Groom, e-mail message to author, 20 September 2010; Seventh Census of the United States, 1850, Florida, Duval County; St. Johns County Court, Minute Book, 1827–1845, 267–268, SAHL; Seventh and Eighth Censuses of the United States, 1850, 1860, Florida, St. Johns County; "Union Army Census of Northeast Florida, 1864 and 1865," Department of the South, Census of the District of Florida, Charles E. Coolidge, Seventh US Infantry, Provost Marshal (hereafter cited as Union Army Census), SAHL.

8. CB, vol. 3, entries 37, 181, vol. 2, entries 3, 193, 258, 556, 645, 751, vol. 4, pp. 3, 8, 23, 66; Sixth Census of the United States, 1840, Florida, St. Johns County, Monroe County; Seventh Census of the United States, 1850, Florida, St. Johns County, Monroe County; DB-H, 201–202, DB-P, 386–389, DB-Q, 309; CCR, 116-19; Compiled Service Records of Volunteer Soldiers Who Served in Organizations from the State of Florida during the Florida Indian Wars, 1835–1858, Microcopy 1086, microfilm roll 25 (2d Sanchez's Florida Mounted Militia), Records of the Adjutant General's Office, Record Group 94, National Archives, Washington, DC; St. Johns County Tax Rolls, 1829–1835, 1845–1861, FSA; Wills and Letters of Administration, vol. 1, 215, CCH; Tax Assessments/Revenue, 1855–1871, City Papers.

9. Interview of Edward Lycurgus, Jacksonville, Florida, 15 December 1936, in *The American Slave: A Composite Autobiography*, vol. 17, *Florida Narratives*, ed. George P. Rawick (Westport, CT: Greenwood, 1972), 204–208. According to antebellum records, Julia Gray was born free circa 1840. Her mother, Barbara or Bobet, had belonged to the estate of Bartolomé de Castro. Julia's father, the free man of color David Gray (alias Fleming), had purchased Bobet's freedom for $500, which he paid in installments from 1824 to 1829. Some time before 1837, the couple solemnized their marriage before a Catholic priest. See: DB-H, 311–312, DB-P, 45; White Baptisms, entry for 2 August 1837, p. 438, Records of the

Cathedral Parish, SAHL; Eighth Census of the United States, 1860, Florida, St. Johns County.

10. Lycurgus, *Florida Narratives*, 204–208.

11. Prince Weedman to George Burt, 7 February 1856, "Slave Letter," Burt Papers, SAHL; Abraham Lancaster, Soldier's Certificate no. 671600, RG 15; Eighth Census of the United States, 1860, Florida, St. Johns County; CM, pp. 61, 63, Records of the Cathedral Parish, SAHL; CB, vol. 4, p. 75; St. Johns County Marriage Licenses, Vol. A, 4, 215, CCH; "Clarke, George F. Last Will and Testament," Clarke Papers, SAHL; Union Army Census.

12. Frank Tannenbaum, *Slave and Citizen: The Negro in the Americas* (Boston: Beacon Press, 1992), 49; Jane Landers, *Black Society in Spanish Florida* (Urbana: University of Illinois Press, 1999), 124–126. An interesting case of a slave suing her owner in order to prevent her from being sold away from her husband can be read in the East Florida Papers, bundle 330R6, reel 151, 1792-19, 19 September 1792, P. K. Yonge Library of Florida History, University of Florida.

13. CM; CB, vol. 3, vol. 4; Marriage Licenses, 1823–1833, SAHL; Marriage Licenses, vol. A, CCH; Records of Trinity Episcopal Church, St. Augustine, Florida, vol. 1, SAHL; Landers, *Black Society*, 125.

14. Handy Growles, alias Goud, Soldier's Certificate no. 469919, RG 15; CB, vol. 4, pp. 17, 48, 57; CM, p. 62.

15. John Mills, Soldier's Certificate no. 490204, RG 15.

16. CB, vol. 3, pp. 317, 327, vol. 4, pp. 32, 40, 42, 50, 53, 61, 63, 71, 75; In Supreme Court, Florida, February Term, 1860, *D. L. Yulee Appellee, Caveator. Ads. Francis Bridier, Executor, Brief of G. R. Fairbanks, Counsel of Appellee* (Jacksonville, FL: Columbus Drew, 1860), 26, Treaty of 1819 (Florida Claims), Spain, International Claims, Records of Boundary and Claims Commissions and Arbitrations, Record Group 76, National Archives, College Park, Maryland.

17. Marriage Licenses, 1830–1840, entries for 21 February 1838 and 15 June 1839, SAHL; CB, vol. 3, pp. 315, 318, 320, 325, 332, 339, vol. 4, entry 45 and pp. 28, 49.

18. Ann Patton Malone, *Sweet Chariot: Slave Family and Household Structure in Nineteenth-Century Louisiana* (Chapel Hill: University of North Carolina Press, 1992), 243; Gary B. Mills, "Piety and Prejudice: A Colored Catholic Community in the Antebellum South," in *Catholics in the Old South: Essays on Church and Culture*, eds. Randall M. Miller and Jon L. Wakelyn (Macon, GA: Mercer University Press), 180, 182; Randall M. Miller, "Slaves and Southern Catholicism," in *Masters and Slaves in the House of the Lord: Race and Religion in the American South, 1740–1870*, ed. John B. Boles (Lexington: University Press of Kentucky, 1988), 128, 138, 230 (n10); John B. Boles, "Introduction," in *Masters*

and Slaves in the House of the Lord, 12; Abel Poitrineau, "Demography and the Political Destiny of Florida During the Second Spanish Period," *Florida Historical Quarterly* 66 (April 1988): 427; Cyprian Davis, *The History of Black Catholics in the United States* (New York: Crossroads, 1990), 42; Cyprian Davis and Jamie Phelps, eds., *"Stamped with the Image of God": African Americans as God's Image in Black* (New York: Orbis, 2003), 20–22, 274n54.

19. Michael V. Gannon, *The Cross in the Sand: The Early Catholic Church in Florida, 1513–1870* (Gainesville: University of Florida Press, 1965), 152; Abraham Lancaster, Soldier's Certificate no. 671600, RG 15; Eighth Census of the United States, 1860, Florida, St. Johns County; St. Johns County Marriage Licenses, vol. A, pp. 4, 215, CCH; CB, vol. 4, p. 75; CM.

20. St. Johns County Marriage Licenses, 15 April 1839, 15 June 1839, 20 February 1843, 16 July 1845, 26 February 1846, 9 May 1856, and 16 June 1841, 29 January 1842, 10 February 1847, CCH; Boles, "Introduction," in *Masters and Slaves*, 12.

21. Blake Touchstone, "Planters and Slave Religion in the Deep South," in Boles, *Masters and Slaves in the House of the Lord*, 35, 99–102, 105, 108–109; Clarence L. Mohr, "Slaves and White Churches in Confederate Georgia," in Boles, *Masters and Slaves in the House of the Lord*, 154–155, 157–159; John W. Blassingame, *The Slave Community: Plantation Life in the Antebellum South*, 2nd ed. (New York: Oxford University Press, 1979), 168–170; Eugene Genovese, *Roll, Jordan, Roll: The World the Slaves Made* (New York: Random House, 1974), 69; Albert J. Raboteau, *Slave Religion: The "Invisible Institution" in the Antebellum South* (New York: Oxford University Press, 1978), 187.

22. Randall M. Miller, "A Church in Cultural Captivity: Some Speculations on Catholic Identity in the Old South," in Miller and Wakelyn, *Catholics in the Old South*, 26; Miller, "Slaves and Southern Catholicism," in Boles, *Masters and Slaves in the House of the Lord*, 138–151; Miller, "The Failed Mission: The Catholic Church and Black Catholics in the Old South," in *The Southern Common People: Studies in Nineteenth-Century Social History*, eds. Edward Magdol and Jon L. Wakelyn (Westport, CT: Greenwood, 1980), 48, 52n14.

23. Augustin Verot, *A Tract for the Times. Slavery & Abolitionism Being the Substance of a Sermon, Preached in the Church of St. Augustine, Florida, on the 4th Day of January, 1861, Day of Public Humiliation, Fasting and Prayer*, new ed. (New Orleans: Catholic Propagator, 1861), 5–6, 15–16, 17–19; Michael V. Gannon, *Rebel Bishop: The Life and Era of Augustin Verot* (Milwaukee: Bruce, 1964), 47.

24. See Daniel L. Schafer, "'A Class of People Neither Freemen nor Slaves': From Spanish to American Race Relations in Florida, 1821–1861," *Journal of*

Social History 26 (Spring 1993): 587–610; St. Johns County Deed Books, Order Book A, Wills and Letters of Administration, vol. 1, all in CCH; Union Army Census; Schafer, "'A Class of People Neither Freemen nor Slaves,'" 591.

25. CCR, 90-12; Seventh Census of the United States, 1850, Florida, St. Johns County.

26. CB, vol. 4, entry 507; Accounts of Jose S. Sanchez as Tax Collector & Papers Relating Thereto: 1839–1848, Joseph Simeon Sanchez Papers, SAHL; Order Book A, 1, 3–4, Wills and Letters of Administration, vol. 1, 163–166, CCH; Clarissa C. Anderson to Miss C. L. Fairbanks, 15 March 1844, Lyman Cochrane to Mrs. Clarissa Anderson, 25 August 1842, Anderson Papers, SAHL; Judgment Record A, 96, CCH; Seventh and Eighth Censuses of the United States, 1850, 1860, Florida, St. Johns County; Supplemental list of Insolvencies and over charges presented to the Board of County Commissioners acting upon assessment return of 1846, "Accounts of Jose S. Sanchez as Tax Collector & Papers Relating Thereto: 1839–1848," Joseph Simeon Sanchez Papers.

27. The Territory v. Tony Papy, 1 November 1845, Territorial Court of Appeals Case Files, Series 73, roll 8, Record Group 970, FSA; DB-M, 136–137.

28. The Territory v. Tony Papy.

29. Ibid.

30. Order Book A, 3–4, Wills and Letters of Administration, vol. 1, 163–166, CCH.

31. Wills and Letters of Administration, vol. 1, 297–298, CCH; Entries for 11 July 1857, 18 December 1858, Minute Book B, 110, 160, City Papers; CB, vol. 4, entry for 6 January 1858, p. 61; Eighth Census of the United States, 1860, Florida, St. Johns County; *Escrituras* (Notarized Instruments), 1784–1821, East Florida Papers, Bundle 365, *Quaderno* 3, microfilm reel 55-A, pp. 122–125, SAHL.

32. Order Book A, 6–7, CCH; Eighth Census of the United States, 1860, Florida, St. Johns County; 26. Account no. 85048, Abraham McQueen, Settled Miscellaneous Treasury Accounts, September 6, 1790–September 29, 1894, Office of the First Auditor, Records of the Accounting Officers of the Department of the Treasury, Record Group 217, National Archives, College Park, Maryland; Entry D35, 6 December 1858, entry D45, 7 December 1858, Negro Passes and Permits, City Papers; William Morris, Soldier's Certificate no. 176225, and Abraham Lancaster, Soldier's Certificate no. 671600, RG 15.

33. CB, vol. 3, entry 243; Order Book A, 8, CCH; Testimony of Antonio Huertas, 10 February 1893, letter 162, Segui-Dallum Papers, SAHL; Inventories, "Old" Book 3: 1840–1861, pp. 200–208, St. Johns County, County Judge, Probate Records, 1784–1933, FSA.

34. Seventh Census of the United States, 1850, Florida, St. Johns County; Ac-

counts to October 27, 1857, "1850s Business Bills & Memos," Burt Papers; CM, entries 60, 70; CB, vol. 4, entry 23, and pp. 23–24 (1851), p. 67 (7 October 1858); Entries D7, 2 January 1857, and D29 [6 December 1858?], Negro Passes and Permits, City Papers; Entry for 11 December 1858, Minute Book B, 158, City Papers.

35. George Vanness Jr., Soldier's Certificate no. 258248, RG 15; Deed Book A, 75, Putnam County Clerk of the Court, Palatka, Florida; Seventh and Eighth Censuses of the United States, 1850, 1860, Florida, St. Johns County.

Chapter 7

1. Edward E. Baptist, *Creating an Old South: Middle Florida's Plantation Frontier before the Civil War* (Chapel Hill: University of North Carolina Press, 2002), 260–261.

2. Account nos.: 94405, Francis P. Fatio Jr.; 74969, Francisco Xavier Sanchez; 74862, George Long, Settled Miscellaneous Treasury Accounts, September 6, 1790–September 29, 1894, Office of the First Auditor, Records of the Accounting Officers of the Department of the Treasury, Record Group 217, National Archives, College Park, Maryland (hereafter cited as RG 217).

3. Account nos.: 95167, Joseph Summerall; 82248, James Dell; 79073, Juan Leonardy; 75008, Catherine Baker, 81651, Francis Richard Jr., RG 217.

4. Account nos.: 83177, George J. F. Clarke; 98273, Prince Whilton, RG 217; Gregg D. Kimball, "African, American, and Virginian: The Shaping of Black Memory in Antebellum Virginia, 1790–1860," in *Where These Memories Grow: History, Memory, and Southern Identity*, ed. W. Fitzhugh Brundage (Chapel Hill: University of North Carolina Press, 2000), 61.

5. Account nos.: 86844, Philip Edinborough; 98271, Domingo Davis; 98272, Sancho Davis; 98273, Prince Whilton; 99008, Scipio Fleming, RG 217.

6. Account nos.: 87746, Margarita Acosta; 82538, Christopher Lopez; 79073, Juan Leonardy; 75214, Francis Pellicer; 75215, Isaac Weeks; 73063, Felipe Solana; 86282, Fernando de la Maza Arredondo Jr.; 73347, Francisco D. and Peter Pons; 73629, Jose Hernandez Cardona; 86225, Henry Yonge; 72942, James Hall; 73915, John Forbes; 74969, Francis X. Sanchez; 98273, Prince Whilton, RG 217; Captain John Williams to Lieutenant Colonel Franklin Wharton, 15 September 1812, vol. 16, Letters Received, 1798–1817, Office of the Commandant, Headquarters, US Marine Corps, Historical Division, Records of the US Marine Corps, Record Group 127, National Archives, Washington, DC; Zephaniah Kingsley, "Address to the Legislative Council of Florida on the Subject of Its Coloured Population," 1823, Manuscript Collection 11, State Library of Florida, Tallahassee;

Joseph H. Alexander, "Swamp Ambush," *Military History* 14 (March 1998): 40, 44; See, for example, the following claims in RG 217: nos.: 86844, Philip Edinborough; 99008, Scipio Fleming; 99162, Abraham Rocho; 85048, Abraham McQueen; 89455, John Howley; 98271, Domingo Davis; 98272, Sancho Davis; 94419, Isaac Bacchus; 94421, John Morrell; 98270, George Clarke. See also Claim of Benjamin Wiggins, Patriot War Papers, St. Augustine Historical Society Research Library, St. Augustine, Florida (hereafter cited as SAHL).

7. Jane Landers, *Black Society in Spanish Florida* (Urbana: University of Illinois Press, 1999), 88–89, 116–117, 144–145; Colored Baptisms (hereafter cited as CB), vol. 1, entries 125, 126, 138, 232, vol. 3, entry 74, and Colored Marriages, 1784–1882 (hereafter cited as CM), entry 38, Records of the Cathedral Parish, SAHL; Account no. 98273, Prince Whilton, RG 217.

8. Account no. 86844, Philip Edinborough, RG 217; Landers, 171.

9. Account nos.: 86844, Philip Edinborough; 99008, Scipio Fleming, RG 217.

10. Account no. 83177, George J. F. Clarke, RG 217.

11. Michael V. Gannon, *The Cross in the Sand: The Early Catholic Church in Florida, 1513–1870* (Gainesville: University of Florida Press, 1965), 152.

12. Seventh and Eight Censuses of the United States, 1850, 1860, Florida, St. Johns County; CB, vol. 3, entries 540–542, vol. 2, pp. 68–69, 198, vol. 4, pp. 14, 16–17, 22–24, 32, 63–64, 71; Deed Book F, 160–162 (hereafter cited, for example, as DB-F, 160–162), DB-P, 317–318, Judgment Record A, 20, DB-E, 202–203, DB-G, 31–36, St. Johns County Courthouse, St. Augustine, Florida (hereafter cited as CCH); St. Johns County Court, Records, box 116, file 19 (hereafter cited, for example, as CCR, 116-19), SAHL; CCR, 98-45; *St. Augustine East Florida Herald*, 8 August 1826; "Union Army Census of Northeast Florida, 1864 and 1865," Department of the South, Census of the District of Florida, Charles E. Coolidge, Seventh US Infantry, Provost Marshal (hereafter cited as Union Army Census), SAHL.

13. CB, vol. 4, pp. 14, 16–17, 22–24, 32, 63–64, 71, vol. 3, p. 14, CM, p. 56; Order Book A, 7–8, CCH.

14. Minute Book B, 16, 20, 27, 74, 76, 78, 195, 205–206, and Petition of R. B. Canovas and Others Asking Weekly Allowance and Shelter for Moseby, 6 January 1860, "Blacks: 1824–1855," both in City of St. Augustine, Papers (hereafter cited as City Papers), SAHL.

15. Minute Book B, 74, 76, 78, and Petition of R. B. Canovas and Others Asking Weekly Allowance and Shelter for Moseby, 6 January 1860, "Blacks: 1824–1855," both in City Papers.

16. Sources for the statistical data were: CB, vols. 3, 4; Joshua Hagaman, Soldier's Certificate no. 503002, Civil War and Later Pension Files, Records of the Veteran's Administration, Record Group 15, National Archives, Washington, DC

(hereafter cited as RG 15); Gary B. Mills, "Piety and Prejudice: A Colored Catholic Community in the Antebellum South," in *Catholics in the Old South: Essays on Church and Culture*, eds. Randall M. Miller and Jon L. Wakelyn (Macon, GA: Mercer University Press), 171–194; Michael V. Gannon, *Rebel Bishop: Augustin Verot, Florida's Civil War Prelate* (Milwaukee: Bruce, 1964; reprint, Gainesville: University Press of Florida, 1997), 26.

17. Report of Haager[?], 13 February 1844, "Blacks: 1824–1855," City Papers; Affidavit of Albert A. Nunes, 21 August 1845, State of Florida v. Johnson, a Slave of the Estate of G. W. Perpall, in "Blacks: 1824–1855," City Papers.

18. Affidavit of Albert A. Nunes, 21 August 1845, State of Florida v. Johnson, a Slave of the Estate of G. W. Perpall, in "Blacks: 1824–1855," City Papers; Affidavit of W. W. Loring, State of Florida v. Brigadier General William W. Worth, 21 August 1845, "Blacks: 1824–1855," City Papers; *St. Augustine Florida Herald & Southern Democrat* (hereafter cited as FHSD), 3 July 1842; E. B. Gould to Francis P. Ferreira, 21 August 1845, "Patrols, 1838–1867," City Papers; Circuit Court Minutes, St. Johns County, vol. A, 1846–1860, entry for 29 July 1846, SAHL.

19. George R. Fairbanks, Patrol Report, 8 August 1849, "Blacks: 1824–1855," City Papers; Detail of City Patrol for night of 29th December 1849, Patrol Report 9th inst. [penciled "Apr. 1840], "Patrols, 1836–1837," City Papers.

20. Items B10, B11, B12, Negro Passes and Permits, City Papers; James M. Denham, *"A Rogue's Paradise": Crime and Punishment in Antebellum Florida, 1821–1861* (Tuscaloosa: University of Alabama Press, 1997), 131.

21. DB-O, 373, 578–579; CCR, 165-23.

22. CCR, 165-23.

23. Ibid.

24. Minute Book B, 244, 247, 256, City Papers; 6 August, 5 October 1857, 13 August 1859, 29 May, 28 October, 29 November, 3 December 1860, Court Dockets, 9 March 1857–9 July 1883, pp. 6, 9, 23, 31–32, City Papers.

25. 31 January, 20 February, 25 June1861, Court Dockets, 9 March 1857–9 July 1883, pp. 43, 47, 51, City Papers; David J. Coles, "Ancient City Defenders: The St. Augustine Blues," in *Civil War Times in St. Augustine*, ed. Jacqueline K. Fretwell (Port Salerno: Florida Classics Library, 1988), 73–74.

26. Mrs. C. C. Anderson to Andrew Anderson, St. Augustine, 8 October 1858, Anderson Papers, SAHL; *St Augustine Examiner* (hereafter cited as SAE), 27 October 1860.

27. Coles, "Ancient City Defenders," 65–66; Minute Book B, 268, 270, 272–273, City Papers.

28. SAE, 18 August 1860.

29. Thomas Graham, "The Home Front: Civil War Times in St. Augustine,"

in *Civil War Times in St. Augustine*, 26; 14, 28 February 1862, Court Dockets, 9 March 1857–9 July 1883, p. 57, City Papers; Patrol Report, 16 May 1837, "Patrols, 1836–1837," City Papers; Thomas Stark to Joseph Simeon Sanchez, 8 April 1847, Joseph Simeon Sanchez Papers, SAHL

30. Daniel L. Schafer, "Freedom Was as Close as the River: African Americans in the Civil War in Northeast Florida," in *The African American Heritage of Florida*, ed. David R. Colburn and Jane L. Landers (Gainesville: University Press of Florida, 1995), 157, 175; Alexander Clark, Soldier's Certificate nos.: 359456, George J. F. Garvin; 370848, Abraham Lancaster; 671600, Julius Shemetella, 174818 and 522752, RG15; Edward Wanton, Company G, Regimental Descriptive Book, vol. 1, 33d United States Colored Infantry, and William Williams, Regimental Descriptive Book, Company A, 34th United States Colored Infantry, Book Records of Volunteer Union Organizations, Records of the Adjutant General's Office, Record Group 94, National Archives, Washington, DC (hereafter cited as RG 94); Abraham McQueen, 85048, RG 217; "Clarke, George F. Last Will and Testament," Clarke Papers, SAHL; CM, p. 63; CB, vol. 3, p. 314; Union Army Census, SAHL; Theodore Shemytillo, Churchill's Escort, Florida Mounted Militia, Compiled Service Records of Volunteer Soldiers Who Served in Organizations from the State of Florida during the Florida Indian Wars, 1835–1858 microfilm roll 39, National Archives, Washington, DC; Seventh Census of the United States, 1850, Florida, Putnam County, St. Johns County; Karen Taylor, e-mail message to author, 13 August 2010; James W. Curtis, *The Descendants of Flora Leslie and George John Frederick Clarke* (Riverside, CA: James W. Curtis, 2004), 25.

31. Samuel Osborn Sr., Samuel Osborn Jr., Regimental Descriptive Book, Company D, 33d United States Colored Infantry, RG 94; Emanuel Osborne, Tony Fontane, Company B, 3rd Regiment, Florida Infantry, Compiled Service Records of Confederate Soldiers Who Served in Organizations from Florida, Microform 251, microfilm rolls 47, 50, National Archives, Washington, DC; Samuel Osborn 1st, Soldier's Certificate nos.: 998312, John W. Welters, alias John Williams; 675241, James A. Lang; 1166518, RG 15; Eighth Census of the United States, 1860, Florida, St. Johns County; Coles, "Ancient City Defenders," 65–66, 73–74; *St. Augustine Record*, 22 February 1998.

32. Mark M. Smith, "Remembering Mary, Shaping Revolt: Reconsidering the Stono Rebellion," *Journal of Southern History* 67 (August 2001): 517, 534; Kimball, "African, American, and Virginian," 59, 62–63, 65, 73–74; Herbert Aptheker, *American Negro Slave Revolts* (New York: Columbia University Press, 1943), 11; Larry Eugene Rivers, *Slavery in Florida: Territorial Days to Emancipation* (Gainesville: University Press of Florida, 2000), 164–165.

33. Denham, *"A Rogue's Paradise,"* 139; Joseph Conan Thompson, "Toward a More Humane Oppression: Florida's Slave Codes, 1821–1861," *Florida Historical Quarterly* 71 (January 1993): 324, 326, 328–330, 332, 338; Lois Virginia Meacham Gould, "In Full Enjoyment of Their Liberty: The Free Women of Color of the Gulf Ports of New Orleans, Mobile, and Pensacola, 1769–1869" (PhD diss., Emory University, 1989), 94–95, 99–100; Julia Floyd Smith, *Slavery and Plantation Growth in Antebellum Florida, 1821–1861* (Gainesville: University of Florida Press, 1973), 111, 118, 120–121; Leedell W. Neyland, "The Free Negro in Florida," *Negro History Bulletin* 29 (November 1965): 42.

34. Steven Hahn, *A Nation under Our Feet: Black Political Struggles in the Rural South, From Slavery to the Great Migration* (Cambridge, MA: Harvard University Press, 2003), 86. For the Twine photograph and background on his life, see "Richard Aloysius Twine: Photographer of Lincolnville, 1922–1927," which constitutes the subject of *The East-Florida Gazette* 11 (February 1990): 1–6, published by the St. Augustine Historical Society and edited by Jean Parker Waterbury.

Chapter 8

1. *Fifth Census; or, Enumeration of the Inhabitants of the United States. 1830 . . .* (1832; reprint, New York: Norman Ross Publishing, 1990), 156–157; Joseph C. G. Kennedy, *Population of the United States in 1860 . . .* (1864; reprint, New York: Norman Ross Publishing, 1990), 51–55.

2. *Fifth Census*, 156–157; *Sixth Census or Enumeration of the Inhabitants of the United States, as Corrected at the Department of State, in 1840* (1841; reprint, New York: Norman Ross Publishing, 1990), 454–457; *The Seventh Census of the United States* (1853; reprint, New York: Norman Ross Publishing, 1990), 396–400; Kennedy, *Population of the United States in 1860*, 51–54.

3. Based on data from: Spanish Land Grants (hereafter cited as SLG), P. K. Yonge Library of Florida History (hereafter cited as PKY), University of Florida, Gainesville, Florida; US Congress, *American State Papers: Documents of the Congress of the United States in Relation to Public Lands, from the First Session of the Twenty-First to the First Session of the Twenty-Third Congress, Commencing December 1, 1828, and Ending April 11, 1834*, ed. Asbury Dickins and John W. Forney (Washington, DC: Gales & Seaton, 1860) (hereafter cited as ASP-PL); St. Johns County Deed Books, St. Johns County Courthouse, St. Augustine, Florida (hereafter cited as CCH); United States Bureau of Land Management Records, Record Group 49 (hereafter cited as RG 49), National Archives, Washington, DC.

4. Russell Garvin, "The Free Negro in Florida before the Civil War," *Florida*

Historical Quarterly 46 (July 1967): 12; Seventh and Eighth Censuses of the United States, 1850, 1860, Florida, St. Johns County, Monroe County; Daniel L. Schafer, *Anna Kingsley*, rev. and expanded ed. (St. Augustine: St. Augustine Historical Society, 1997), 41–42.

5. Deed Book M, 444–446, 417–418 (hereafter cited, for example, as DB-M, 444–446, 417–418), St. Johns County Courthouse, St. Augustine, Florida (hereafter cited as CCH); DB-N, 259–262; *St. Augustine Ancient City* (hereafter cited as AC), 23 October 1852; DB-Q, 174.

6. Jane L. Landers, "Black Society in Spanish St. Augustine, 1784–1821," (PhD diss., University of Florida, 1988), 127; Landers, *Black Society in Spanish Florida* (Urbana: University of Illinois Press, 1999), 151–152, 336n52; Testamentary Proceedings of Don Francisco Xavier Sanchez, 31 November 1807, Records of Testamentary Proceedings, 1756–1821, East Florida Papers, microfilm reel 41, PKY; Book or Register of City Lots, St. Augustine Historical Society Research Library, St. Augustine, Florida (hereafter cited as SAHL); DB-A, 12–16, 68, 76–81; DB-AA, 118–120; DB-H, 34; Order Book A, 85–89, CCH.

7. St. Johns County Court, Records, box 158, file 51 (hereafter cited, for example, as CCR, 158-51), SAHL; "The Claim of Susanna Sanchez," Patriot War Claims, SAHL; Escrituras (Notarized Instruments), East Florida Papers, Library of Congress microfilm reel 168, 1820, pp. 3–5 and 1821, pp. 628–630, SAHL; DB-P, 155–156; Jose Sanchez, Claim no. 351, Private Land Claims, Florida, RG 49; CCR, 166-28.

8. CCR, 158-51; DB-P, 155–156; Chancery Book B, 1854–1876, 202–203, 215–216, CCH; Jose Sanchez, Claim no. 351, RG 49.

9. See Frank Marotti Jr., "Edward M. Wanton and the Settling of Micanopy," *Florida Historical Quarterly* 73 (April 1995): 456–477. Edward M. Wanton's will can be found in Escrituras, East Florida Papers, Library of Congress microfilm reel 168, 1820, pp. 71–76; CCR, 111-31.

10. CCR, 111-31.

11. Ibid.

12. *St. Augustine Florida Herald & Southern Democrat* (hereafter cited as FHSD), 20 February 1840; DB-O, 84, 216–217; DB-I&J, 26–27; DB-O, 153–156, 162–163, 474–475.

13. DB-O, 187; Wills & Letters of Administration, vol. 1, 209–210, CCH; St. Johns County, County Judge, Probate Records, 1784–1933, Inventories, "Old" Book 3: 1840–1861, pp. 95–96, Florida State Archives, Tallahassee, Florida (hereafter cited as FSA); United States v. Clarke's Heirs, 41 US 228.

14. DB-O, 593–599; "Clarke, George F. Last Will and Testament," Clarke Papers, St. SAHL; Order Book A, 2, CCH.

15. DB-G, 87–93; DB-B&L, 29–30; DB-M, 502–503, 361–363; DB-N, 341.

16. CCR, 122-9; CCR, 117-14; Account nos.: 83177, George J. F. Clarke; 83763 George J. F. Clarke surviving partner of Clarke & Garvin, Settled Miscellaneous Treasury Accounts, September 6, 1790–September 29, 1894, Office of the First Auditor, Records of the Accounting Officers of the Department of the Treasury, Record Group 217, National Archives, College Park, Maryland (hereafter cited as RG 217).

17. DB-O, 449; DB-P, 32; CCR, 117-14.

18. DB-R, 173; DB-O, 502–503; DB-P, 43–44, 101–102, 132–134.

19. Return Books, 1845, 1850, 1855, Tax Rolls, St. Johns County, FSA.

20. St. Johns County Tax Rolls, 1861, FSA; Tax Assessments, 1856–1859, 1861, Tax Assessments/Revenue, 1855–1871, City of St. Augustine, Papers (hereafter cited as City Papers), SAHL; "Last Will and Testament of Mrs. Frances Kerr Translated from the Spanish by Margaret Booth," File, SAHL; DB-I&J, 5; Order Book A, 1; Marriage Licenses, 1830–1840, 8, SAHL; "Union Army Census of Northeast Florida, 1864 and 1865," Department of the South, Census of the District of Florida, Charles E. Coolidge, Seventh US Infantry, Provost Marshal (hereafter cited as Union Army Census), SAHL; Colored Marriages (hereafter cited as CM), entry 54, Records of the Cathedral Parish, SAHL; St. Johns County Marriage Licenses, vol. A, 16, SAHL; Site 8SJ2512, Historical Structures Form, Florida Master Site File, SAHL; Colored Baptisms (hereafter cited as CB), vol. 3, p. 286, Records of the Cathedral Parish, SAHL; Fifth, Sixth, Seventh, and Eighth Censuses of the United States, 1830, 1840, 1850, 1860, Florida, St. Johns County; Wills and Letters of Administration, vol. 1, 167, 235, CCH; Tax Receipts for Haager Kerr, 1857, 1858, File, SAHL; David Nolan, *The Houses of St. Augustine* (Sarasota, FL: Pineapple Press, 1995), 14; DB-G.

21. CB, vol. 3, entries 545, 549, 563, 644, 645; Tax Assessments, 1866, 1867, City Papers; Wills and Letters of Administration, vol. 1, 424, CCH; Eighth Census of the United States, 1860, Florida, St. Johns County, Monroe County; Pablo Rodgers, Soldier's Certificate no. 826153, Civil War and Later Pension Files, Records of the Veteran's Administration, Record Group 15, National Archives, Washington, DC (Hereafter cited as RG 15); Rosita Alvarez to Sabrina Andreu, Deed, 1869, Stephens Papers, SAHL; Account no. 85048, Abraham McQueen, RG 217.

22. Tax Assessments, 1850, 1852, 1861, City Papers; Mortgage Record A, 80, 105–106, 389–391, CCH; DB-P, 250, 265–266.

23. St. Johns County Tax Rolls, 1854, 1860, 1861, FSA; Marotti, "Edward M. Wanton," 458, 460; DB-K, 341–344; DB-P, 45; Eighth Census of the United States, 1860, Florida, St. Johns County.

24. AC, 4 May, 26 October, 2 November, 16 November 1850; DB-P, 230–231, 266–267; Wills and Letters of Administration, vol. 1, 209–210, 288, CCH; Miscellaneous Record A, 99, 118, CCH; Return Books, 1850, 1852, Tax Rolls, St. Johns County, FSA; AC, 4 May 1850, 26 October 1850, 2 November 1850, 16 November 1850; DB-P, 230–232, 266–267, 286–287; DB-Q, 174; Miscellaneous Record A, 35, 118, CCH; CCR, 11–31; Joseph Lawton to George R. Fairbanks, 25 January 1844, "Fairbanks, G. R., Letters to: 1836-1858 #1," Miscellaneous Manuscripts Collection, PKY; Judgment Record A, 7, CCH.

25. DB-G, 220–221; DB-B&L, 63; DB-M, 176–177, 314–317; DB-D, 11–14; DB-P, 264–265; Ledger B, Account Book, Dr. Seth Peck, 10 May 1837–15 May 1841, 80 and Ledger C, Account Book, Dr. Seth Peck, c. June 1839–21 July 1841, 62, Peck Papers, SAHL; St. Johns County, Tax Rolls, 1845–1861, FSA; Wills & Letters of Administration I, 158, 436–437, CCH; CB, vol. 3, p. 316; SLG, Confirmed, microfilm roll 50-G, entry E-10, PKY; CCR, 117-14, 122-9, 352-14; Passes—1838, "Blacks: 1824–1855," City Papers.

26. CCR, 174-51; Judgment Record A, 104, CCH; Account Book, Ledger B, Dr. Seth Peck, c. June 1839–21 July 1841, and Dr. John E. Peck, 1844–1859, Peck Papers; CCR, 122-9, 117-14, 98-66; Circuit Court Minutes, St. Johns County, vol. A, 1846-–860, 11, 36, SAHL; CCR, 160-53, 122-5, 98-58.

27. CCR, 160-53, 122-5, 98-58; SLG, Confirmed, microfilm reel 50-I, entry G-4, PKY; DB-M, 289–292; DB-N, 542–543; DB-O, 108, 138–139; William Garvin, Claim no.196, RG 49; Mrs. C. C. Anderson to Miss C. L. Fairbanks, 11 October 1842, "Correspondence: 1841," and Anderson to Fairbanks, 11 March 1842, "Correspondence: 1842," Anderson Papers, SAHL.

28. DB-O, 449, 624; DB-R, 173; 21.Whitwell to Peck, 30 May 1868, Peck Papers.

29. David Nolan, *Fifty Feet in Paradise* (New York: Harcourt Brace Jovanovich, 1984), 40–55.

30. Whitwell to Peck, 30 May 1868, Peck Papers; Account Book, Ledger C, Dr. Seth Peck, 148, and Dr. John E. Peck, 1844–1859, 7, and W. W. Dewhurst to W. Wade Hampton, 31 May 1907, Peck Papers.

31. Whitwell to Peck, 30 May 1868, Peck Papers; DB-O, 108; DB-N, 542–543; CCR, 95-17; CCR, 144-31; DB-P, 2; Miss C. C. Anderson to Miss C. L. Fairbanks, 11 March 1842, and Anderson to Fairbanks, 15 March 1844, Anderson Papers.

32. Thomas Clarke, Claim no. 72, George J. F. Clarke, Claim no. 66, RG 49.

33. Felicia M. F. Garvin to John M. Fontane, 17 February 1842, "Correspondence 1842 Appraisements, Business, etc.," Joseph Simeon Sanchez Papers, SAHL; Whitwell to Peck, 30 May 1868, Peck Papers; George J. F. Clarke, Claim nos.

104, 65–66, 70, 80, 104; William Garvin, Claim nos. 190, 196; Clarke & Atkinson, Claim no. 74; Thomas Clarke, Claim no. 72, RG 49.

34. CCR, 117-14; "Clarke, George F. Last Will and Testament," Clarke Papers; DB-O, 593–599; *St. Augustine News* (hereafter cited as SAN), 24 February 1844.

35. CCR, 117-14; DB-G, 87–93; DB-P, 32.

36. CCR, 117-14; DB-M, 361–363; DB-N, 341; Order Book A, 2, CCH; "Clarke, George F. Last Will and Testament," Clarke Papers.

37. CCR, 122-5, 98-58; DB-M, 304–305; SAN, 24 June 1843, 9 April 1842, 9 August 1845; FHSD, 18 February 1842.

38. Alvarez Ledger, 1839, 5, 27, SAHL; Ledger B, Dr. Seth Peck, May 10, 1837–May 15, 1841, 109, 124, Peck Papers; Inventories, "Old" Book 3, Probate Records, 1784–1933, County Judge, St. Johns County, 24, 64, 160–161, FSA.

39. SAN, 2 August 1845; *Jacksonville News*, 19 December 1845.

40. CCR, 117-14; "Clarke, George F. Last Will and Testament," Clarke Papers; DB-O, 593–599; SAN, 24 February 1844.

41. Account Book, Dr. Jonathan E. Peck, 1844–1859, 95, Peck Papers; City Poor—1825–1893, City Papers; Minute Book B, Council Meetings, November 16, 1854–July 31, 1871, 53, 226–228, City Papers; Return Book, 1855, Tax Rolls, St. Johns County, FSA; "Accounts to October 27, 1857," Burt Papers, SAHL.

42. CB, vol. 3, entry 41; "Clarke, George F. Last Will and Testament," Clarke Papers; Louise Biles Hill, "George J. F. Clarke, 1774–1836, *Florida Historical Quarterly* 21 (January 1943): 204–208; *St. Augustine Tatler*, 27 January 1894, SAHL.

43. Compiled Service Records of Volunteer Soldiers Who Served in Organizations from the State of Florida during the Florida Indian Wars, 1835–1858, Microcopy 1086, microfilm rolls 10, 14, 25–26, 39–41, Records of the Adjutant General's Office, Record Group 94, National Archives, Washington, DC; Militia and Troop Lists, and Index, Claims, Florida War, both in State Claims Relating to the Florida Indian Wars, State Claims, Land Files and Miscellaneous Division, Records of the Accounting Officers of the Department of the Treasury, Record Group 217, National Archives, College Park, Maryland.

44. *St. Augustine East Florida Herald*, 29 November 1824, 25 July 1825; CCR, 150-11, 98-25.

45. Melvin Patrick Ely, *Israel on the Appomattox: A Southern Experiment in Black Freedom from the 1790s through the Civil War* (New York: Alfred A. Knopf, 2004), 87–89, 351–354.

46. Return Book, 1835, Tax Rolls, St. Johns County, FSA; "Petition of Sampson Williams," 5 December 1835, Licenses: Liquor—1825–1826, City Papers; "Clarke, George F. Last Will and Testament," Clarke Papers.

47. Whitwell to Peck, 30 May 1868, Peck Papers; Deed Record D, 390, Deed Record E, 42–43, 87, Local and State History Department, Monroe County Public Library, Key West, Florida; Frederick A. Clarke to James Washington Clarke, 26 April 1854, "Blacks: 1824–1855," City Papers.

48. Eunice A. Clarke, Widow of Fred A. Clarke, Private, Captain Warbass' Company L, 2 Washington Territory Volunteers, Certificate 7777, Indian Wars Pension Files, Records of the Veterans Administration, Record Group 15, National Archives, Washington, DC; Oscar Osburn Winther, *The Old Oregon Country: A History of Frontier Trade, Transportation, and Travel* (Stanford: Stanford University Press, 1950), 75, 128, 165; Weldon W. Rau, *Surviving the Oregon Trail, 1852* (Pullman: Washington State University, 2001), 212–215; miscellaneous materials graciously provided by Sandra Carter of Heritage Quest Research Library, Sumner, Washington; James W. Curtis, *The Descendants of Flora Leslie and George John Frederick Clarke* (Riverside, California: James W. Curtis, c. 2004), 21, 29, and photograph between pages 29 and 30; Michael Cook, e-mail message to author, 18 December, 2009.

49. Thomas Graham, "The Home Front," in *Civil War Times in St. Augustine*, ed. Jacqueline K. Fretwell (Port Salerno: Florida Classics Library, 1998), 19, 26, 41–43; C. F. Woolson, "The Ancient City," Part 2, *Harper's New Monthly Magazine*, vol. 50, no. 296 (January 1875): 178.

50. Sharon Wells, *Forgotten Legacy: Blacks in Nineteenth Century Key West* (Key West: Historic Key West Preservation Board, n.d.), 20; *Key West Historic Memorial Sculpture Garden: Key West's 36 Most Influential People & Their Times* (Key West: Friends of Mallory Square, n.d.), 20; Jeanne E. English, *English Family Research* 1 (February 1991): 1–5; Jeanne E. English to author, 16 May 2003; Telephone interview with Jeanne E. English, 2 September 2002.

51. Rayford W. Logan and Michael R. Winston, *Dictionary of American Negro Biography* (New York: W. W. Norton, 1982), 264–265; Curtis, *Descendants of Flora Leslie*; Elva Heastie Gamble to author, 5 September 1998. Emily Jane Ball-Groom, a great, great, great grandchild of the free woman of color Phoebe Dupont and the Jewish settler Theodore Shemetella, supplies further evidence of antebellum St. Augustine's African American potential. She is a writer, businesswoman, government administrator, and community leader. Her family distinguished itself by higher education and community service. See Emily Jane Ball-Groom, *And, Yet Another Day: Journey of My Soul* (n.p.: Emily Jane Ball-Groom, 2010), 19, 182, 243.

52. Telephone interviews with Dr. Yvonne Daniel, 6 April 2000, Attorney Kirby Payne, 17 September 2000, and Mrs. Orville Payne, 17 September 2000 and 12 October 2000; T. H. Breen and Stephen Innes, *"Myne Owne Ground":*

Race & Freedom on Virginia's Eastern Shore, 1640–1676 (New York: Oxford University Press, 1980), 114.

53. Jon Meacham, *American Lion: Andrew Jackson in the White House* (New York: Random House, 2008), 95–96, 123, 359.

54. David R. Colburn, *Racial Change and Community Crisis: St. Augustine, Florida, 1877–1980* (New York: Columbia University Press, 1985), 21–24, 207, 217–221. For an uplifting account of how another community handled race, see Anna-Lisa Cox, *A Stronger Kinship: One Town's Extraordinary Story of Hope and Faith* (New York: Little, Brown, and Company, 2006).

55. Robert L. Paquette, *Sugar Is Made of Blood: The Conspiracy of La Escalera and the Conflict between Empires over Slavery in Cuba* (Middleton, CT: Wesleyan University Press, 1988), 219–220, 228–229. For a briefer, more recent study, see Jane G. Landers, *Atlantic Creoles in the Age of Revolutions* (Cambridge, MA: Harvard University Press, 2010), 204–230.

56. Charles R. Gallagher, "The Catholic Church, Martin Luther King Jr., and the March in St. Augustine," *Florida Historical Quarterly* 83 (Fall 2004): 150.

Bibliography

Archival Sources

Department of Archives, Nassau, Bahamas

Duplicate Governor's Despatches

Florida State Archives, Tallahassee, Florida

St. Johns County Probate Records
Tax Rolls, Monroe County
Tax Rolls, Putnam County
Tax Rolls, St. Johns County
Territorial Court of Appeals Case Files

Heritage Quest Research Library, Sumner, Washington

Miscellaneous Materials

Library of Congress, Washington, DC

American Colonization Society Records
Duncan Clinch Letterbook
East Florida Papers

Local and State History Department, Monroe County Public Library, Key West, Florida

Deed Records
Nelson English Biographical File
St. Mary Star of the Sea Catholic Church Baptismal Registries

Manuscript Division, New York Historical Society

Buckingham Smith Papers

Monroe County Courthouse, Key West, Florida

Deed Books

National Archives, College Park, Maryland

Record Group 56, General Records of the Department of the Treasury
Record Group 59, Records of the Department of State
Record Group 76, Records of the Boundary and Claims Commissions and Arbitrations
Record Group 206, Records of the Solicitor of the Treasury
Record Group 217, Records of the Accounting Officers of the Department of Treasury

National Archives, Washington, DC

Record Group 15, Records of the Veterans' Administration
Record Group 29, Records of the Bureau of the Census
Record Group 46, Records of the US Senate
Record Group 127, Records of the US Marine Corps
Record Group 233, Records of the US House of Representatives

P. K. Yonge Library of Florida History, University of Florida, Gainesville, Florida

East Florida Papers
Miscellaneous Manuscripts Collection
Spanish Land Grants

Putnam County Courthouse, Palatka, Florida

Deed Books

St. Augustine Historical Society Research Library, St. Augustine, Florida

Alvarez Ledger
Anderson Papers
Book or Register of City Lots
Burt Papers
Calhoun Putnam Papers
City of St. Augustine Papers
Clarke Papers
East Florida Papers
Historical Structures Forms, Florida Master Site File
Joseph Simeon Sanchez Papers

Patriot War Papers and Patriot War Claims
Peck Papers
Records of the Cathedral Parish
Records of the Presbyterian Church
Records of Trinity Episcopal Church
Report of the Census for Jacksonville, Fernandina, and St. Augustine (November 1864)
Segui-Dallum Papers
Stephens Papers
St. Johns County Circuit Court Minutes
St. Johns County Court Cases
St. Johns County Court Minute Book, 1827–1845
St, Johns County Marriage Bonds, 1823–1833
St. Johns County Marriage Licenses, 1830–1840
St. Johns County Marriage Records, 1823–1880
Venancio Sanchez Papers
Vertical Files
William Whitwell Dewhurst Papers

St. Johns County Courthouse, St. Augustine, Florida

Chancery Books
Deed Books
Judgment Records
Marriage Licenses
Miscellaneous Records
Mortgage Records
Order Books
Wills and Letters of Administration

State Library of Florida, Tallahassee, Florida

Florida Collection

Newspapers

British and Foreign Anti-Slavery Reporter
Jacksonville News
New-Hampshire Sentinel
New-York Daily Tribune
St. Augustine Ancient City

St. Augustine East Florida Gazette
St. Augustine East Florida Herald
St. Augustine Examiner
St. Augustine Florida Herald
St. Augustine Florida Herald & Southern Democrat
St. Augustine News
St. Augustine Record
St. Augustine Tatler

Personal Interviews and Correspondence

Jane Ball-Groom
Michael Cook
James W. Curtis
Dr. Yvonne Daniel
Jeanne E. English
Elva Heastie Gamble
Kirby Payne
Orville Payne
Karen Taylor

Books and Periodicals

Abel, Annie Heloise, and Frank Klingberg, eds. *A Side-Light on Anglo-American Relations, 1839–1858: Furnished by the Correspondence of Lewis Tappan and Others with the British and Foreign Anti-Slavery Society*. Lancaster, PA: Association for the Study of Negro Life, 1927.

Alexander, Joseph H. "The Ambush of Captain John Williams, U.S.M.C.: Failure of the East Florida Invasion 1812-1813." *Florida Historical Quarterly* 56 (January 1978): 280–296.

———. "Swamp Ambush in Florida." *Milwaukee History* 14 (March 1998): 38–45.

Ancestry.com. "Some Descendants of Jose Sanchez de Ortigosa y de Giles and Juana Theodora Perez y de Lansarote." Rootsweb. http://rootsweb.ancestry.com/~flsags/josesanchez.htm (accessed 10 November 2011).

Aptheker, Herbert. *American Negro Slave Revolts*. New York: Columbia University Press, 1943.

Ball-Groom, Emily Jane. *And, Yet Another Day: Journey of My Soul*. N.p.: Emily Jane Ball-Groom, 2010.

Baptist, Edward A. *Creating an Old South: Middle Florida's Plantation Frontier before the Civil War*. Chapel Hill: University of North Carolina Press, 2002.

Barr, Ruth B., and Modeste Hargis. "The Voluntary Exile of Free Negroes of Pensacola." *Florida Historical Quarterly* 17 (July 1938): 3–14.

Bates, Thelma. "The Legal Status of the Negro in Florida." *Florida Historical Quarterly* 6 (January 1928): 159–181.

Bentley, Jerry H., Renate Bridenthal, and Kären Wigen, eds. *Seascapes: Maritime Histories, Littoral Cultures, and Transoceanic Exchanges*. Honolulu: University of Hawai'i Press, 2007.

Berlin, Ira. *Many Thousands Gone: The First Two Centuries of Slavery in North America*. Cambridge, MA: Harvard University Press, 1998.

———. *Slaves without Masters: The Free Negro in the Antebellum South*. New York: Pantheon, 1975. Reprint, New York: New Press, 1992.

Blassingame, John W. *The Slave Community: Plantation Life in the Antebellum South*. Rev. ed. New York: Oxford University Press, 1979.

Boles, John B., ed. *Masters and Slaves in the House of the Lord: Race and Religion in the American South, 1740–1870*. Lexington: University Press of Kentucky.

Bolt, Christine, and Seymour Drescher. *Anti-Slavery, Religion and Reform: Essays in Memory of Roger Anstey*. Folkestone, England: Wm. Dawson & Son, 1980.

Bordewich, Fergus M. *Bound for Canaan: The Epic Story of the Underground Railroad: America's First Civil Rights Movement*. New York: HarperCollins, 2005.

Bowser, Frederick P. "Colonial Spanish America." In *Neither Slave nor Free: The Freedman of African Descent in the Slave Societies of the New World*, ed. David W. Cohen and Jack P. Greene, 19–58. Baltimore: Johns Hopkins University Press, 1972.

Breen, T. H., and Stephen Innes. *"Myne Owne Ground": Race & Freedom on Virginia's Eastern Shore, 1640–1676*. New York: Oxford University Press, 1980.

Brown Jr., Canter. *Ossian Bingley Hart, Florida's Loyalist Reconstruction Governor*. Baton Rouge: Louisiana State University Press, 1997.

———. "Race Relations in Territorial Florida, 1821-1845." *Florida Historical Quarterly* 73 (January 1995): 287–307.

———. *Tampa Before the Civil War*. Tampa: University of Tampa Press, 1999.

Browne, Jefferson B. *Key West: The Old and the New, A Facsimile Reproduction of the 1912 Edition*. Gainesville: University of Florida Press, 1973.

Brundage, W. Fitzhugh, ed. *Where These Memories Grow: History, Memory, and Southern Identity*. Chapel Hill: University of North Carolina Press, 2000.

Bryant, William Cullen. *Letters of a Traveller; or, Notes of Things Seen in Europe and America*. 3rd ed. New York: George P. Putnam, 1851.

Buker, George E. "The Americanization of St. Augustine." In *The Oldest City: St. Augustine Saga of Survival*, ed. Jean Parker Waterbury, 151–179. St. Augustine: St. Augustine Historical Society Research Library, 1983.

Bushnell, David. "The Republic of Florida: An Overview." In *La Republica de las Floridas: Texts and Documents*, comp. David Bushnell, 7–18. Mexico City: Pan American Institute of Geography and History, 1986.

———, comp. *La Republica de las Floridas: Texts and Documents*. Mexico City: Pan American Institute of Geography and History, 1986.

Carter, Clarence Edwin, ed. *Territorial Papers of the United States*. Vols. 22–26, *Florida Territory*. Washington, DC: Government Printing Office, 1956–1962.

Cobley, Alan Gregor. "That Turbulent Soil: Seafarers, the 'Black Atlantic' and Afro-Caribbean Identity." In *Seascapes: Maritime Histories, Littoral Cultures, and Transoceanic Exchanges*, ed. Jerry H. Bentley, Renate Bridenthal, and Kären Wigen, 153–168. Honolulu: University of Hawai'i Press, 2007.

Cohen, David W., and Jack P. Greene, eds. *Neither Slave nor Free: The Freedman of African Descent in the Slave Societies of the New World*. Baltimore, MD: Johns Hopkins University Press, 1972.

Colburn, David R. *Racial Change and Community Crisis: St. Augustine, Florida, 1877–1980*. New York: Columbia University Press, 1985.

Colburn, David R., and Jane L. Landers, eds. *The African American Heritage of Florida*. Gainesville: University Press of Florida, 1995.

Coles, David J. "Ancient City Defenders: The St. Augustine Blues." In *Civil War Times in St. Augustine*, ed. Jacqueline K. Fretwell, 65–90. Port Salerno: Florida Classics Library, 1988.

Cornelius, Janet Duitsman. *Slave Missions and the Black Church in the Antebellum South*. Columbia: University of South Carolina Press, 1999.

Cox, Anna-Lisa. *A Stronger Kinship: One Town's Extraordinary Story of Hope and Faith*. New York: Little, Brown, 2006.

Craton, Michael, and Gail Saunders. *From the Ending of Slavery to Twenty First Century*. Vol. 2 of *Islanders in the Stream: A History of the Bahamian People*. Athens: University of Georgia Press, 1998.

Crider, Robert Franklin. "The Borderland Floridas, 1815–1821: Spanish Sovereignty under Siege." PhD diss., Florida State University, 1979.

Curtis, James W. *The Descendants of Flora Leslie and George John Frederick Clarke*. Riverside, CA: James W. Curtis, c. 2004.

Cusick, James G. *The Other War of 1812: The Patriot War and the American Invasion of Spanish East Florida*. Gainesville: University Press of Florida, 2003.

Davis, Cyprian. *The History of Black Catholics in the United States*. New York: Crossroads, 1990.

Davis, Cyprian, and Jamie Phelps, eds. *"Stamped with the Image of God": African Americans as God's Image in Black*. New York: Orbis, 2003.

Denham, James M. *A Rogue's Paradise: Crime and Punishment in Antebellum Florida, 1821–1861*. Tuscaloosa: University of Alabama Press, 1997.

Dewhurst, William W. *The History of St. Augustine, Florida*. 1885. Reprint. Rutland, VT: Academy Books, 1968.

Dunn, Marvin. *Black Miami in the Twentieth Century*. Gainesville: University Press of Florida, 2002.

Ely, Melvin Patrick. *Israel on the Appomattox: A Southern Experiment in Black Freedom from the 1790s through the Civil War*. New York: Alfred A. Knopf, 2004.

English, Jeanne E. *English Family Research* 1 (February 1991): 1–5.

Florida Historical Records Survey. *Ordinances of the City of St. Augustine*. Vol. 1. Jacksonville: Florida Historical Records Survey, 1941.

Fretwell, Jacqueline K., ed. *Civil War Times in St. Augustine*. Port Salerno: Florida Classics Library, 1988.

Gaddis, John Lewis. *Surprise, Security, and the American Experience*. Cambridge, MA: Harvard University Press, 2004.

Gallagher, Charles R. "The Catholic Church, Martin Luther King Jr., and the March in St. Augustine." *Florida Historical Quarterly* 83 (Fall 2004): 149–172.

Gannon, Michael V. *The Cross in the Sand: The Early Catholic Church in Florida, 1513–1870*. Gainesville: University of Florida Press, 1965.

———. *Rebel Bishop: Florida's Civil War Prelate*. Milwaukee: Bruce, 1964. Reprint. Gainesville: University Press of Florida, 1997.

———, ed. *The New History of Florida*. Gainesville: University Press of Florida, 1996.

Garvin, Russell. "The Free Negro in Florida before the Civil War." *Florida Historical Quarterly* 46 (July 1967): 9–17.

Genovese, Eugene. *Roll, Jordan, Roll: The World the Slaves Made*. New York: Random House, 1974.

Gould, Virginia. "In Full Enjoyment of Their Liberty: The Free Women of Color of the Gulf Ports of New Orleans, Mobile, and Pensacola, 1769–1860." PhD diss., Emory University, 1989.

Graham, Thomas. *The Awakening of St. Augustine: The Anderson Family and the Oldest City, 1821–1924*. St. Augustine: St. Augustine Historical Society, 1978.

———. "The Home Front: Civil War Times in St. Augustine." In *Civil War*

Times in St. Augustine, ed. Jacqueline K. Fretwell, 19–46. Port Salerno: Florida Classics Library, 1998.

Great Britain, Foreign and Commonwealth Office. *British and Foreign State Papers: 1841–1842*. Vol. 30. London: James Ridgway and Sons, 1858.

Griffin, Patricia C. "The Halifax-Mosquitoes Plantation Corridor: An Overview." *Florida Anthropologist* 52 (March–June 1999): 5–23.

———. "Mullet on the Beach: The Minorcans of Florida, 1768–1788." Special issue, *El Escribano: The St Augustine Journal of History* 27 (1990).

———. "The Spanish Return: The People-Mix Period 1784–1821." In *The Oldest City: St. Augustine Saga of Survival*, ed. Jean Parker Waterbury, 125–150. St. Augustine: St. Augustine Historical Society, 1983.

Griffin, Patricia C., and Diana S. Edwards. "Richard Aloysius Twine: Photographer of Lincolnville, 1922–1927." [unpublished manuscript]. St. Augustine Historical Society Research Library, St. Augustine, FL.

Hahn, Steven. *A Nation under Our Feet: Black Political Struggles in the Rural South, from Slavery to the Great Migration*. Cambridge, MA: Harvard University Press, 2003.

Hall, Claude H. *Abel Parker Upshur: Conservative Virginian, 1790–1844*. Madison: State Historical Society of Wisconsin, 1964.

Hazouri, Kim. "From Jose Mariano Hernandez to Joseph Martin Hernandez: 1788–1856." [unpublished manuscript]. St. Augustine Historical Society Research Library, St. Augustine, FL.

Hebel, Ianthe Bond. "The Samuel Williams Family." *Journal of the Halifax Historical Society* 2, no. 1 [1952?]: 30–31.

Hill, Louise Biles. "George J. F. Clarke, 1774–1836." *Florida Historical Quarterly* 21 (January 1943): 197–253.

Howard, Rosalyn. *Black Seminoles in the Bahamas*. Gainesville: University Press of Florida, 2002.

Jacobsen, Matthew Frye. *Whiteness of a Different Color: European Immigrants and the Alchemy of Race*. Cambridge, MA: Harvard University Press, 1998.

Jervey, Edward D., and C. Harold Huber. "The Creole Affair." *Journal of Negro History* 65, no. 3 (Summer 1980): 196–211.

Johnson, Howard. *The Bahamas in Slavery and Freedom*. Kingston, Jamaica: Ian Randle, 1991.

Johnson, Walter, ed. *The Chattel Principle: Internal Slave Trades in the Americas*. New Haven, CT: Yale University Press, 2004.

Johnson, Whittington B. *Race Relations in the Bahamas, 1784–1834: The Nonviolent Transformation from a Slave to a Free Society*. Fayetteville: University of Arkansas Press, 2000.

Kane, Joseph Nathan. *The American Counties*. 3rd ed. Metuchen, NJ: Scarecrow Press, 1972.

Kennedy, Joseph C.G. *Population of the United States in 1860; Compiled from the Original Returns of the Eighth Census* . . . 1864. Reprint, New York: Norman Publishing, 1990.

Key West Historic Memorial Sculpture Garden: Key West's 36 Most Influential People & Their Times. Key West, FL: Friends of Mallory Square, n.d.

Kimball, Gregg D. "African, American, and Virginian: The Shaping of Black Memory in Antebellum Virginia, 1790-1860." In *Where These Memories Grow: History, Memory, and Southern Identity*, ed. W. Fitzhugh Brundage, 57–78. Chapel Hill: University of North Carolina Press, 2000.

Kingsley, Zephaniah. *A Treatise on the Patriarchal or Cooperative System of Society*. . . . 2nd ed. 1829. Reprint, Freeport, NY: Books for Libraries Press, 1970.

Kingston, Clara Talley. "Sarah Warner Fish." *El Escribano: The St. Augustine Journal of History* 24 (1987): 63–84.

Kirk, Cooper C. "A History of the Southern Presbyterian Church in Florida, 1821–1891." PhD diss., Florida State University, 1966.

Klein, Herbert S. *Slavery in the Americas: A Comparative Study of Virginia and Cuba*. Chicago: University of Chicago Press, 1966.

Klos, George. "Blacks and the Seminole Removal Debate, 1821–1835." In *The African American Heritage of Florida*, ed. David R. Colburn and Jane L. Landers, 128–156. Gainesville: University Press of Florida, 1995.

Kluger, Richard. *Seizing Destiny: How America Grew from Sea to Shining Sea*. New York: Alfred A. Knopf, 2007.

Knetsch, Joe. "The Development of Amelia Island in the Second Spanish Period: The Impact of George J. F. Clarke." Address given to the Amelia Island Museum of History, Fernandina Beach, FL, March 26, 1999.

Landers, Jane G. *Atlantic Creoles of Color in the Age of Revolutions*. Cambridge, MA: Harvard University Press, 2010.

———. *Black Society in Spanish Florida*. Urbana: University of Illinois Press, 1999.

———. "Black Society in Spanish St. Augustine, 1784–1821." PhD diss., University of Florida, 1988.

———. "Traditions of African American Freedom and Community in Spanish Colonial Florida." In *The African American Heritage of Florida*, ed. David R. Colburn and Jane Landers, 17–41. Gainesville: University Press of Florida, 1995.

———, ed. *Colonial Plantations and Economy in Florida*. Gainesville: University Press of Florida, 2000.

Laumer, Frank. *Massacre!* Gainesville: University of Florida Press, 1968.

Lisenby, Julie Ann. "The Free Negro in Antebellum Florida, 1821–1861." Master's thesis, Florida State University, 1967.

Logan, Rayford W., and Michael R. Winston. *Dictionary of American Negro Biography*. New York: W. W. Norton, 1982.

Macdougall, Donald V. "Habeas Corpus, Extradition and a Fugitive Slave in Canada." *Slavery & Abolition* 7, no. 2 (September 1986): 118–128.

Magdol, Edward, and Jon L. Wakelyn, eds. *The Southern Common People: Studies in Nineteenth-Century Social History*. Westport, CT: Greenwood Press, 1980.

Mahon, John K. *History of the Second Seminole War*. Gainesville: University of Florida Press, 1967.

Mahon, John, and Brent R. Weisman. "Florida's Seminole and Miccosukee Peoples." In *The New History of Florida*, ed. Michael Gannon, 183–206. Gainesville: University Press of Florida, 1996.

Malone, Ann Patton. *Sweet Chariot: Slave Family and Household Structure in Nineteenth-Century Louisiana*. Chapel Hill: University of North Carolina Press, 2002.

Marotti Jr., Frank. "Edward M. Wanton and the Settling of Micanopy." *Florida Historical Quarterly* 73 (April 1995): 456–477.

Meacham, Jon. *American Lion: Andrew Jackson in the White House*. New York: Random House, 2008.

Meyer, Marjorie. "Venancio Sanchez: Nineteenth Century St. Augustine Citizen." Master's thesis, Arkansas State Teachers College, 1959.

Miller, Randall M. "A Church in Cultural Captivity: Some Speculations on Catholic Identity in the Old South." In *Catholics in the Old South: Essays on Church and Culture*, ed. Randall M. Miller and Jon L. Wakelyn, 11–52. Macon, GA: Mercer University Press, 1983.

———. "Slaves and Southern Catholicism." In *Masters and Slaves in the House of the Lord: Race and Religion in the American South, 1740–1870*, ed. John B. Boles, 127–152. Lexington: University Press of Kentucky, 1988.

———. "That Failed Mission: The Catholic Church and Black Catholics in the Old South." In *The Southern Common People: Studies in Nineteenth-Century Social History*, ed. Edward Magdol and Jon L. Wakelyn, 37–54. Westport, CT: Greenwood Press, 1980.

Miller, Randall M., and Jon L. Wakelyn, eds. *Catholics in the Old South: Essays on Church and Culture*. Macon, GA: Mercer University Press, 1983.

Mills, Gary B. "Piety and Prejudice: A Colored Catholic Community in the Antebellum South." In *Catholics in the Old South: Essays on Church and Cul-*

ture, ed. Randall M. Miller and Jon L. Wakelyn, 171–194. Macon, GA: Mercer University Press, 1983.

Mohr, Clarence L. "Slaves and White Churches in Confederate Georgia." In *Masters and Slaves in the House of the Lord: Race and Religion in the American South, 1740–1870*, ed. John B. Boles, 153–172. Lexington: University Press of Kentucky, 1988.

Morgan, Robert J. *A Whig Embattled: The Presidency under John Tyler*. Lincoln: University of Nebraska Press, 1954.

Neyland, Leedell W. "The Free Negro in Florida." *Negro History Bulletin* 29 (November 1965): 27–28, 42–43, 45.

Nolan, David. *Fifty Feet in Paradise*. New York: Harcourt Brace Jovanovich, 1984.

———. *The Houses of St. Augustine*. Sarasota, FL: Pineapple Press, 1995.

Panagopoulos, E. P. *New Smyrna: An Eighteenth Century Greek Odyssey*. Gainesville: University of Florida Press, 1966.

Paquette, Robert L. *Sugar Is Made of Blood: The Conspiracy of La Escalera and the Conflict between Empires over Slavery in Cuba*. Middleton, CT: Wesleyan University Press, 1988.

Parker, Susan R. "Men Without God or King: Rural Settlers of East Florida, 1784–1790." *Florida Historical Quarterly* 69 (October 1990): 135–155.

———. "Success through Diversification: Francis Philip Fatio's New Switzerland Plantation." In *Colonial Plantations and Economy in Florida*, ed. Jane G. Landers, 69–82. Gainesville: University Press of Florida, 2000.

Parry, Clive, ed. *The Consolidated Treaty Series*. Vol. 70. Dobbs Ferry, NY: Oceana, 1969.

Patrick, Rembert W. *Florida Fiasco: Rampant Rebels on the Georgia-Florida Border, 1810–1815*. Athens: University of Georgia Press, 1954.

Poitrineau, Abel. "Demography and the Political Destiny of Florida during the Second Spanish Period." *Florida Historical Quarterly* 66 (April 1988): 420–443.

Porter, Kenneth W. "The Early Life of Luis Pacheco *Ne* Fatio." *Negro History Bulletin* 7 (December 1943): 52, 54, 62, 64.

———. "Florida Slaves and Free Negroes in the Seminole War, 1835–1842." *Journal of Negro History* 28, no. 4 (October 1943): 390–421.

———. "Negro Guides and Interpreters in the Early Stages of the Seminole War, Dec. 28, 1835–March 6, 1837." *Journal of Negro History* 35, no. 2 (April 1950): 174–182.

———. "Negroes and the East Florida Annexation Plot, 1811–1813." *Journal of Negro History* 30, no. 1 (January 1945): 9–29.

———. *The Negro on the American Frontier*. New York: Arno Press, 1971.

———. "Three Fighters for Freedom." *Journal of Negro History* 28, no. 1 (January 1943): 51–72.

Ortiz, Puig, and Jos Augusto. *Emigración de Libertos Norteamericanos A Puerto Plata En La Primera Mitad Del Siglo XIX: La Iglesia Metodista Wesleyana*. Santo Domingo: Editora "Alpha y Omega," 1978.

Raboteau, Albert J. *Slave Religion: The "Invisible Institution" in the Antebellum South*. New York: Oxford University Press, 1978.

Rau, Weldon W. *Surviving the Oregon Trail, 1852*. Pullman: Washington State University Press, 2001.

Rawick, George P., ed. *Florida Narratives*. Vol. 17 of *The American Slave: A Composite Biography*. Westport, CT: Greenwood Press, 1972.

Riley, Sandra. *Homeword Bound: A History of the Bahama Islands to 1850 with a Definitive Study of Abaco in the American Loyalist Plantation Period*. Miami: Island Research, 1983.

Rivers, Larry Eugene. *Slavery in Florida: Territorial Days to Emancipation*. Gainesville: University Press of Florida, 2000.

Rugemer, Edward B. "Robert Monroe Harrison: British Abolition, Southern Anglophobia and Texas Annexation." *Slavery & Abolition* 28, no. 2 (August 2007): 169–191.

Schafer, Daniel L. *Anna Kingsley*. Revised and expanded ed. St. Augustine: St. Augustine Historical Society, 1997.

———. *Anna Madgigine Jai Kingsley: African Princess, Florida Slave, Plantation Slaveowner*. Gainesville: University Press of Florida, 2003.

———. "'A Class of People Neither Freemen nor Slaves': From Spanish to American Race Relations in Florida, 1821–1861." *Journal of Social History* 26, no. 3 (Spring 1993): 587–609.

———. "Freedom Was as Close as the River: African Americans and the Civil War in Northeast Florida." In *The African American Heritage of Florida*, ed. David R. Colburn and Jane L. Landers, 157–184. Gainesville: University Press of Florida, 1995.

———. "'A Swamp of an Investment'?: Richard Oswald's British East Florida Plantation Experiment." In *Colonial Plantations and Economy in Florida*, ed. Jane G. Landers, 11–38. Gainesville: University Press of Florida, 2000.

———. "U.S. Territory and State." In *The New History of Florida*, ed. Michael Gannon, 207–230. Gainesville: University Press of Florida, 1996.

Schick, Tom W. *Emigrants to Liberia, 1820 to 1843: An Alphabetical Listing*. Newark: University of Delaware Press, 1971.

Smith, Julia Floyd. *Slavery and Plantation Growth in Antebellum Florida, 1821–1860*. Gainesville: University of Florida Press, 1973.

Smith, Mark M. *Debating Slavery: Economy and Society in the Antebellum American South*. Cambridge: Cambridge University Press, 1998.

———. "Remembering Mary, Shaping Revolt: Reconsidering the Stono Rebellion." *Journal of Southern History* 67, no. 3 (August 2001): 513–534.

Stagg, J. C. A. "George Mathews and John McKee: Revolutionizing East Florida, Mobile, and Pensacola in 1812." *Florida Historical Quarterly* 85 (Winter 2007): 269–296.

Stowell, Daniel W., ed. *Balancing Evils Judiciously: The Proslavery Writings of Zephaniah Kingsley*. Gainesville: University of Florida Press, 2000.

Tannenbaum, Frank. *Slave and Citizen*. New York: Alfred A. Knopf, 1946. Reprint. Boston: Beacon Press, 1992.

Tebeau, Charlton W. *A History of Florida*. Coral Gables, FL: University of Miami Press, 1971.

Thomas, David Y. "The Free Negro in Florida before 1865." *South Atlantic Quarterly* 10 (October 1911): 335–345.

Thompson, Arthur W. *Jacksonian Democracy on the Florida Frontier*. Gainesville: University of Florida Press, 1961.

Thompson, Joseph Conan. "Toward a More Humane Oppression: Florida's Slave Codes, 1821–1861." *Florida Historical Quarterly* 71 (January 1993): 324–338.

Tornero Tinajero, Pablo. *Relaciones de Dependencia Entre Florida Y Estados Unidos (1783–1820)*. Madrid: Ministerio de Asunto Exteriores, 1979.

Touchstone, Blake. "Planters and Slave Religion in the Deep South." In *Masters and Slaves in the House of the Lord: Race and Religion in the American South, 1740–1870*, ed. John B. Boles, 99–126. Lexington: University Press of Kentucky, 1988.

Troutman, Phllip. "Grapevine in the Slave Market: African American Geopolitical Literacy and the 1841 Creole Revolt." In *The Chattel Principle: Internal Slave Trades in the Americas*, ed. Walter Johnson, 203–233. New Haven, CT: Yale University Press, 2004.

Turley, David M. "'Free Air' and Fugitive Slaves: British Abolitionists versus Government over American Fugitives, 1834–1861." In *Anti-Slavery, Religion and Reform: Essays in Memory of Roger Anstey*, ed. Christine Bolt and Seymour Drescher, 163–182. Folkestone, England: Wm. Dawson & Son, 1980.

United States Census Office. *Fifth Census; or Enumeration of the Inhabitants of the United States. 1830*. 1832. Reprint, New York: Norman Ross Publishing, 1990.

———. *The Seventh Census of the United States*. 1853. Reprint, New York: Norman Ross Publishing, 1990.

———. *Sixth Census or Enumeration of the Inhabitants of the United States, as Corrected at the Department of State, in 1840*. 1841. Reprint, New York: Norman Ross Publishing, 1990.

United States Congress. *American State Papers: Documents of the Congress of the United States in Relation to Public Lands, from the First Session of the Twenty-First to the First Session of the Twenty-Third Congress, Commencing December 1, 1828, and Ending April 11, 1834*. Vol. 6. Asbury Dickins and John W. Forney, eds. Washington, DC: Gales & Seaton, 1860.

Verot, Augustin. *A Tract for the Times. Slavery & Abolitionism Being the Substance of a Sermon, Preached in the Church of St. Augustine, Florida, on the 4th Day of January, 1861, Day of Public Humiliation, Fasting and Prayer*. New ed. New Orleans: Catholic Propagator, 1861.

Warner, Lee H. *Free Men in An Age of Servitude: Three Centuries of a Black Family*. Lexington: University Press of Kentucky, 1992.

Waterbury, Jean Parker. "Richard Aloysius Twine: Photographer of Lincolnville, 1922–1927." *East Florida Gazette* 11 (February 1990): 1–6.

———. ed. *The Oldest City: St. Augustine Saga of Survival*. St. Augustine: St. Augustine Historical Society Research Library, 1983.

Weber, David J. *The Spanish Frontier in North America*. New Haven, CT: Yale University Press, 1992.

Weeks, William Earl. *John Quincy Adams and American Global Empire*. Lexington: University Press of Kentucky, 1992.

Wells, Sharon. *Forgotten Legacy: Blacks in Nineteenth Century Key West*. Key West: Historic Key West Preservation Board, n.d.

Willis, Sandra, transcriber. "1850 Census of St. Johns County, FL." Rootsweb. http://www.rootsweb.ancestry.com/~flstjohn/resources/1850Census/index.htm (accessed 10 November 2011).

———. "Putnam, FL 1860 Census." USGenWeb Census Project. http://files.usgwarchives.net/fl/putnam/census/1860 (accessed 10 November 2011).

Winther, Oscar Osburn. *The Old Oregon Country: A History of Frontier Trade, Transportation and Travel*. Stanford: Stanford University Press, 1950.

Wilson, Gil. "An African American Flight for Freedom." *Ancient City Genealogist* 3, no. 1 (1992): 16–18.

Woolson, C. F. "The Ancient City." Part 2. *Harper's New Monthly Magazine* 50, no. 296 (January 1875): 165–185.

Wyllys, Rufus Kay. "The East Florida Revolution of 1812–1814." *Hispanic American Historical Review* 9, no. 4 (November 1929): 415–445.

Wyly-Jones, Susan. "The 1835 Anti-Abolition Meetings in the South: A New Look at the Controversy Over the Abolition Postal Campaign." *Civil War History* 47, no. 4 (December 2001): 289–309.

Index

Page numbers in italic refer to figures.